Second Edition

Writing in the Social Sciences

A Guide for Term Papers and Book Reviews

Jake Muller

OXFORD
UNIVERSITY PRESS

OXFORD
UNIVERSITY PRESS

Oxford University Press is a department of the University of Oxford.
It furthers the University's objective of excellence in research, scholarship,
and education by publishing worldwide. Oxford is a registered trade mark of
Oxford University Press in the UK and in certain other countries.

Published in Canada by
Oxford University Press
8 Sampson Mews, Suite 204,
Don Mills, Ontario M3C 0H5 Canada

www.oupcanada.com

Library and Archives Canada Cataloguing in Publication

Muller, Jake, author
Writing in the social sciences : a guide for term papers and book reviews
/ Jake Muller. — Second edition.

Includes bibliographical references and index.
ISBN 978–0–19–900986–2 (pbk.)

1. Social sciences—Authorship. 2. Report writing. 3. Book reviewing.
I. Title.

PE1479.S62M85 2015   808.06'63   C2014-907919-2

Cover image: © iStock/shuoshu

Oxford University Press is committed to our environment.
This book is printed on Forest Stewardship Council® certified paper
and comes from responsible sources.

Printed and bound in Canada

1 2 3 4 — 18 17 16 15

Contents

Acknowledgements

This second edition continues my inquiry to show how to create and organize the kind of research and writing that students need for mainstream social sciences. Over the decades I have learned quite a bit from my students, especially some of the difficulties they encountered in research and writing. I have tried to help solve some of their problems, and in the process learned quite a lot. For instance, the use of the building blocks helped them to understand quickly the general concepts in a course. I want to thank them for all the questions and problems that they posed to me. Without them this book would never have happened.

I want to thank Leona Wells, First Nations Access Coordinator, Northwest Community College, and Don Wells for providing me with the local Kitsumkalum First Nation's traditional territory name for "Terrace": *Manganeex*, which means "climbing steps." Most of the writing for this book took place in Manganeex. The name is also an apt metaphor for learning, both for me and for my students.

As with the previous edition, I want to thank the excellent staff at Oxford University Press, including Darcey Pepper, Lisa Peterson, and Leah-Ann Lymer. It was a pleasure to work with them to create this edition. Part of this process involved the anonymous comments by the reviewers. Their advice and comments helped to make this a better book. I also want to thank Colleen Ste Marie for her excellent job of copyediting this book. To all of them, thank you.

As part of this edition, I had discussions with librarians about their work in assisting students to find appropriate academic research sources. Here I wish to thank Peggy Ellis, associate librarian, at Western University (rebranded from the University of Western Ontario) for taking the time to discuss this with me. As well, the library staff at Western University made me feel quite welcome while I was undertaking research. At Northwest Community College, I want to thank Melanie Wilke, librarian, for discussing with me appropriate academic sources for student research papers. Neither of them are responsible, however, for my wayward application of their suggestions. I am also very grateful for the interlibrary loan assistance provided by Penny Llewellyn, at Northwest Community College. She saved me hours of reference work. As well, I am much indebted to Simon Thompson, college professor of English at Northwest Community College, for assisting me with referencing. Without his help, it would have been difficult for me to obtain some current referencing in college essay writing.

It would not have been possible to do research at Western University without the great hospitality of Pete Muller and Lynn Muller. Thank you both for everything.

Finally, this book has been a long project. Barbara Hammer was there from the beginning. She helped put the manuscript together to be considered for publishing with her editorial work and grammar corrections. She offered insights, suggestions, and omissions that made the then manuscript a better proposal. Her wit and humour continued from the previous edition to the present one. I am very grateful to her for her understanding, love, and support throughout these editions.

Jake Muller

Introduction

Preparing for Your Social Science Term Paper and Book Review

In this introduction you will learn about the following:

1. How this book will help you write a term paper or book review
2. How this book is organized
3. Basic knowledge and skills about reading and writing
4. Building blocks of research and writing: concept, definition, and evidence/example
5. Fundamental expectations about your new research and writing role
6. Specific requirements you will need to follow in your term paper

1. How Will This Book Help Me Write a Term Paper or Book Review?

The aim of this book is to help you to research and write your first social science term paper or book review (or article critique) at a community college or university. You will find this book helpful if you are

- a social science student (for example, anthropology, political science, psychology, sociology);
- a student in an applied or career program (for example, education, criminology, social work); or
- a senior high school student preparing for community college or university courses.

This book is a supplement (or complement) to the subject matter being taught. In fact, you can read and work on the book on your own.

What you will get from this book is guidance about the following:

- A starting argumentative format and process for researching and writing a social science term paper or undertaking a book review (or article critique)
- Some ways to adapt this format and process to suit various social science instructors, each of whom may require you to write different kinds of argumentative term papers or book reviews (or article critiques)

- Some ways of adding to this beginning format or arrangement for future term papers or book reviews
- Three common referencing styles to help you document your research sources:
  1. *The Publication Manual of the American Psychological Association* (APA) (2010, 6th edition)
  2. *The Chicago Manual of Style* (CMS) (2010, 16th edition)
  3. *American Sociological Association Style Guide* (ASA) (2010, 4th edition)
- Ways these formats and processes can be used to evaluate and grade your term paper or book review (or article critique)

To write a *term paper* you should

- read this Introduction and make sure you understand it,
- skim through chapters 1 to 5 to get an overview, and then
- work through chapters 1 to 5.

To write a book review or article critique you should

- read this Introduction and make sure you understand it,
- skim through Chapters 1 to 6 to get an overview, and then
- work through Chapter 6 in detail.

(If there is something that you do not understand in Chapter 6, look it up in chapters 1 to 5, where more information is presented.)

As a student you will become part of the general social science community of researchers and writers. You will learn new responsibilities or a new role as you undertake one of the above assignments for your instructor.

The general word *instructor* is used throughout this book to refer to the person for whom you are writing your term paper or book review (or article critique). She or he may also be your professor, teacher, teaching assistant, or tutorial assistant.

2. How Is This Book Organized?

The organization of this book is based on a practical process to research and write a term paper (or book review or article critique). The process involves determining which research material to use, learning how to do your research and writing, and then working on doing it. This introduction starts you on this process of what you will need to know and do, such as basic writing skills, the building blocks of research and writing, and the requirements of your instructor. Next, Chapter 1 presents a basic social science argumentative format and process. The items of this starting format and process are used to create a standard outline for a term paper consisting of individual arguments (as in Appendix E). From individual arguments, you can then go on to create an outline consisting of headings/themes (as in Appendix F).

For this basic argumentative form, the research process is arranged as two priorities. The first priority research is presented in Chapters 2 and 3. They start the manual-like character of this book. Chapter 2 starts with creating an aim and arguments, which are recorded in your outline. You can either stop there, or carry on with the steps to create headings/themes. Chapter 3 presents three different reference styles (APA, CMS, and ASA) to document your research sources. The second priority research is presented in Chapter 4, which is concerned with preparing the introduction, defining concepts in the aim, organizing individual arguments or headings/themes, drafting a conclusion, and including further references. The inclusion of these second priority items completes the outline and the research. Chapter 5 takes you through the steps of writing a coherent term paper based on the completed outline, whether it is for individual arguments or headings/themes. The chapter also includes some final suggestions that you can consult before submitting your term paper to meet your instructor's requirements.

Chapter 6 presents a similar research and writing process to write a book review or article critique, using the outline in Appendix E.

TIPS This book provides links to websites that may change, be redirected, or be removed. Wherever possible, we will also present the name of the organization that maintains the site. If a particular link no long works, you can use this name (for example, college, university, professional association, or organization) to locate the organization's general website. Once you have located that, you can then search for the new link or information you are seeking. As well, you can check out this book's website at Oxford University Press (http://www.oupcanada.com/Muller2e), where any links will be updated if they do change.

3. What Do I Need to Know about Reading and Writing?

Your instructor will expect you to have the basic reading and writing skills that are vital for researching and writing a social science term paper (or book review or article critique). You must be able to read efficiently *and* effectively. Reading efficiently is necessary to find information and material for your research. (See the building blocks of research and writing that are offered in the next section.) Reading effectively, which is crucial to research and writing, includes the following:

- Understanding what you are reading and looking up unfamiliar words
- Being able to think critically to evaluate what you are reading
- Knowing how you will use the information in your term paper

In addition, you must know and be able to use basic writing skills to present your research clearly to your instructor. These basic writing skills include the following:

- Spelling
- Grammar

- Punctuation
- Sentences
- Paragraphs

As well, you must write logically and coherently, arranging your ideas and material in a consistent sequence. Your instructor must be able to follow the organization of your writing.

Read through the following sections and determine if you are able to understand them. In particular, try to answer the questions that appear in each section (except the section on paragraphs). The answers are provided in Appendix A. If you have problems with these questions, you should brush up on the grammar and style tips provided in Appendix B.

Spelling

You must be able to spell commonly used words and know how to use them correctly. Words that are considered common are those that are found in general-use dictionaries. You should thus obtain or have access to the following:

- A recent, university-level dictionary, such as *The Canadian Oxford Dictionary* or the *Gage Canadian Dictionary*
- A thesaurus—a book that contains a list of *synonyms* (meaning "similar") and *antonyms* (meaning "opposite")

Word-processing software also has these features. In addition, search engines allow you to look up words. MSN *Bing*, for example, has language tools, including a dictionary, thesaurus, and spell checker. Google *Chrome* has a dictionary button that allows you to view various definitions.

You may be familiar with websites that allow you to look up the meaning of words and other aspects, for example, http://www.dictionary.com. However, these dictionaries may be out of date or may present one kind of English spelling only, such as US English. For a quick set of multiple Web-based definitions, try the Google search engine by entering "define: <word you are looking up>" (e.g., "define: adolescent"). This Google search will present you with a number of results pertaining to the meaning of *adolescent*.

Try looking up the following words in a dictionary:

- *teen* or *adolescent*
- *runaway*
- *alcohol*
- *abuse*

Some word-processing software allows you to select various kinds of English spelling. You will need to turn this feature on for your particular country, such as Canada. This will help to highlight some of the spelling differences between Canadian English and American English, such as *cheque* and *check*. Current computer spell checkers have difficulty with the correct spelling of a word in the context of a sentence. For example, you must know the difference in spelling between *there* and *their* in a sentence.

Can you identify the following spelling errors in the context of the sentence?

1. The parents hid there alcohol from they're kids.
2. There teen did not no to phone home.

Grammar

Grammar refers to the ways that words are used in sentences. Your instructor will understand what you are writing about only when you use correct grammar.

Can you identify the grammar mistakes in the following? Remember, the answers are in Appendix A and additional tips appear in Appendix B. Can you determine the singular and plural agreement errors?

3. A teen ran away from homes.
4. Many teens ran away from their home.

Can you identify the use of a singular verb for a whole group and a plural verb for a group acting individually?

5. The family are worried about their runaway teen.
6. The family is worried about its runaway teen.

Can you correct the following unclear or vague pronoun reference?

7. The parents are going out drinking and partying, and are staying out late. She doesn't like them.

How would you correct this sentence, which is not grammatically parallel?

8. She was lying, cheating, and had to steal to survive.

Punctuation

Punctuation refers to the use of conventional marks, such as a comma or a period, to make your writing clear. Your instructor will assume that you have a good command of proper punctuation.

Where would you use a comma in the following sentence?

9. A runaway teen may require food and shelter and clothing.

Where would you use a colon and quotation marks in the sentence below?

10. The detox worker stated the policy clearly, You must follow the rules of this clinic or you will not be allowed to stay.

The general rule for a student is to keep the punctuation simple. This will be easier if you keep your sentences simple.

Sentences

You must be able to write *complete* sentences that have a subject and a verb. You should keep your sentences short when you first start to write a social science term paper. Short sentences will help you to avoid run-on sentences.

Can you reword this sentence fragment into a complete sentence?
11. The runaway teen's family.

Can you reword this run-on sentence into a proper sentence?
12. She ran away from home and didn't know where she would live and what she would be doing.

Paragraphs

The last item of the required basic writing skills is paragraphs. To write in paragraphs means that you are able to write in separate but related sentences. To make a paragraph, these related sentences must include a beginning sentence, a middle sentence or sentences, and an end sentence. Here are the main features:

- The first sentence of the paragraph is the *topic sentence*, which presents one main idea or point.
- The other sentences follow by clarifying the words of the topic sentence.
- A final sentence ends the clarification or provides a *transition* (connection) to the next paragraph.

Two common problems for students are (1) paragraphs with too many points or (2) paragraphs that are one sentence. Both make it difficult for the reader to understand what the writer is presenting. Too many points or ideas in a paragraph can be resolved by using more paragraphs. Writing more sentences to clarify your point or idea can expand a vague one-sentence paragraph.

This completes the list of basic writing skills that your instructor will assume that you already have. If you had problems understanding these and found it difficult to answer the questions correctly, you are probably not ready to write a social science term paper or book review.

If you lack these skills, take an English writing course to improve your ability to understand and write clearly. You do not want to put yourself in a situation where you are trying to learn basic writing skills while you are also struggling to understand the material of a social science course(s). You will feel overwhelmed.

TIPS Check out the writing and learning resources available on your community college or university website. Many of these resources are also available through the library.

If you feel that you have a good understanding of these basic writing skills, you are ready to write a social science term paper or book review. Remember, though, that you must continue to develop your writing knowledge and skills beyond the elementary ones presented here.

4. Can I Recognize the Building Blocks of Research and Writing?

Most social science researchers and writers take for granted that you are familiar with presenting an idea, stating what that idea means, and providing evidence or an example of it. They might use more formal language, however. That is, the idea is referred to as a *concept*, the meaning of the idea becomes the *definition* of the concept, and the support for the concept and definition is called *evidence/example*.

Concept (C), definition (D), and evidence/example (E) are used like an unwritten code in research and writing. When all the items of this code are used, they form a basic unit and process for presenting knowledge. Here, they are referred to simply as essential building blocks that are used in undertaking research and writing. *You will see these building blocks used in this book.* Use Table I.1 below to help you visualize and remember these building blocks.

Table I.1 Building Blocks Used in Social Science Research and Writing

Everyday Language	Social Science Language	How to Remember Them?
Idea	Concept	C
Meaning	Definition of concept	D
Example	Evidence/example of concept and definition	E

See if you can recognize these items (C, D, and E) in the following writing sample:

Brym, Roberts, Lie, and Rytina (2013) write the following:

Ageism is prejudice about, and discrimination against, older people. Ageism is evident, for example, when older men are stereotyped as "grumpy" (p. 314).

Here is how these authors have used the writing method:

- C: The *concept* here is "ageism." Setting it in bold helps to identify it.
- D: The *definition* of the concept is "prejudice about, and discrimination against, older people."
- E: The *evidence/example* is "older men are stereotyped as 'grumpy.'"

You can use these building blocks in various ways. For example, you can follow a process that starts with a concept and ends with evidence/example, or you can start with evidence or example and end with a concept. As well, some authors may omit parts of these building blocks, such as the definition of a concept. Finally, you can add to the building blocks by using more than one concept, definition, and evidence/example. They may be used to create parts of a term paper, including a thesis statement or aim and supporting points and evidence.

These building blocks (C, D, and E) are introduced to you so that you are aware of and will recognize them (together or separately) in the research and writing of other authors. In turn, you will use them in your own research and writing of your term paper (or book review or article critique). It takes considerable practice to identify an author's use of C, D, and E. You can use your textbook(s) and readings for practice.

To help you get started, see if you can recognize the variety of ways that they are used in the following writing samples. Check Appendix C to see how you did.

Can You Recognize the Concept, Definition, and Evidence/Example in These Samples?

Sample 1

Maureen Baker (2008) writes the following:

The Canadian government also uses the concept of household in gathering statistics relating to family and personal life. Household refers to people sharing a dwelling, whether or not they are related by blood, adoption, or marriage. For example, a boarder might be part of the household, but not necessarily part of the family. Table 8.1 shows the percentage of Canadians living in various family types in 2001, compared to 1981. (p. 221)

Sample 2

Myers (2014) writes the following:

Adolescence—the years spent morphing from child to adult—starts with the physical beginnings of sexual maturity and ends with the social achievement of independent adult status. (p. 140)

Sample 3

Macionis and Gerber (2011) write the following:

. . . many academic disciplines are taking a global perspective, the study of the larger world and our society's place in it. What is the importance of a global perspective for sociology?

First, global awareness is a logical extension of the sociological perspective. Since sociology shows us that our place in society shapes our life experiences, it stands to reason that the position of our society in the larger world system affects everyone in Canada. Consider Canada's ambivalent relation to the United States—the destination of 85% of our exports—and our nation's attempts to come to terms with the economic powers of China and India. (p. 6)

Sample 4

Steckley and Letts (2013) write the following:

Socialization is a learning process, one that involves learning how to be a social person in a given society, and it brings changes in an individual's sense of self. This applies both in the earliest socialization that an individual undergoes in childhood, generally known as primary socialization, and in socialization that occurs later in life, which is sometimes known as secondary socialization. (p. 91)

5. What Will My Instructor Expect from Me in My Research and Writing Role?

Your instructor will expect the following from you as you carry out your new research and writing role:

- That you will understand and follow your instructor's directions
- That you will be an ethical author who will not plagiarize
- That you will learn proper referencing to avoid plagiarism

If you do not meet these expectations, you will lose marks and possibly fail your assignment.

You Must Understand and Follow Your Instructor's Directions

It may seem obvious that your instructor will assume that you are following her or his directions in writing your term paper or book review. This means that you understand the given instructions and that you will carry them out to the best of your abilities. If you do not understand any aspect of the requirements, then the onus is on you to talk to or confer with your instructor.

You Must Be an Ethical Author Who Will Not Plagiarize

In carrying out these requirements, your instructor expects you to do your own work. What this means for you is this: *everything in your social science term paper, book review, or article critique will be considered your work unless you include a reference to someone else's work.*

You are the author of your term paper or book review (or article critique) and will receive credit for doing that work.

To conduct yourself ethically means that you will *not* commit the following:

- Copy part or all of another student's work
- Download, copy, and paste from the Internet
- Buy or pay someone else to write your term paper or book review
- Sell your term paper or book review

The above are all examples of unethical conduct in writing a term paper or book review. They are also examples of plagiarism. Plagiarism means that you are trying to take credit for someone else's work. You are also participating in plagiarism if you are helping someone else achieve credit for work that she or he did not do. All instructors consider plagiarism to be stealing.

> ## Reminder
> Take all necessary writing and referencing steps to avoid plagiarism. Most institutions have strict disciplinary policies in response to plagiarism. Penalties may include a failing grade or a potential expulsion from the student's institution.

To avoid plagiarism and unethical conduct, you need to understand the distinction between a student who helps you by editing your work (called *peer editing*) and one who rewrites part of it. Peer editing generally refers to the process whereby another student points out your specific writing errors in spelling, punctuation, grammar, and sentences. Being made aware of these errors is helpful to you in order to improve your writing. However, you must make these corrections yourself. When you do so, you are conducting yourself ethically because you are doing your own work. If someone else, such as a student or friend, however, *rewrites* any part of your work, such as a sentence or a paragraph, then that is not your work. You would be claiming credit for writing that you did not do and that is not yours. This is also considered plagiarism and is unethical. You must know and use this distinction whenever someone helps you with your work.

You Must Learn Proper Referencing to Avoid Plagiarism

For a social science term paper based on research, you are expected to include *references*. These reference sources are from other authors whose ideas and research you are using for the purpose of your term paper (or other work).

When you provide a reference source or document your research sources, your instructor will know that you are using someone else's ideas or information in your term paper and giving that author credit. *You are expected to do this*. Indeed, using and giving credit to sources that assist you demonstrates to your instructor that you have done a lot of work for your term paper.

You will, however, run into serious problems with your instructor if you do not follow the proper referencing of someone else's ideas or research in your term paper (or book review). When you do *not* provide a reference for an idea or information that is not yours, you are saying, essentially, that this is your idea or information. Remember, anything in your term paper (or book review or article critique) is considered your work by your instructor. When you do not document your reference sources, your instructor will assume that you are trying to take credit for someone else's work and she or he will accuse you of plagiarism. And many colleges and universities subscribe to software companies (for example, Turnitin) that detect plagiarism and unethical work.

To avoid plagiarism you *must* provide references for the following:

- Someone else's words, ideas, or information
- Quotes, paraphrasing, summary, or a condensed version of another author's work
- Mimicking someone's structure, organization, theme, or paragraph

In other words, when you use someone else's work (their words, ideas, or information)—even when you reword their work in your own words (by paraphrasing, summarizing, or condensing it)—you *must* provide a reference to that author. You must also include a reference if you follow the author's organization of idea(s), even for a paragraph, to avoid committing plagiarism. If you have any doubts about what to do, talk to your instructor *before* you hand in your work.

Because your instructor will not accept ignorance of plagiarism as an acceptable excuse, you must learn how to avoid it. This book will help you to avoid plagiarism. It will show you how to reference properly according to the APA, CMS, and ASA formatting styles. In addition, this book will show you how using an outline will help you to

- record every source in your outline, and
- keep track of your sources in one place.

6. What Specific Requirements Must I Follow in My Term Paper?

Your instructor will inform you about specific requirements for your term paper. (See Chapter 6 for requirements for book reviews and article critiques.)

Instructors in the social sciences and related fields of study require students to follow certain formatting and referencing styles. Many follow *one* of the three styles that are presented here:

- The *Publication Manual of the American Psychological Association* (APA)
- The *Chicago Manual of Style* (CMS)
- The *American Sociological Association Style Guide* (ASA)

You will need to know which *one* of these styles your instructor requires you to use. The style chosen has implications for a number of items in your term paper, including the following:

- The title page
- Headers
- An abstract (if required)
- The page on which your text starts
- In-text citations
- Quotations
- References page

Record the general style that you are required to use. As well, instructors often adapt these styles to suit the needs of their course(s), in which case, you will require detailed information of how your particular instructor does so. You must record and follow these requirements.

Due Date

Your instructor will give you a deadline for handing in your term paper. It is your responsibility to meet all deadlines and timelines, so be sure to record all due dates and times.

Some instructors impose penalties if you submit your work after the date and time it is due. If you have a problem with the deadline, you should contact your instructor *before* your work is due.

Length

Your instructor may stipulate the required length of your social science term paper in the following ways:

- Number of pages (for example, 6–8 pages or 10–12 pages)
- Number of words (for example, 1200–1500 words or 2500 words)
- Number of arguments (for example, five arguments or eight arguments)

This book presents a social science term paper based on *arguments* (this will be clarified starting with the next chapter). You must present enough arguments within your term paper to fulfill your instructor's page or word requirement. As a student you may not know how many arguments to include because there are various factors that will affect your term paper length, such as writing style and ability to clarify ideas.

 TIPS Have more arguments than necessary to fulfill page or word requirements. It is easier to reduce arguments by keeping the most convincing ones than it is to search for more arguments later.

For most students, a short five-argument term paper may take anywhere from 6 to 10 pages while a longer eight-argument one usually takes 8 to 12 pages to complete. Again, there are various writing factors that influence the total number of pages or words.

Standard Outline

Most instructors strongly recommend that you create and use an outline to write your term paper. This book will help you use a standardized outline to write your first social science term paper. This involves the following steps:

- Use or create a computer file of a standardized outline from Appendix E or F of this book to get started.
- Use this outline not just as an exercise but also as a template for writing your term paper.
- Change or adapt this standard outline as directed by your instructor.

You should also find out the following from your instructor:

- Is your outline to be handed in? If so, what is the due date and time?
- Is the outline to be attached to your term paper?

Title Page

Most instructors require a title page for a term paper. Students are generally required to include some or all of the following items on a title page. For now, record (so that you will remember) which of the following are required to be on your title page (see Chapter 5 for examples):

- A page header
- The title of the term paper
- Your name
- Your student number
- The course name and number, and the section number
- Your instructor's name
- The name of your college or university
- The date (by which the term paper must be submitted) and time if submitted online

If you are unsure about any of these requirements, contact your instructor for clarification.

Abstract

An *abstract* is a brief summary of your term paper on a separate page after the title page. Check to see if you are required to include one. If yes, then follow the APA, CMS, or ASA style for length and format (presented in Chapter 5).

References

A *reference* refers to the research source that you consult and use in your term paper. Your instructor may require you to have the following:

- A minimum number of sources (books or periodicals)
- Acceptable kinds of sources (they should contain quality information and will most likely come from various fields of study, including the one you are studying)

If you have any doubts about the acceptability of a source (for instance, a Web-based source), consult your instructor *before* you write your term paper.

A *referencing style* refers to a particular way of formatting your sources inside and at the end of your term paper (see Chapter 3 for details). All instructors will require you to learn one referencing style. You must learn it to reference or *document* the sources that you use in your writing. For a social science term paper, you must learn to find, use, and record references. This book will help you learn how to do this.

All three styles have guidelines concerning what to include and how to present in-text citations and the references page. These are pointed out in Chapter 3, where reference styles are presented. Chapter 5 offers examples of reference pages. In general:

- APA style is different from CMS and ASA styles.
- CMS style in this book is limited to the social science way of doing

referencing, which uses the author/date system. We do not include foot-notes or endnotes, which are common in humanities courses.

- ASA style is based in large part on the comprehensive CMS style, although some differences exist. Whenever there are particulars of style that are not outlined in ASA style, instructors tend to use CMS style.

Computer software exists to help you with referencing your sources of research and formatting them correctly according to a particular style. Such software, includ-ing *RefWorks*, *EndNote*, and *MyBib*, is referred to generally as reference management software. Many college and university libraries use referencing software. Check with your librarian to see if it is *up-to-date*.

Page Numbers

Each referencing style has a way to number its pages. The APA style is different from that of CMS and ASA, which are similar. Your instructor's referencing style will deter-mine how your pages are numbered. You may also require some detailed informa-tion from your instructor on these styles. For example:

- APA page numbering starts with the title page as page 1 and ends with the last page of the references. If your instructor requires something more or different, record this.
- CMS and ASA page numbering start with the text of your term paper as page 1 and end with the last page of the references. Here, too, if your instructor requires something more or different, record this.

Page numbering examples are provided in Chapter 5.

Margins, Font Size, and Type

To ensure that all students meet the required length of the term paper, given in terms of pages, your instructor will usually stipulate the margins, font size, and type required. The following are generally required:

- Margins: one inch or 2.54 cm
- Font size: 12 point
- Font type: Times New Roman

Clarify the acceptable font size and type with your instructor *before* writing your term paper or book review.

Lastly, once your instructor has stated the specific requirements for your term paper, book review, or article critique, your instructor will assume that you are now starting to work on it.

Chapter Summary

How this book will help you write a term paper or book review:

- It will introduce you to a starting argumentative format and process for researching and writing a social science term paper, book review, or article critique.
- It will teach you some ways to adapt this format and process for various instructors who may require a different kind of argumentative term paper, book review, or article critique.
- This book will present you with some ways to add to this starting format and process for future term papers, book reviews, or article critiques.
- It will present some common APA, CMS, and ASA referencing styles to document your research.
- It will inform you of some ways that your instructor might use this basic argumentative format and process to evaluate and grade your term paper, book review, or article critique.

How this book is organized:

- This book is organized according to a practical process approach to researching and writing a term paper (or book review or article critique). It presents a basic social science argumentative format and process with a corresponding outline. Research is arranged into priorities so that once they are completed so is your research outline. Three (APA, CMS, and ASA) referencing styles are offered to document your research. The starting point for research and writing is individual arguments. This book will show you how to create headings/themes from individual arguments. The completed outline is then used to write your individual argument or headings/themes term paper. How to write a coherent term paper and fulfill instructor requirements completes the writing of a term paper. A similar process is presented for writing a book review or an article critique.

The basic knowledge about reading and writing and required skills you must have:

- You must know how to read to understand and critically evaluate information.
- You must have basic writing skills of spelling, grammar, punctuation, sentences, and paragraphs.
- You will have to decide if you have the basic reading and writing skills to research and write a social science term paper or book review.

Building blocks of research and writing: concept, definition, and evidence/example

- Learn how social scientists use concept (C), definition (D), and evidence/example (E) so that you can use them in your research and writing.

The fundamental expectations about your new research and writing role:

- You must follow your instructor's directions for your term paper or book review over those of this book.
- You must be aware that everything you write in your term paper or book review is considered your work unless you reference it.
- You must provide a reference source for someone else's words, ideas, information, or how these materials are organized and presented by someone else.
- If you do not provide a required reference source for the preceding, your instructor will accuse you of plagiarism.
- You must conduct your research and writing ethically (do your own work; do not simply copy and paste material; do not buy or sell your work).

Specific requirements to record for your term paper:

- You must record the specific requirements for your term paper, including due date; length; standard outline; title page (based on one of the three reference styles: APA, CMS, or ASA); abstract (based on a reference style); references (based on a reference style); page numbers; and margins, font size, and type. (See below.)

✔️ Checklist for Term Paper Requirements

Basic knowledge about reading and writing and required skills:

☐ Do you have the basic reading and writing skills to write a social science term paper (or book review)?

Building blocks of research and writing: concept, definition, and evidence/example

☐ Do you know the meaning of concept (C), definition (D), and evidence/example (E)?
☐ Can you recognize their use in research and writing so that you can use them as well?

Fundamental expectations about your new research and writing role:

☐ Do you know that the entire term paper or book review is considered your work unless you refer to someone else's work?

☐ Do you know what plagiarism means, what it involves, and the serious consequences that might result if you plagiarize?

☐ Do you know how to conduct yourself ethically and how to research and write ethically?

Specific requirements to record for your term paper:

For due date:

☐ What day and time must your term paper be submitted?

For length:

☐ Is the length of your term paper based on the number of words, pages, or arguments?

☐ How many words, pages, or arguments are required?

For standard outline of term paper:

☐ Is a standard outline required as per Appendix E or F?

☐ Are any changes required to this standard outline as directed by your instructor?

☐ Does your outline have to be submitted?

☐ What is the outline due date and time, if the outline is required to be submitted?

For title page:

☐ Is a page header required?

☐ Did you record any particular requirements for a title?

☐ Is your student name and your number required?

☐ Is your course name and number plus section number required?

☐ Is your instructor's name required?

☐ Is your college or university name required?

☐ Is the due date required?

For abstract:

☐ Is an abstract required for your term paper?

☐ What style (APA, CMS, or ASA) must be used?

For references:

☐ What is the minimum number of references required?

☐ What are acceptable/unacceptable kinds of references?

☐ What referencing style (APA, CMS, or ASA) must be used?

continued

For page numbering:
- ☐ What referencing style does your instructor require (APA, CMS, or ASA)?
- ☐ Does your page number 1 start with the title page or the text of your term paper?

For margins, font size, and type:
- ☐ Does your paper have one-inch or 2.54 cm margins?
- ☐ What font size is required (for example, 12 point)?
- ☐ What font type is required (for example, Times New Roman)?

Recommended Websites

Purdue University
Purdue OWL for grammar:
https://owl.english.purdue.edu/owl/section/1/5/

Purdue OWL for writing and research:
http://owl.english.purdue.edu

Purdue OWL to understand paragraphs:
http://owl.english.purdue.edu/owl/resource/606/01/

University of Waterloo
University of Waterloo Library, on plagiarism, by Christine Jewel:
https://www.youtube.com/watch?v=sWrFrB9EsAo

University of Wisconsin at Madison
Writing Center, on writing and research:
http://www.wisc.edu/writing/Handbook/index.html

Recommended Readings

Engkent, L., & Engkent, G. (2013). *Essay do's and don'ts: A practical guide to essay writing.* Don Mills, ON: Oxford University Press.
Messenger, W.E., de Bruyn, J., Brown, J., & Montagnes, R. (2012). *The Canadian writer's handbook: Essentials edition.* Don Mills, ON: Oxford University Press.
Norton, S., & Green, B. (2011). *Essay essentials with readings* (5th ed.). Scarborough, ON: Thomson/Nelson.

Chapter 1

Learn the Basic Social Science Argumentative Format and Process

To start you on your way to research and write a social science term paper, you will need to learn the following:

1. The basic social science argumentative format and process
2. The argumentative roots of the basic social science argumentative format and process
3. How to choose one of three kinds of term papers
4. How to use a standardized social science outline for your research priorities and for writing your term paper
5. How to visualize the basic social science research and writing process

1.1 What Is the Basic Social Science Argumentative Format and Process?

A basic social science argumentative format and process for writing a term paper (or a book review or an article critique) is presented below (notably 1 to 5). This is followed by the meaning of these words or *terms*.

The Basic Social Science Argumentative Format and Process

1. Aim
2. Definition of concepts
3. Organization of arguments or headings/themes
4. Presentation of arguments or headings/themes
5. Conclusion
6. In-text citations (APA, CMS, or ASA style)
7. References (APA, CMS, or ASA style)

We elaborate on all seven of these items in future chapters (especially in Chapters 2 to 4).

Following is the general meaning of each of the preceding terms:

1. *Aim*: We use the word *aim* to refer to the term paper's overall purpose or focus. A student should write the aim of the term paper in a sentence or, alternatively, as a question. Hence, the aim sentence or question presents the overall purpose and guides your entire term paper.

2. *Definition of concepts*: The aim sentence or question will contain key ideas or concepts. These ideas or concepts are defined so the reader can understand their meaning and use. "Definition of concepts" thus refers to clarifying the meaning of the words that present these key ideas, thoughts, or mental images. You will use the meaning or definition of these concepts in your aim for your entire term paper.

3. *Organization of arguments or headings/themes*: This refers to the sequence or order of arguments. Your term paper will contain arguments that you will arrange in a logical manner to support your aim. The same applies to the headings or themes of your term paper.

4. *Presentation of arguments* (or simply *arguments*) *or headings/themes*: The word *argument*, which generally means "to persuade," includes two parts: (1) point and (2) evidence. The word *point* refers to the reason for presenting your argument, concerning your aim. In other words, the point of the argument is the idea that you are putting forward. The *evidence* is the information, fact, result, or example that you are using to substantiate the point. In order to be called an argument, a statement must consist of a point and the evidence to support that point.

    The presentation of *headings or themes* consists of arguments that have been grouped together because they have something in common or are seen to be related to each other. (In some cases, only one argument may be presented.) Both the individual arguments and headings/ themes must appear in the same order as is stated in the previous section on the organization of arguments or headings/themes. Individual arguments and those grouped into headings or themes are used to substantiate the aim.

5. *Conclusion*: This refers to the summary and end of the term paper. Your social science term paper must have a conclusion. The conclusion consists primarily of your aim and how your arguments supported the aim.

6. *In-text citations*: The in-text citations are those research sources that are used in your term paper and formatted according to American Psychological Society (APA), *Chicago Manual of Style* (CMS), or American Sociological Society (ASA) style.

7. *References*: This refers to the full text of all your research sources that are used in your term paper and formatted according to the required APA, CMS, or ASA style. The word *bibliography* is used sometimes to refer to all the sources that you may have consulted for your social science term paper but not used in writing it. The references page is the last part of your term paper and thus appears at the end of your paper.

Here is some clarification of the terms *social science*, *format*, and *process* in the phrase "basic social science argumentative format and process."

- *Social science*: We use this term in its broadest meaning to include all the disciplines or fields (and related applied fields) that study people (behaviour, social interactions, and groups) in society. Other possible terms could be *behavioural science* or *life science*.

- *Format*: This refers to the individual items or parts in our list on p. 19. The word *basic* in this format means that these items are the minimum number that you must use. To use the basic social science argumentative format to research and write a term paper, then, means that you must include all seven items.

- *Process*: We use the word *process* in two general ways: (1) to refer to the writing process and (2) to refer to the research process. In the first, *process* refers to the sequence of writing the items or parts in the social science format. In the second, *process* refers to the sequence of research. The research process is divided into first and second priorities. The first priority process starts the research, and the second one ends it.

In the first outline for your term paper, you will use all the items in the basic social science argumentative format and process. The first outline starts with individual arguments, which you can then go on to group into headings/themes.

You should be able to tell from the preceding terms and their meaning where the building blocks for research and writing are being used. Here is Table 1.1 to help you:

Table 1.1 Where Do You Use the Building Blocks in the Basic Social Science Argumentative Format and Process?

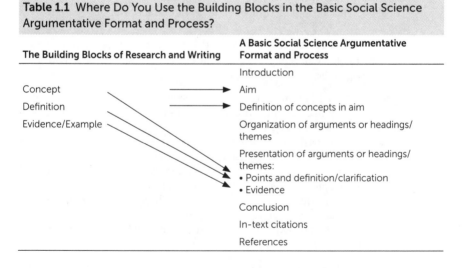

The Building Blocks of Research and Writing	A Basic Social Science Argumentative Format and Process
	Introduction
Concept	Aim
Definition	Definition of concepts in aim
Evidence/Example	Organization of arguments or headings/themes
	Presentation of arguments or headings/themes: • Points and definition/clarification • Evidence
	Conclusion
	In-text citations
	References

The building blocks are used here in a hierarchical way, starting with the *aim*, where only concepts are used. Similarly, only definitions are used in the *definition of concepts in the aim*. The aim and definitions are supported by *arguments*, consisting of *points* that contain concepts and their definitions and *evidence*. Despite this hierarchy, the aim and definitions along with their supporting arguments are interdependent. A weakness in one will have an impact on the other.

1.2 What Are the Argumentative Roots of the Basic Social Science Argumentative Format and Process?

The basic social science argumentative format and process is part of a *general argumentative tradition* of research and essay writing. Writers and researchers have carried on this argumentative research tradition or rhetoric tradition for centuries (Booth, Colomb, & Williams, 2008, pp. 9–15). The basic social science format and process is part of this larger argumentative community and discourse. Knowing how the social science argumentative format and process relates to the argumentative tradition will show you the following:

- That the starting items (the words and phrases) of the basic social science argumentative format and process come from the earlier, argumentative tradition (Corbett & Connors, 1999) and that they are not unique or original; they are a basic part (a start or foundation) of more aspects in the argumentative tradition
- That the items in the basic social science argumentative format and process are similar (despite using some different words) to those of the argumentative essay
- How much of an argumentative essay you are starting with by using the basic social science argumentative format and process
- What you still need to learn about writing arguments for a more advanced social science term paper (or book review or article critique)

The argumentative research tradition and basic social science argumentative format and process for writing a term paper are essentially similar. The two main differences are as follows:

1. The traditional argumentative essay presents a thesis or a claim that is supported by reasons and evidence. This kind of an essay uses argument in a general way to refer to the thesis or claim supported by reasons and evidence. The basic social science argumentative format and process, on the other hand, starts with a different and more specific use of the term *argument*. Here, argument is used to refer to points (or reasons) and evidence *to support an aim (or thesis)*. That is, an argument consists of points as well as evidence to support that point. These specific arguments are made in order to support a thesis or claim.

2. The basic argumentative format and process for writing a term paper *starts with fewer parts or items* than the traditional argumentative essay.

In the general argumentative tradition, the overall essay or term paper is referred to as an *argument*. The author's overall argument consists of a *claim* or a position taken on an issue. This claim or position is supported by reasons and evidence to make the claim convincing (Gooch & Seyler, 2013, pp. 16–24). A claim may also be called a *thesis* (Gooch & Seyler, 2013, p. 16). The thesis statement or claim refers to the sentence in which the author presents a stance or position on a topic or issue. The thesis statement is the overall argumentative position that the author will try to persuade the reader to accept.

The basic social science format and process for a term paper also has a general stance or position that is stated in the *aim* sentence. The aim is similar to a thesis and claim since all refer to the position that an author takes on a topic or issue. One difference between these two approaches, however, is in the use of the word *argument*. In the basic format and process, the word *argument* is limited to points and evidence. Such a use of *argument* would only refer to the reasons and evidence in the general argumentative tradition and not to a general use to refer to the overall argument being advanced. Hence, the word *argument* is used in a specified way in the basic format and process to help students learn the starting features for creating a generalized argument. As students become more experienced in creating and using arguments, they should be able to state that the general argument they are advancing is expressed in the aim sentence (as is the case in the general argumentative essay).

Furthermore, an argumentative research essay uses "information and analysis to support a thesis, to argue for a claim" (Gooch & Seyler, 2013, pp. 19–22). Research is undertaken to provide *reasons* and *evidence* to make a claim convincing (Gooch & Seyler, 2013, p. 19). Essentially, the claim or thesis of the essay is supported by reasons and analysis that are based on information and evidence.

The basic social science argumentative format and process is slightly different in its use of words to support an aim. An *argument* is used to support the aim. Remember that an argument consists of points and evidence. The meaning of *point* includes "reason." The meaning of *evidence* to support points or reasons is identical for both approaches. So, for the basic format and process, an argument consists of a point and evidence to support an aim. In the argumentative research essay, the emphasis is on reasons and evidence to support a thesis or claim. The difference between the two approaches is that the word *argument* is used in the basic format and process to get students started and used to thinking that they are presenting arguments to support an aim (or thesis). As well, arguments can be grouped into headings or themes, based on what they have in common, to support the aim.

In addition, the basic social science argumentative format and process consists of fewer parts than the general argumentative tradition. A typical argumentative research essay, according to Kirszner and Mandell (2011), begins with an introduction that contains a thesis statement on a particular issue. The body presents the reasons and evidence that support the thesis (*inductively*, i.e., from specific reasons and evidence to a general thesis; or *deductively*, i.e., from a general thesis to specific reasons and evidence). As well, arguments against the thesis and a rejection of those arguments are also presented. The conclusion restates the thesis, but is worded differently, and includes a strongly worded closing statement (pp. 12–14).

A term paper that is written by following the basic social science argumentative format and process has an introduction that includes an aim sentence (or thesis) on an issue or topic. Unlike the argumentative research essay, the introduction also includes defining concepts in the aim sentence and states how the arguments or groups of arguments are organized to demonstrate the aim. Initially, the aim is developed from arguments (using *inductive* reasoning). *Deductive* reasoning is added later. The first kind of argument is usually limited to those that support the aim. Arguments that oppose the aim, and their rejection, are added later. The conclusion restates the aim sentence, summarizes the arguments, and clarifies how the arguments supported the aim. Unlike an argumentative research essay, there is no strongly worded closing statement.

Table 1.2 summarizes the relationship between these two approaches:

Table 1.2 The Argumentative Tradition and the Basic Social Science Argumentative Format and Process

Argumentative Research Tradition	Basic Social Science Argumentative Format and Process
Introduction • Introduce the issue. • Provide thesis statement.	*Introduction* • Introduce the aim. • Provide aim sentence. • Define concepts. • Organize arguments or headings/themes.
Body • Use inductive reasoning: evidence to support the thesis. • Use deductive reasoning: thesis that requires supporting evidence. • State arguments against thesis and refute them.	*Body* • Use arguments or headings/themes to create aim (inductive). • Later, add arguments or headings/themes against aim and refute those arguments or headings/themes. • Later, add deductive reasoning.
Conclusion • Restate thesis. • Add a strongly worded closing statement.	*Conclusion* • Restate aim. • Restate arguments or headings/themes and how they supported the aim.

As Table 1.2 highlights, the basic social science argumentative format and process is a starting point for you to learn the argumentative research style:

- In the basic format and process, you expand the introduction to include the aim sentence (thesis statement), define the concepts in the aim sentence, and state how the arguments or headings/themes have been organized.
- You limit the argument or headings/themes section of the basic format and process to inductive reasoning until you become more familiar with making arguments or grouping them into headings/themes and creating an aim sentence. Once you become comfortable with this, and gain more experience, you can then add deductive reasoning.
- As well, you must learn to add arguments against your thesis or aim and provide reasons for rejecting those arguments or headings/themes. Indeed, your term paper may not be considered an argumentative research essay until you include these.
- Like the argumentative research essay, your conclusion in the basic format and process also focuses on restating the aim. However, in the basic format and process, you are also required to restate your arguments or headings/themes and how each supported your aim sentence.

Because the basic format and process is similar to the argumentative research essay, you are able to do the following:

- Look for and recognize the words or similar ones (and their meaning) from the basic format and process in the research of other writers. Knowing to look for and to recognize, for example, an aim in a book, periodical, and online source will help you be more efficient in your research.
- Write your views and research in a factual manner. This point is best expressed by Booth et al. (2008). Their view is that you should write your essay or term paper as if you, along with your reader, were seeking a co-operative answer to an issue or question (p. 106). Thus, the *tone* of your argumentative term paper should be friendly and neutral, not antagonistic or coercive.

TIPS Once you have learned the basic social science argumentative format and process, see if you can find these parts in your textbook or readings. Check to see how they are used and what more you can learn about their use in your field of studies.

Some writers on argumentative essays encourage you to develop an outline from your research notes (Reinking et al., 2010, pp. 417–419). However, as a student you may have difficulty creating your first outline. You are still learning to construct convincing arguments that support an aim and need an outline format that emphasizes arguments. Therefore, creating your own outline may be quite unfamiliar to you.

A standard social science outline was created to help you get started. All parts of the basic social science argumentative format and process are included in this outline. Here are some benefits to using a common outline in starting your research:

- There is one place (or file) to record your arguments and all other aspects of your term paper (or book review or article critique).
- The outline allows you to keep track of your arguments (points and evidence) and note where more research may be needed.
- The research information within the outline can easily be revised and reorganized.
- Your research is already recorded and organized based on the way that your term paper will be written, so you will be in good shape to start writing it.

After you have gained some experience using a common outline, you are expected to develop your own for a term paper (or for a book review or article critique).

Before you start your research, you need to consider which one of three general kinds of term papers to write. The basic social science argumentative format and process is used to show you the research and writing that is involved in each one of these term papers.

1.3 How Do I Choose One of the Three Kinds of Term Papers?

You will need to decide which *one* of the three kinds of term papers you plan to write. These three general kinds are as follows:

a. All the arguments or headings/themes are advanced to support the aim.
b. A majority of arguments or headings/themes support the aim while a minority oppose it.
c. There is a balance of arguments or headings/themes equally supporting and opposing the aim (the point and counterpoint type of essay).

TIPS If you are unsure what kind of term paper your instructor requires, read about these three kinds to understand them. Decide *after* reading about them which one or which variation of which kind is required. If you are unsure, contact your instructor right away.

A. All Arguments or Headings/Themes Support the Aim

Some instructors may begin by asking you to write a short argumentative term paper with a small number of arguments, such as up to five arguments. The reasons for such a short term paper may be as follows:

• To learn the various parts of the social science format
• To focus more on creating convincing arguments
• To practise writing this kind of a research term paper

Social science students should know how to write such a starting term paper. The basic social science argumentative format and process is repeated here to show you the general requirements for this kind of term paper.

• *Aim*: You must have a properly worded aim. It may be a sentence or a question to be answered. The aim must be worded to suit your course, discipline, or field of studies.
• *Definition of concepts in the aim*: The concepts in your aim will normally be defined according to your course, discipline, or field of studies. You must find and use these definitions accordingly.
• *Organization of arguments or headings/themes*: You must arrange your arguments or headings/themes that support your aim in a sequence, from first to last.
• *Presentation of arguments or headings/themes*: Your instructor may specify the number of arguments that you are required to have in support of your aim. A short paper may have up to five arguments while a longer paper may have up to eight. You must fulfill this requirement. For each argument, you must present a point and evidence to support that point, and each argument must be worded clearly to relate to your aim. The number of

arguments to be grouped into headings/themes must also be fulfilled. The headings/themes must relate clearly to your aim. If your instructor does not specify the number of arguments but states the number of words or pages, then you must have enough arguments to fulfill that requirement.

- *Conclusion*: Your conclusion must state how each of your arguments or headings/themes supported the aim.

- *References*: You must use the minimum number of references, as required by your instructor, in your term paper. Some instructors require fewer references for the first social science term paper (about six) and more for the second one (ten to twelve). Although these are a minimum, having a few more than the required number is preferable. A longer term paper that has more arguments and references will result in a greater understanding of the material.

B. The Majority of Arguments or Headings/Themes Support the Aim While the Minority Oppose It

For this kind of a term paper, the majority of arguments or headings/themes support the aim sentence. A minority of arguments or headings/themes, usually one or two, then oppose or contradict the aim. Each argument that opposes the aim is in turn argued against, or refuted, to show that the opposing argument has little or a negligible effect on the aim. The same is true for headings or themes. You should refute each opposing argument after it is presented. In other words, state that the argument has minimal impact on the aim and give a specific reason for rejecting it.

This term paper begins in a similar way to the previous one. The requirements for the *aim* and *definition of concepts in the aim* are the same. Some differences start, however, with organization of arguments or headings/themes.

- *Organization of arguments or headings/themes*: The arguments, or arguments grouped into headings or themes, that support the aim are presented first. Arrange their sequence the same way as in the previous kind of term paper and state the arguments in general terms.

  As mentioned, follow this with a brief reference to the arguments or headings/themes opposed to the aim sentence. State these arguments or headings/themes and provide a general reason or reasons why they have a minimal or negligible effect on the strength of the aim sentence.

- *Presentation of arguments or headings/themes*: Present a majority of arguments or headings/themes in support of the aim. For example, for a five-argument term paper, you could present three to four arguments in support of the aim and one to two arguments in opposition to it. For two to three headings or themes in support of the aim, you could present one opposed to it.

  A reason(s) for rejecting an opposing argument may or may not be presented as an argument. If you present a reason for rejecting an opposing argument and it is only a point then it is not a complete argument and should not count as one of your arguments. However, if your reason contains all the features of an argument (point and evidence), then you will tend to be more convincing. Your reason then should count as one of the total arguments required for an argumentative term paper.

- *Conclusion:* Begin your conclusion by restating the aim. Then, write a short sentence or two for each argument or group of arguments, stating how they supported the aim sentence. Follow with the arguments that oppose the aim.

    You might conclude this kind of a term paper with a statement to the effect that there were valid arguments that opposed your aim. However, their impact was negligible, and most of the arguments clearly supported the aim.

- *References:* You will need more references for this type of term paper than for the previous kind. This is because introducing opposing arguments or headings/themes and then refuting them generally requires providing reference sources for them.

C. A Balance of Arguments or Headings/Themes Supports and Opposes the Aim

The final kind of social science term paper presented here is one where there is a balance of arguments or headings/themes between those that support an aim and those that oppose it. This kind of term paper can also be seen as presenting both sides of an issue or problem.

Before starting this kind of term paper, you must find out

- if your instructor expects you to remain *neutral* in presenting both sides of an issue, or
- if you are expected to take a position and present both sides.

Most instructors prefer you to choose one side of arguments over the other. Depending on your instructor's requirements, there are three different ways to construct this kind of term paper:

1. Start with a neutral aim sentence or pose a neutral question, present both sides of it, and make a neutral conclusion. This shows the instructor that you have a good grasp of both sides of an issue. You also demonstrate your ability to remain neutral on the issue.
2. Start from a neutral standpoint, examine both sides, and then state in the conclusion which side of the aim or question you are taking. In this kind of a term paper, you can show not only a good grasp of both sides of an issue but go one step further by deciding that one side of the arguments is more persuasive than the other.
3. Present an issue, point out that there are two sides to that issue, and state your position on it. In other words, you state your position clearly at the beginning of the term paper, present both sides of the issue, and then affirm your final stance in the conclusion. Although this kind of a term paper is similar to the previous one, the difference is that the side you take is stated at the outset.

Become familiar with how you take a stance in these three types of term papers, the major part of which is to present both sides of an issue. Determine which way your instructor wants you to set up your term paper. Since all three are related, learn to shift from one to another.

- *Aim*: Word your aim sentence as neutrally as possible. At this point, each one of the three ways will create a different term paper. In the first way, or neutral stand, add that the objective is to present both sides of the issue so that the reader can decide which side to take. In the second way, after both sides have been presented fairly, suggest that one side will be favoured because of the persuasiveness of the arguments. In the third way, state that although both sides will be presented, you clearly prefer one.
- *Definition of concepts in the aim*: Define the concepts in the aim sentence, whether written as an issue or as a question. Define those concepts in a convincingly neutral manner that does not favour one side over the other, thereby demonstrating to your instructor your ability to remain neutral.

    If the favoured side uses a recognized concept from the course (or from the discipline or field of studies), then you will need to define that concept as well. However, if the side you choose uses everyday language, this is not necessary.
- *Organization of arguments or headings/themes*: There are two ways for you to organize these. They are as follows:
    1. *Separate the supporting and opposing arguments or headings/themes.* This is referred to as the *block method* (Davis et al., 2013, p. 107). Present all the arguments of one side followed by those of the other side. Unless directed by your instructor, decide for yourself which side to present first. You can start by presenting the arguments that oppose the issue followed by those that support it, or vice versa. However, write both sides of the issue *convincingly*. For the opposing arguments (grouped into headings or themes), follow the pattern of presenting the least important group of arguments first and end with the most important one. Use this pattern with the supporting groups of arguments as well.
    2. *Integrate the supporting and opposing arguments or headings/themes to show the preference for one side over the other.* This is referred to as the *point-by-point method* (Davis et al., 2013, p. 107). As in the first way, you can start with either supporting or opposing arguments. Continue to present one argument (or groups of arguments as headings or themes) advocating one side of the issue (the opposing side) followed by an argument for the supporting side throughout the paper.

        Although there are two general ways to present arguments or headings/themes (*separated* and *integrated*), try to use the integrated way in your paper in order to demonstrate a more knowledgeable, convincing understanding and analysis of the issue.
- *Presentation of arguments or headings/themes*: Present an equal number of arguments or headings/themes for and against an issue. For a five-argument term paper, this would mean presenting two arguments in support of the aim and two arguments opposed to it. One argument could then present the reason for favouring one side over the other. For headings/themes, this might involve two to three headings/themes for and against and an argument that is made in favour of one side over the other.

- *Conclusion*: You can have three possible conclusions for a balance-of-arguments or a headings/themes paper based on your aim.
  1. In the first way, you can remain neutral and offer no opinion about either side of the issue. Typically, you can leave it up to the reader (in this case, your instructor) to decide which side is more convincing. The main emphasis in your paper has been on presenting arguments or headings/themes on both sides of the debate with a minimum of bias toward either side. An instructor who requires this kind of a term paper is interested in determining your ability to remain neutral on an issue or problem.
  2. You can arrive at the second way to conclude after starting with a neutral stance in the aim sentence, presenting both sides, and then stating which side you favour. Provide a reason for preferring one side over the other. Typically, you would do this by finishing the statement, "This side was more convincing because . . ."
  3. The third and final way for you to conclude this kind of a term paper is to reaffirm the side that you supported at the start. In other words, restate the side that you supported in the aim sentence (issue or problem). You still present individual or grouped arguments for both sides, but the arguments you favoured refute those that you opposed. Hence, in the conclusion you reaffirm the position that you supported at the outset of the term paper, based on the persuasiveness of those arguments.
- *References*: Just as with the previous kind of term paper, more references than a term paper where all arguments support the aim are required here for the same reason (i.e., because introducing opposing arguments or headings/themes and then refuting them generally requires providing reference sources for them).

This section has presented three general kinds of argumentative term papers for you to consider writing. Here are some suggestions to help you decide which kind of term paper to write:

- If your instructor directs you to write a certain kind of essay, then you must do that. Use the basic social science argumentative format and process to help you.
- If your instructor gives you no direction, then she or he is most likely expecting type (b) (where a majority of arguments support the aim and a minority oppose it).
- If you have considerable writing experience you might try (c) (where a balance of arguments equally supports and opposes an aim).

1.4 How Do I Use a Standard Social Science Outline for My Research Priorities and to Write My Term Paper?

There are three general steps involved in the overall process of writing your term paper:

- Create your outline.
- Work on research priorities and record all aspects in your outline.
- Write your term paper based on your completed outline.

Create Your Outline

- Create and use a computer file of the standard example outline provided in Appendix E or F. (You might omit any unnecessary formatting, such as page or line borders.)
- Include all parts of the standard outline: from the title page to the references page. Leave some space to complete each section.
- Be sure to include all headings and subheadings in the outline that you create (for example, for the Arguments section include point and evidence for each argument in your outline).
- You can also print your outline and take it with you to do research. Remember to record your research in your computer file outline.

Work on Research Priorities and Record All Aspects in Your Outline

- The basic social science argumentative format and process is separated into two related parts referred to simply as the first-priority items and the second-priority ones.
- The first-priority and second-priority items are listed below.

Research Priorities

First Priority
- Aim
- Presentation of arguments or headings/themes (steps 1 and 2; see p. 58)
- In-text citations
- References

Second Priority
- Definition of concepts
- Organization of arguments or headings/themes (step 3; see p. 112)
- Conclusion
- In-text citations
- References

- Start your research with the first-priority items and record them in your outline until you have completed them (see details in chapters 2 and 3).
- Make any changes in the first-priority items as your research progresses. For headings or themes, there are two additional steps to work on to begin grouping arguments (see Chapter 2, p. 58).
- Revise your first-priority items before you start your second-priority ones.

- Research your second-priority items, record the research in your outline, and complete these items. For headings or themes, this is referred to as step 3, which is the final step for the outline. Make any changes as necessary (see details in Chapter 4).
- Once the second-priority items are finished, your outline is complete.

Some advantages to working with research priorities include the following:

- You can start working on parts of your term paper right away as you read or are being taught the chapters.
- By concentrating only on completing the first priority items, you have a smaller list of items to work on (by not having to worry about the second-priority items), you will know what to do for the second priority items, and you won't be wasting your time in making unnecessary changes to the second-priority aspects.

In general, using research priorities from the basic social science argumentative format and process is a relatively efficient and effective way to complete your outline and then write your term paper.

Write Your Term Paper Based on Your Completed Outline

- You should plan on two general steps to write your term paper: (1) write a *draft* from your completed outline, and then (2) *revise* your draft (details in Chapter 5).
- The completed outline gives you the main parts and the sequence to write a rough draft for your term paper.
- Following is the list of items you will need to write your draft with an added introduction to arouse interest in your aim.

Writing the Term Paper Draft

- Introduction to aim: "The (subject area/topic/issue) is important because . . ."
- Aim: "The aim of this paper is to demonstrate . . ."
- Definition of concepts: "The concepts in the aim that will be defined are . . ."
- Organization of arguments or headings/themes: "The sequence of the arguments or headings/themes will be as follows . . ."
- Presentation of arguments or headings/themes: "The first argument or heading/theme to demonstrate the aim (restate aim) is . . ."
- Conclusion: "In conclusion, this paper has demonstrated that (restate aim) . . ."
- In-text citations: Set in APA, CMS, or ASA style throughout term paper.
- References: Set in APA, CMS, or ASA style.

- All parts of your written draft must be related through the use of *transitions* that connect your sentences, paragraphs, and ideas (see suggestions in Chapter 5).
- Once you have written a draft, revise it to make sure that it is complete, coherent, and unified, without basic writing errors.
- After you have revised your draft, complete the other parts, including proper formatting, the abstract (if required), and the title page.
- Completing all these parts will produce your final copy, which you will submit to your instructor.

1.5 How Can I Visualize the Basic Social Science Research and Writing Process?

Table 1.3 and Figure 1.1 will help you visualize the basic social science research and writing process, consisting of individual arguments or headings/themes of arguments. (Table 1.3 is meant to be read one column at a time.)

Table 1.3 The Individual Arguments or Headings/Themes Arguments Term Paper

Know the Basic Social Science Argumentative Format and Process	*Work On* Research Priorities, Using a Standard Outline	*Write* the Social Science Term Paper
1. Aim	*First Priority:*	Introduction to aim
2. Definition of concepts	Aim	Aim
3. Organization of arguments or headings/themes	Presentation of argument or headings/thems (Step 1 and Step 2)	Definition of concepts
4. Presentation of arguments or headings/themes	In-text citations	Organizaton of arguments or headings/themes
5. Conclusion	References	Presentation of arguments or headings/themes
6. In-text citations	*Second Priority:*	Conclusion
7. References	Definition of concepts	(In-text citations throughout term paper)
	Organization of arguments or headings/themes (Step 3)	References
	Conclusion	
	In-text citations	
	References	

Figure 1.1 is a flow chart to help you visualize the various steps that are involved in researching and writing your term paper. This chart helps you to

- plan the sequence of your research and writing, and
- keep track of where you are and what you need to do.

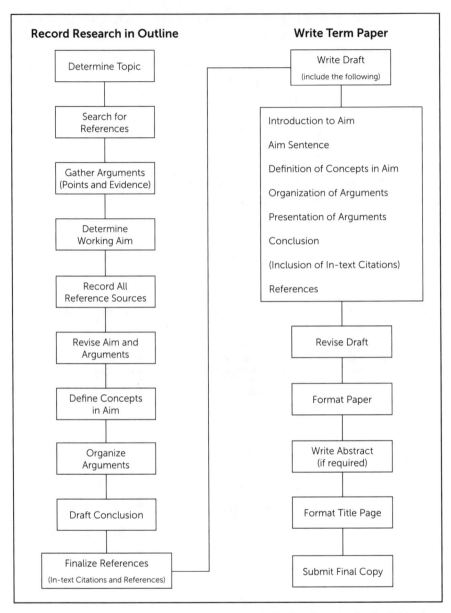

Figure 1.1 A Basic Social Science Research and Writing Process for Individual Arguments

Next, Table 1.4 and Figure 1.2 will help you create, organize, and use headings/themes to research and write a basic social science argumentative term paper. In particular, Table 1.4 shows you how to create and organize headings/themes starting with individual arguments. There are three general steps involved:

1. *Create individual arguments using point and evidence.* You already know how to word points with evidence of individual arguments from the previous section. See Step 1 of Table 1.4 below.

2. *Create headings or themes; group related points of arguments.* Use your wording of the points of each argument to give them a *heading/theme* based on what they are about or have in common. (Remember that the wording of each heading/theme must relate clearly to your aim.) Table 1.4 refers to the name of each group of related arguments simply as Name A, Name B, and Name C. The names of A, B, and C are the words of each heading/theme that contain the related arguments from the previous step. An individual argument would be by itself and have a name as a heading or theme, as is shown in Name C.

3. *Organize the headings/themes into a sequence.* Usually, there is a reason provided for the sequence of the headings/themes. Organize your headings/themes according to this reason. Table 1.4 shows how the name or wording of each heading/theme is organized into a sequence, from the first heading to the third heading. That is, the heading/theme with Name C is made the first heading, Name A becomes the second heading, and Name B is considered to be the third heading. Also, for each heading/theme organize the individual arguments/points into a sequence as shown in Table 1.4, Step 3, below the name/wording of each heading/theme. For instance, notice that the third heading with Name B contains individual arguments arranged 1, 2, and 3 in support of this heading from the previous sequence of 1, 6, and 2. Now, both the headings/themes and their individual supporting arguments are organized into a sequence.

Table 1.4 How to Create and Organize Headings/Themes

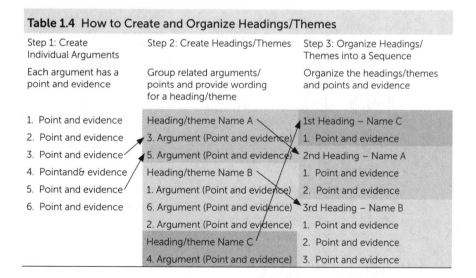

Step 1: Create Individual Arguments	Step 2: Create Headings/Themes	Step 3: Organize Headings/Themes into a Sequence
Each argument has a point and evidence	Group related arguments/ points and provide wording for a heading/theme	Organize the headings/themes and points and evidence
1. Point and evidence	Heading/theme Name A	1st Heading – Name C
2. Point and evidence	3. Argument (Point and evidence)	1. Point and evidence
3. Point and evidence	5. Argument (Point and evidence)	2nd Heading – Name A
4. Pointand& evidence	Heading/theme Name B	1. Point and evidence
5. Point and evidence	1. Argument (Point and evidence)	2. Point and evidence
6. Point and evidence	6. Argument (Point and evidence)	3rd Heading – Name B
	2. Argument (Point and evidence)	1. Point and evidence
	Heading/theme Name C	2. Point and evidence
	4. Argument (Point and evidence)	3. Point and evidence

Figure 1.2 expands on the previous flow chart (Figure 1.1) to help you visualize how to research and write a term paper using headings/themes.

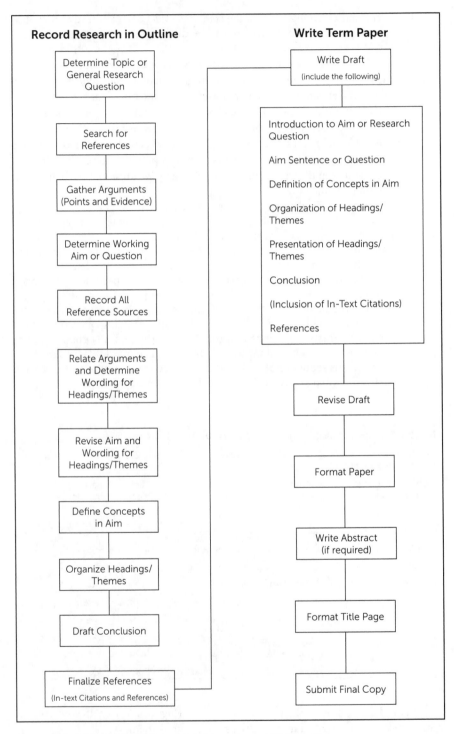

Figure 1.2 A Basic Social Science Research and Writing Process:
Use of Headings/Themes

As you gain more experience through course work, research and writing is not as straightforward as it appears in these beginning diagrams. You may change one part, which will involve returning to another, and so forth. You may write and re-write what you have written several times or more. That is the nature of the creative process in research and writing. The diagrams, with their basic items and steps, will help you start that journey.

Chapter Summary

Learn the basic social science argumentative format and process:

- Include the aim, definition of concepts, organization of arguments or head-ings/themes, presentation of arguments or headings/themes, conclusion, in-text citations, and references.
- Learn how the building blocks are part of the basic social science argumen-tative format and process.

Consider writing one of three kinds of term papers:

1. Where all arguments or headings/themes support the aim
2. Where a majority of arguments or headings/themes support the aim while a minority oppose it
3. Where there is a balance of arguments or headings/themes

Use a standard social science outline for research priorities and for writing your term paper:

Create a social science outline.

- Create a computer file of the standardized outline from Appendix E or F.
- Include all headings and subheadings.

Work on research priorities to complete the outline.

- Start and complete first-priority items and then complete second-priority ones.

Write your term paper based on the completed outline.

- Use your completed outline to write a draft of your term paper, with transitions.
- Revise your draft (that is, proofread, check for coherence).
- Format your term paper.
- Write an abstract (if required).
- Include a title page.

Visualize your research and writing:

- There are two ways to research and write the term paper: individual arguments or those grouped into headings/themes.
- Use diagrams to plan your research and writing.
- Use a chart of research and writing to check where you are in the process and to see what still needs to be completed.

✓ Checklist for Term Paper Research and Writing

Do you know the basic social science argumentative format and process?

☐ Do you know how the items of the building block for research and writing are used in the basic social science argumentative format and process?

☐ Do you know what to add to the basic social science argumentative format and process from the argumentative research essay?

Which kind of term paper will you write?

a. One where all arguments or headings/themes support the aim
b. One where the majority of arguments or headings/themes support the aim while a minority oppose it
c. One where there is a balance of arguments or headings/themes

Do you know how you will use the standard social science outline?

☐ Did you create your required social science outline using Appendix E or F with any changes required by your instructor?

☐ Did you make a backup copy of your completed outline file in a separate storage device?

☐ Do you know whether you will use your outline to create individual arguments or use the three steps to create headings/themes?

☐ Can you visualize your research and writing?

☐ Can you follow the diagram plans to do your research and writing?

☐ Are you ready to start with priority-one items in the next two chapters?

Recommended Websites

Dartmouth College
Institute for Writing and Rhetoric: An overview of materials from topic, argument, and logic to writing style
http://writing-speech.dartmouth.edu/learning/materials-first-year-writers/logic-and-argument

Colorado State University
Writing at CSU: An overview of writing arguments
http://writing.colostate.edu/guides/guide.cfm?guideid=53

Recommended Readings

Alfano, C.L., & O'Brien, A.J. (2011). *Envision: Writing and researching arguments* (3rd ed.). Boston, MA: Longman.

Campbell, M., & Gregor, F. (2008). *Mapping social relations: A primer in doing institutional ethnography*. Toronto, ON: University of Toronto Press.

Henderson, E., & Moran, K.M. (2014). *The empowered writer: An essential guide to writing, reading, & research* (2nd ed.). Don Mills, ON: Oxford University Press.

Kirszner, L.G., & Mandell, S.R. (2011). *Introducing practical argument: A text and anthology*. Boston, MA: Bedford/St. Martin's.

Kirszner, L.G., & Mandell, S.R. (2012). *Patterns for college writing: A rhetorical reader and guide* (12th ed.). Boston, MA: Bedford/St. Martin's.

Muth, F.M. (2006). *Researching and writing: A portable guide*. Boston, MA: Bedford/St. Martin's.

Chapter 2

Research to Create an Aim, Arguments, and Headings/Themes

To start you on your research for your term paper, this chapter highlights the first-priority items of the basic social science argumentative format and process. It will show you how to create an aim and arguments and then how to combine those arguments to create headings/themes. Here is a general list of what you will learn and do:

1. Start by deciding on a topic, subject area, or question.
2. Learn how to create an aim.
3. Research to create arguments.
4. Develop your aim from your arguments and combine arguments to create headings/themes.

2.1 How Do I Choose a Topic, Subject Area, or Question?

Before you start on a topic, you should know what the word *topic* means. You must also determine if you are to choose your own topic or if your instructor will be choosing the topic for you.

2.1.1 You Must Know the Meaning of *Topic*

When you start your first social science term paper, you will hear the word *topic*. According to Davis et al. (2013), a topic is a general area of interest that needs to be developed (pp. 161–164). For Corbett and Connors (1999), a topic is a general subject area that you explore in depth (pp. 27–31). In other words, a topic is a general area of interest or subject matter that will be explored or developed into a possible term paper.

There are other words besides the word *topic* that are used to indicate a general interest to be explored, including the following:

- Subject area
- Problem area
- General issue

Here are two examples worded as topics, subject areas, problem areas, or general issues:

- Teen runaways
- Alcohol abuse

Another way to word a topic is as a question. Here are some examples:

Topic Worded as Question

For teen runaways:

- What about teens who run away?
- Where do teens run to?

For alcohol abuse:

- Who abuses alcohol?
- When do people abuse alcohol?

For a student, having a general topic (or subject area, problem area, issue, or question) is helpful. It gives you a place to start your research. There are two ways to get a topic: (1) your topic is assigned, or (2) you are free to choose your own topic.

2.1.2 You Are Assigned a Topic

An assigned topic means that your instructor may require you to do a research term paper on a certain topic. The reasons for this might be as follows:

- Because the topic is an important part of your course work
- So you can learn a certain part of your course work in more detail

There are at least two noteworthy benefits to you of having an assigned topic:

1. You know that the topic is *part of* and *fits in* with your course.
2. The *words* of your assigned topic are part of your course or field of studies.

Both of these benefits also apply when you are allowed to choose your own topic.

2.1.3 You Choose Your Own Topic

An instructor may allow you to choose your own topic for one of the following reasons:

- You may be more motivated to explore your own interests.
- You will learn how your personal interests can be turned into professional ones related to your course work or studies.

If you are allowed to choose your own topic for your term paper, you *must* still fulfill the previous requirements:

- Your topic must be part of and fit in with your course.
- The words of your topic must be part of the course or subject area that you are studying.

Your chosen topic will mean different things to instructors who teach different courses, subjects, or fields of studies called a *discipline* (which refers to a branch of knowledge like anthropology, psychology, or sociology). Various instructors will look at your topic from the point of view of their field of studies. Your topic must fit into their discipline and be worded accordingly. The professional wording used in a discipline is referred to as the *discourse* (or dialogue). To guide you, here are examples of teen runaways and alcohol abuse and possible wording for different courses:

Possible Wording of Topics for Different Disciplines

Course/discipline	Teen runaways	Alcohol abuse
Anthropology	Culture of teen runaways	Alcohol abuse in different cultures
Psychology	Personality traits of teen runaways	Alcohol abuse and perception
Sociology	Social relations of teen runaways	Alcohol abuse and the family
Social services	Shelter for teen runaways	Helping those who abuse alcohol go to detox

Note that the wording for each one of these general examples (teen runaways, alcohol abuse) differs depending on the course. That is, the same example is worded differently to suit each course.

The words used in the topics, so far, are everyday, common words. These words may or may not be used by researchers. Social science researchers may use different words in their discourse. For example:

- The everyday word *teen* may be substituted by the research word *adolescent*.
- The everyday words *alcohol abuse* might become *chemical dependence*.

You can find different synonyms for your topic by looking in dictionaries and encyclopedias for your field of studies, which we will present later in this chapter.

Instead of coming up with just one topic, you should have at least two to three topics. This is in case you have difficulty finding enough research references for your chosen topic in the time you have to do your term paper. There may be a variety of reasons for not finding as many research references as your instructor requires, such as that the research is written in another language or that the material is not readily available. Hence, you would then move on to your second choice and research it.

Once you have a number of possible topics for your term paper, you should consult with your instructor about them. Your instructor will be able to help you with possible words and ideas for your topic that are part of your course work. Pay

TIPS Consider doing a term paper from the point of view of a participant you are researching. For instance, think about writing a term paper from the perspective of a runaway teen or the parents of such a teen. As well, you might consider writing a paper from the point of view of a community or social service worker who is helping a runaway teen. Check with your instructor to see if researching and writing this kind of a term paper would be acceptable.

particular attention to your instructor's comments about your topic(s) even if they seem minor to you. These comments are meant to help you with your wording, ideas, and research.

The overall benefit of having a topic(s) is that it helps you get started on your research. However, *a topic is not an aim*. A topic is a good place to start your term paper, but you still have to develop your topic into an aim.

2.2 How Do I Create an Aim?

To create an aim for your term paper, you have to know the meaning of *aim* in the social sciences and how to write it in a sentence or question. Once you understand these basics, you can then go on to create your first aim from your arguments.

2.2.1 You Must Learn the Meaning of *Aim*

In the previous chapter the word *aim* was used in a general way to refer to the overall position or stance for your term paper. The word *aim* was used instead of *thesis*, although both have the same general meaning. You should know that there are other similar words that are used in the social sciences, including these:

- Purpose
- Focus
- Theme

Each one of these words can readily be substituted for *aim*. The reason these words, including *aim*, are used instead of *thesis* is to emphasize that there are additional requirements in the social sciences to present your overall opinion or focus. A beginning meaning for an *aim* in the social sciences is this:

- "The use of two differently worded ideas from a field of studies that express a general stance or position supported by convincing arguments."

This section will clarify what is assumed in understanding an aim. We refer to these assumptions as *principles* (which means that they are ways, actions, or conditions to follow) in order to create an aim in the social sciences.

There are four principles that you must know and follow to create an aim. These principles are related but will be presented one at a time:

1. Your aim must include two ideas written in words or phrases.
2. These two ideas must be a part of your course or field of studies.
3. The two ideas must be different.
4. You must state a relationship between these two different ideas that present an overall position.

Following, we clarify each one of these principles.

1. Your Aim Must Include Two Ideas or Concepts Written in Words or Phrases

An aim in the social sciences must have at least two ideas that are written in words or phrases:

*   The words *teen runaway* are not an aim because there is only one idea.
*   The phrase *alcohol abuse* is not an aim because there is only one idea.

Likewise, an attempt to turn one idea into a question for an aim will also not be acceptable.
Example:

> Who are teen runaways?
> What is alcohol abuse?

These are not acceptable aims because two ideas must be presented in an aim. Here are examples of two ideas for possible aims:

> Teen runaways and homelessness
> Teen runaways and deviant behaviour
> Alcohol abuse and memory loss
> Alcohol abuse and Fetal Alcohol Spectrum Disorder (FASD)

For the above, *teen runaways* is one idea and *deviant behaviour* is another. Likewise, *alcohol abuse* is one idea and *memory loss* is another. While there must be *at least* two ideas in your aim, as a starting point this book presents only two.

2. You Must Word the Two Ideas to Be Part of Your Course or Field of Studies

The main reason that the ideas in your aim must be worded in a particular way is that each course or field of studies has its own basic language or *discourse*. The general language for each field of studies consists of concepts. Recall that a *concept* is a word or phrase that expresses an idea. That an idea is a concept (or vice versa) was introduced to you as part of the building blocks for doing research and writing. Your two ideas must be worded in the language of concepts that come from your course, field of studies, or discipline. If they do not, then you have to reword them to make them relevant. Your instructor may be able to help you by suggesting some concepts to consider in creating an aim relevant to your studies. If it is not possible to reword the aim, find another topic and develop another aim.

3. The Two Ideas or Concepts Must Be Different

Your aim must contain two *different* ideas or concepts. Notice that the examples from the first principle that presented two ideas were different. That is,

- the idea or concept of teen runaway is *different* from deviant behaviour;
- the concept of alcohol abuse is *different* from memory loss.

Your social science term paper will be about two different ideas or concepts and their relationship.

4. You Must State a Relationship between These Two Different Ideas or Concepts that Presents an Overall Position

The relationship between these two different ideas or concepts will be your overall position, or stand, which you will present in your aim. The wording of the relationship between your two different ideas or concepts will be your central idea, which you want to communicate to your instructor in your term paper.

Examples:

> Teen runaways will most likely be socialized into a deviant lifestyle.
> Teen runaways tend to come from dysfunctional families.
> Abusing alcohol may develop into memory loss.
> Alcohol abuse is likely to lead to spousal abuse.

Each of these examples presents something about how you see these two different ideas as related. Your aim must be worded to say something about the relationship between these two ideas or concepts. What you say in your aim about that relationship is your overall stance or position for your term paper.

2.2.2 You Must Learn How to Create an Aim Sentence

You should write your first aim as a proper sentence or question. Your sentence or question has to include all four of the preceding principles in order to be considered a proper aim by your instructor. As well, you should include a key word in your aim sentence or present your question in such a way that it indicates clearly to your instructor that this is your aim.

Following are some examples of aim sentences:

> The aim of this term paper is to show that teen runaways may be socialized into a deviant lifestyle.

> The purpose of this paper is to highlight that alcohol abuse may result in a child with FASD.

Following are examples of aims presented as questions:

> The main question addressed in this paper is this: Do teen runaways become street kids?

> Does alcohol abuse contribute to spousal abuse? That is the central problem of this term paper.

Note that there are two things that you need to convey to your instructor about your aim sentence or question:

- You must have a properly worded sentence or question. It must be grammatically correct so that your instructor can understand it.
- You have to say that this is your aim sentence or main question. *Your instructor should have no doubt what your aim is.*

Here are some *problems to avoid* in writing your aim sentence or central question:

- Do not use similar words to *aim* (such as *purpose, focus,* or *theme*) anywhere else in your term paper. Doing this may indicate that you have more than one aim and will make your case confusing to read.
- Do not omit any of the principles of creating an aim. This will weaken the aim for your term paper.
- You *must* have an aim sentence or main question for a social science research term paper.

2.2.3 You Must Learn How to Create Your Aim from Your Arguments

One way to create an aim is this:

- Start by creating arguments using reference sources from research.
- Then, develop a corresponding aim sentence about your arguments.

This way of creating an aim is called either the *bottom-up approach* (Norton & Green, 2011, pp. 30–36) or the *inductive approach* (Reinking et al., 2010, pp. 313–314). Both terms have a similar meaning. That is, both approaches involve the general process of going from specific arguments to a general aim for your term paper. Particular arguments about a topic are created first, and then an aim is developed about these arguments. The inductive or bottom-up approach is the one used here.

The benefits of starting this way are that

- the aim is based on the kind of arguments that have been created using research reference sources, and
- there are arguments to support the aim.

The wording of your aim will be based on the kind of arguments that you created from researching various reference sources. This avoids the problem of developing an arbitrary aim on a topic and then discovering little information on that topic. Also, your arguments will determine the stance or position of your aim. As a student you will learn that it is your arguments that will determine your view despite any preconceived notions that you might have about your topic.

Reminder

If your instructor has approved your topic of teen runaways, from a participant's perspective, your aim must also be based on the arguments that you create. That is, the arguments that you create about a participant will determine your aim.

As well, different kinds of arguments on a topic will lead to a different aim. That is why another student working on the same topic as you but with different arguments will have a different aim.

Your arguments may change or be altered based on your research, which will subsequently involve changing your aim (view, opinion, or stance). The arguments and aim are thus interrelated. Your aim must have supporting arguments; and your arguments must have a corresponding aim.

As you gain more research and writing experience through additional courses, you might begin with a possible aim and then search for related arguments. This research process is called a *top-down approach* (Norton & Green, 2011, pp. 36–41) or a *deductive approach* (Reinking et al., 2010, p. 315). Both approaches have a similar meaning, and both refer to undertaking research as a process that starts from a general aim, which then seeks particular arguments to support it.

This deductive approach is very useful if you already have some familiarity with research and reference sources, especially in a particular area of interest. Essentially, you would have some prior knowledge of research and reference sources to guide you. As a student, you will need to learn the deductive approach in addition to the inductive one presented here. Knowing both the inductive and deductive approaches is vital for further research.

One idea that both approaches use is that of a *working aim* or *tentative thesis*:

- A working aim (or tentative thesis) means that your stance, position, or view of the ideas being researched is preliminary or tentative.
- A working aim is a guess of what your aim might be, knowing that it will likely be revised or reworded, depending on the arguments that you present.
- For the inductive approach to research, you might refer to your first attempt at wording your aim as a *working aim* to see how the wording relates to the kind of arguments you have. It may take several tries at a working aim to be able to finalize your aim in relation to your arguments.
- For the deductive approach, a similar process exists. Starting with a working aim on a topic, your arguments will determine the final wording of your aim.

Both approaches use the idea of a working aim to help finalize the wording of an aim based on the actual arguments being presented.

A working aim is helpful because it indicates what your thinking is about the ideas in an aim. As a researcher, you must be open-minded and flexible enough to revise your thinking based on the arguments that you actually have.

2.3 How Do I Research to Create Arguments?

This section presents what is generally meant by an *argument* and offers suggestions on where you can obtain arguments. Use the building blocks to help you create arguments. The following sections point out various ways to use the building blocks or parts of them. Record and keep track of your arguments in your first social science outline, including your reference sources. As your arguments are created, you can then suggest a working aim. After you have made the required number of arguments and have a working aim to go with them, review your work so far with your instructor.

2.3.1 You Must Learn the Meaning of *Argument*

In the previous chapter, the word *argument* was used to refer to reasons or points and their supporting evidence to advance an aim. An argument consists of two related parts:

- The point being made
- The evidence to support that point

Both parts are required to make an argument. A single argument, then, consists of one point and the evidence to support that point to convince the reader (your instructor).

The words *point* or *reason* in an argument refer to a sentence that presents at least two or three ideas (or concepts). That is, a point or reason will usually be a statement or sentence that consists of at least two or three ideas. As a start, the number of ideas in a point is kept small deliberately to make them manageable.

The point of an argument will usually contain the two ideas of the aim sentence plus one further idea. For example, here is an aim sentence:

> The aim of this paper is to show that teen runaways are very likely to be involved in deviant behaviour.

The two main ideas in the aim are *teen runaways* and *deviant behaviour*.

Here is an example of a point in an argument about the aim sentence:

> Teen runaways are highly likely to be involved in the deviant behaviour of stealing.

The additional idea (or concept) to the aim sentence is the point that is being made about *stealing*. That is, stealing is one kind of deviant behaviour that involves teen runaways.

The point that you are presenting should always be clear so that the reader understands it. You can clarify your point by *defining* the concept or key word(s) that you used or by explaining what the point means. For instance, the point about stealing can be clarified as referring to theft, to taking something that does not belong to you. You can then reword your point as follows by using your clarification:

> Teen runaways are highly likely to be involved in the deviant behaviour
> of taking something that does not belong to them.

The definition or meaning of a concept clarifies the point and helps the reader to understand it better.

As a point for an argument, there must also be supporting evidence to the point about stealing. Essentially, this added idea of the point in the argument is linked to (or must relate to) the ideas in the aim.

There are a number of things to note about the use of the word *point*:

- Other words in place of the word *point* that can be used are *reason* or *main point*. It is in this way that you can use the phrase: *The point of this argument is . . .*
- Recall that one argument consists of a point and supporting evidence. Only one point or reason is required for one argument.
- As well, Norton and Green (2011) highlight that each point must be distinctive from any other point. That is, each point must have a separate meaning and cannot overlap with any other point (p. 42). Each point that you present must be different from the rest.

As well, a point or reason in an argument is different from the evidence supporting it. According to Booth et al. (2008), *evidence* is a statement of a shared and public fact (p. 131). A fact is offered to support the point of your argument and would not be questioned by your instructor (p. 131). Evidence is thus *different* from the point that you present.

Your instructor may use other words besides *evidence*. Here is a list of some of these words:

> Information, statistics, quantitative data, qualitative data, case studies, personal experience, proof, or illustrations.

These words suggest the various kinds of evidence, results, or findings, sometimes referred to as facts, that you will need.

Can you use personal experience as evidence?

- Some instructors will permit, even encourage, the use of personal experience as an example of a point while others will not.
- You will have to check with your instructor to see if descriptions of personal experience are within the boundary of acceptable evidence for your course or studies.

Based on this brief meaning of *evidence*, you may wonder how much evidence is enough in order to make your point convincing. Here are some guidelines about using evidence for your first social science term paper:

- You must have a least one fact for evidence.
- If you do not have any evidence for a point, then you do not have an argument. What you have is an opinion. An entire term paper consisting only of points is not acceptable because it lacks evidence to create arguments.
- If your term paper consists predominantly of descriptions of an event, issue, or people, without making a number of points, then you do not have an acceptable term paper. Here, your term paper would lack points to create arguments.
- Having one or two more facts ensures that you have corroborating evidence to support each point.
- For now, a limit on research evidence would be no more than two or three findings per point.

> **Reminder**
>
> You may have to produce any evidence from Internet or digital material that your instructor requests. Always make and keep a copy of such material to verify its existence to your instructor.

There is an important assumption about the evidence presented in support of a point. It is taken for granted that the evidence must be shown to relate to the point being made. The evidence does not speak for itself. You have to state how the evidence relates to the point.

> **What to Include in the Point and Evidence of an Argument**
>
> - The point being made with a concept(s)
> - The clarification/definition of the concept(s) of the point
> - The evidence to support the point being made
> - The explanation/relation of the evidence to the point

You should now be able to recognize how the concept, definition, and evidence/example are part of creating an argument.

2.3.2 You Must Look for Quality Research Sources

Before you start your research, whether online or in your college library, keep in mind that you are looking for quality sources. (See Appendix D for tips on selecting appropriate academic sources for a research paper.) One excellent indicator of a quality source is that it has undergone peer review. A *peer review* means that a number of scholars or specialists in the subject area have critically evaluated the work and recommended that it be published. Peer reviews provide a variety of checks on a work, such as accuracy and professional standards. They help to control the quality of what is published. Other sources will be useful to you as well. You may need to verify with other works the information that these sources provide.

Your overall research goal is to look through a variety of sources, most likely books and articles, that you think will be useful to create a working bibliography. The word *bibliography* refers to the list of research sources that you consulted on the topic of your term paper. The word *references* refers to the list of research sources that you actually used in writing your term paper. Searching online or in the library to create this list of sources that you *may* use is your *working bibliography*.

Reminder

A term paper topic written from a participant's viewpoint will be more convincing if you have research sources. Find and relate research sources to your participant's ideas and descriptions.

You should search for a variety of sources on your topic whether online or in print. Your search will most likely involve sources from related fields of study. Search for quality sources among the following:

Books or E-Books
Books may be in print or available online as e-books. Look for reputable, scholarly publishers, such as Oxford, Pearson.

- Check the preface and introduction for the author, the book's purpose, and the research methodology.
- Quality information is also indicated by books with reference sources and a bibliography. Books without these may contain less reliable information.
- Many people write books that may relate to your topic, such as a journalist's investigation of a topic or a politician's autobiography. Use such information appropriately and double-check it as necessary.

Journal and Periodical Articles
There are two general kinds of sources for articles: journal articles and articles in general periodicals. Both are usually available in print and online.

- The word *journal* refers to the professional magazines in which social scientists publish their work and research findings. All fields of study have professional associations that publish academic research articles in their journals. Many are peer reviewed and have high-quality standards. (Ask your instructor for some of the names of journals that might be useful in writing your term paper.)
- Many related fields to the one that you are studying may have useful articles in their journals. You should also consult articles in these related fields.

- An article in a general periodical, on the other hand, is meant to be read by the layperson. Articles in general periodicals present information on current topics, questions, and opinions. (Examples are *Psychology Today*, *The Economist*.)
- You can check the index of topics in the *Readers Guide to Periodical Literature*. You will find this index in the reference section of your library.

Government Publications and Reports

Various levels of government, from local to federal, and their departments produce reports and statistical information.

- There are numerous official publications about laws, policies, issues, and regulations.
- There are government census data (for every 5 or 10 years) although you will have to look elsewhere for more current information.
- You must assess government information (or an organization hired to produce a study for the government) based on the purpose, research methods, and data-collection method.

Newspaper and Magazine Articles

Most well-known magazines (e.g., *Time*, *Newsweek*) and newspapers (e.g., *The New York Times*, *The Globe and Mail*) are online and can be consulted for current events. You may use such information to explore a current issue or problem in depth.

Websites

There is an overwhelming amount of material available on the Internet. Many students simply start their research by typing the keywords of their topic into a search engine to see what happens. Here are some online results using the keywords *teen runaways*:

- *Google*: Over 2 million results, yielding general information and available help.
- *Google Scholar*: Over 7000 results, yielding various books, PDF sources, and no sequence of years; using the limiter "Since 2013" yielded 38 results, including literature and music.

Here are some results using the keywords *street kids*:

- *Google*: Over 1 billion results.
- *Google Scholar*: Almost 500,000 results; using "Since 2013" yielded over 2000 results.

The information from the preceding two results was interesting but not really useful for a social science term paper. Simply doing a number of Google searches does not really count as research. The next section will suggest how to use the Internet for research and how to find better-quality information on it.

2.3.3 Where Do I Research to Create Arguments?

While the nature of research has changed and will continue to do so as technology evolves, at present there are two general ways for you to obtain points and evidence for arguments:

- Internet research
- Library research

On the Internet

There are different ways to use the Internet for your research. If your social science topic is unfamiliar, you can use the Internet to learn something about that topic or to get a brief overview of an unfamiliar topic. (An overview of your topic means to obtain some background information that will help you to understand it.)

Start with the correct spelling and general meaning of the words of a topic. As well, attempt to determine the importance and extent of some of the major issues or problems of your topic. To get started you can use

- dictionaries, and
- encyclopedias.

Dictionaries: You can use a dictionary for the correct spelling of the words in your topic(s) and what your topic means. There are three kinds of dictionaries to note:

1. A general-use dictionary gives you the correct spelling of a word and what it means in everyday use. Examples include the following:

   http://dictionary.reference.com

   http://www.yourdictionary.com

   http://www.alphadictionary.com/index.shtml

   http://www.merriam-webster.com

Reminder

You do not need to reference words that you looked up and used from a general-use dictionary since anyone can look up that definition.

2. A dictionary specific to a field of studies gives you the spelling and meaning of a word used in a specific field of studies. Examples include the following:

   An online dictionary of anthropology: http://www.anthrobase.com/Dic/eng/

An online dictionary of psychology: http://allpsych.com/dictionary/

An online dictionary of social sciences (Canadian emphasis): http://bitbucket.icaap.org/dict.pl?alpha=P/

3. A dictionary on specific topics of a field of studies or related fields gives you the spelling and meaning of a word within a specified topic. An example:

An online dictionary of street drug slang: http://www.drugs.indiana.edu/drug-info/street-drug-slang-dictionary

Encyclopedias: An encyclopedia contains essays that you can use to help you understand your topic. Just like dictionaries, there are three general kinds of encyclopedias (you will most likely have to sign up to use encyclopedias on specific fields and topics):

1. A general-use encyclopedia gives the everyday understanding of topics or problems. Examples include the following:

http://www.encyclopedia.com/

http://en.wikipedia.org/wiki/Main_Page/

Table 2.1 Wikipedia—A Free Online General-Use Encyclopedia

Do	Avoid
use it to get a start on a topic, such as • a general meaning of your topic, • some of the issues involved, or • possible ideas.	using it as a reference source in your term paper because the evidence has not been peer reviewed, so the evidence may not be credible.

2. An encyclopedia for specific fields of study gives the understanding of a topic or problem specific to a field of studies.

An online encyclopedia for psychology:
http://www.psychology.org/links/

An online encyclopedia for sociology:
http://www.sociologyencyclopedia.com/public/

3. An encyclopedia on specific topics for a field of studies or related fields gives you the understanding of a topic or problem related to fields of study.

An encyclopedia of women's studies:
http://gem.greenwood.com/wse/wseIntro.jsp

An online encyclopedia of drug abuse:
http://www.nlm.nih.gov/medlineplus/ency/article/001945.htm

 TIPS If you are unsure about using a dictionary or an encyclopedia as an acceptable reference source, ask your instructor before your paper is due or cite it to avoid plagiarism.

Boolean operators: To assist you in finding information, you will need some basic familiarity with Boolean logic to search online or in your library. Boolean logic refers to the ways that words can be combined for your search. The most common beginning words are *and*, *or*, and *not*.

Table 2.2 Boolean Operators and Their Meaning

Operator	Meaning
And or + sign	Link two words using the word *and* or the + (*plus*) sign to narrow your search.
Example	Street+children
	Your search is narrowed to those sources where these words are kept together.
Or or – *sign*	Use *or* or the – (*minus*) sign to find sources that contain one or the other word.
Example	Street–children
	Your search is expanded to sources that contain street and sources that contain *children*.
Not	Use *not* to narrow a search.
Example	Street+children not China
	Your search will contain all street children except those with *China*.
Asterisk *	Use * at the end of a word to find the variations of a word. This includes the singular and plural forms of the same word.
Example	Street+child* finds *street child, street children, street childhood*, and so on.
Parentheses ( )	Use parentheses to group search terms together to create more complex searches.
Example	(street kid* OR child*)

Evaluate the Quality of Your Internet Research Sources

Not all online information is of the reliable or valid quality that you will require. You will have to evaluate your research sources to determine the quality of information that is provided. (See also Appendix D.) Following are some general guidelines to help you assess websites and the information that they provide.

Is it an identifiable and reputable source? Determine if the source hosting the website is easily identifiable and reputable. For instance, is the website hosted by an identifiable

- scholarly association (e.g., American Sociological Association [ASA], Canadian Sociological Association [CSA])?

- educational institution (e.g., a community college or university)?
- government or government department, at local to federal levels?
- academic publisher (e.g., Oxford, Pearson)? (Note that many scholarly publishers of introductory textbooks have reputable websites listed in them.)
- reputable organization (e.g., scientific, business, labour)?

Avoid all other websites for your research term paper, such as those with no author, those that are racist or sexist, etc.

Is there peer review of the website's information? More reliable information will come from websites that indicate that their information is peer reviewed. Check to see if you can determine this easily. However, information from sites that are not peer reviewed is also of value. You may need to check with your instructor about these sites.

Is the information current? Check the date of the website as well as the dates of the articles to determine if the information is current.

Did you compare information? Compare the information from one website with another to see if you can confirm the information. Check to see why the information holds up from these sites or why there is a difference if it does not.

> ## Reminder
> Many college and university library websites have statements and guidelines on evaluating Internet sources for research. Check out your local college or university library website to see if it contains additional material to what we provide here. Contact your instructor if you are unsure about any website or reference source before you write your term paper.

How to Read Your Sources to Obtain Arguments

You will need time and effort to read your sources to determine how they will relate to your topic or part of your topic. There are a number of ways to help you determine whether the books, articles, and online sources will provide you with the points and evidence that you are looking for to create credible arguments. (Recall that you are also using concept, definition, and evidence/example to find information for your arguments.)

Here is a quick summary of how to read your sources to determine if they might be useful to you. (The following information has been adapted from Booth et al., 2008, pp. 76–77.)

Table 2.3 How to Read Sources

Source	Skim or read . . .
Book	• Index (check for keywords and pages on your topic) • First and *last* paragraphs in chapters with keywords • Introduction and summary chapters • Last chapter, especially first and last two or three pages
Edited book	• Introduction • Chapter titles and first and last page of relevant chapters • Bibliography for more books or articles on your topic
Article	• Abstract, introduction, and conclusion • First and last page of article with no headings • First and last paragraph of sections
Online source	• Abstract, introduction, overview, summary

For those websites where you found relevant material

- save the websites in your outline, and
- record the URL and date retrieved as necessary for referencing.

In the Library

The books and journal articles by reputable publishers available at your library, in print and online, have been screened to ensure that they meet the standards of their respective discipline or profession. This will help you find appropriate social science sources relatively efficiently.

Here are some helpful ways to do your library research:

- Take tours or services offered by your library to learn where different materials are kept (e.g., books, general periodicals, government documents, reference materials) and how to use them.
- Ask librarians to assist you in finding information (e.g., reference desk, help desk, online assistance).
- Search your library online for various sources, including books and articles on your topic.
- Use the library's online catalogue (it contains a list of all of the library's holdings). Use the keywords of your topic to search for materials. Try various keywords (e.g., *teen runaways, runaway teens, street kids, homeless youth*).
- If your search is unsuccessful on your chosen topic, ask for assistance. Librarians are familiar with key search words as well as the location of material and sources to help you. Many college and university libraries have online help.
- Check interlibrary loan since not all libraries carry the same books. Ask how long it will take to get a book from another library.
- Use electronic databases (these contain millions of journal articles provided by online services like EBSCO or ProQuest). Start with a general term, then narrow your search to your specific topic. You will get a list of abstracts or

summaries of articles and reference source information. More full-length articles will be provided that you can save or email to yourself.

More specific tips for selecting appropriate academic sources for a research paper are presented in Appendix D.

Remember to use concept(s), definition(s), and evidence/example(s) to help you pinpoint what you need on your topic.

2.3.4 Record Your Arguments and References in Your Outline

Record and save all relevant information in your outline. For material that you are uncertain about keeping, create a separate file or folder for your topic and save it there. Recording information on file cards or index cards allows you to easily re-organize arguments (points and evidence), which you can then transfer to a computer or digital device. Finally, using a laptop or digital device may tempt you to record too much information so be forewarned about having to spend more time than you had originally planned going through information.

This book recommends two general steps to help you create arguments or headings/themes and record their references in your outline:

1. Create a draft of your arguments or headings/themes in the outline.
2. Revise your draft arguments or headings/themes in the outline.

Create Draft Arguments or Headings/Themes in Outline

You can write a term paper that consists of individual arguments or one that contains headings/themes. A term paper consisting of headings/themes starts with individual arguments and then goes on to organize these individual arguments into headings/themes. We use a three-step process to describe the creation of individual arguments that are then grouped and organized into headings/themes.

*   *Step 1*. Create individual arguments.
*   *Step 2*. Create headings/themes using Step 1. Group similar arguments or points and word them with what they are about or what they have in common.
*   *Step 3*. Organize the headings/themes and the points within each (from Step 2). This step is discussed in Chapter 4.

Consider the start of creating individual arguments or headings/themes in your outline as a rough draft. Recall that your overall goal is to create one or two arguments more than what you need, along with reference sources. Here are some suggestions to help you do this:

*   Decide if a book or journal article is relevant to your topic and interest. If in doubt, hang on to it or save it.
*   Record all your references as a working bibliography in your outline (add the library call number for those materials that have them in case you have to return them and take them out again).

- Make sure that the total number of reference sources in your working bibliography is more than the required minimum.
- If you are unable to get the minimum number of reference sources for your first topic (for whatever reason), then go to your second topic and repeat the previous process.
- If you find too many reference sources, narrow your topic.

How to limit your topic

- Look for material on only one side (or one part) of your topic, problem, or issue.
- Look for material on either the positive (pro) or negative (con) part.

Example: Look for either the positive or negative side of a government program(s) to help homeless youth.

Record your points, evidence, and their sources in the following ways (from Muth, 2006, pp. 107–112):

Table 2.4 Quote, Paraphrase, Summarize

	Quote	Paraphrase	Summarize
Meaning	Copy exact words.	Restate something in your words.	Shorter version, presenting only main points
Reason	Support your point or evidence in words of original.	Present information in your words, using fewer words.	Much shorter than original
Do not . . .	quote long passages, or copy and paste.	follow sentence or pattern of original.	summarize unfairly.

Do not worry about the sequence of your points and evidence for now. Concentrate on creating arguments. If you have too many arguments, then limit yourself to only one kind.

If you have too many arguments (i.e., 10–12 for a 5-argument paper):

- Look for patterns in your arguments.
- Break your arguments into general groups.
- Do your paper on only one part or group of your arguments.

Table 2.5 is an example of too many arguments (for a five-argument term paper) on runaway teens, consisting of eleven arguments that have been grouped into two: the reasons to be street kids and what happens to them on the street:

Table 2.5 Example of Too Many Arguments

Reasons for becoming street kids	What happens to runaway teens living on the street
• Conflict with parents • Emotional abuse • Neglect • Physical abuse • Sexual abuse	• Stealing • Panhandling • Dealing drugs • Doing drugs • Violence • Prostitution

Suggestions:

- Use the arguments from *either* the reasons for running away or from what happens to runaway teens living on the street.
- Note that *now you are only dealing with one part of your topic*. You may decide to do the other part (or different parts) of this topic for a future term paper.
- *The change in arguments has led to a change in emphasis of the term paper. The focus is now on street kids rather than on teen runaways.*

Here is an example of draft arguments. The arguments have been condensed to save space (references omitted).

An Example of Draft Individual Arguments

1. Point: no point
   Evidence: info on runaway population
2. Point: stealing, theft
   Evidence: percentage data
3. Point: dealing drugs
   Evidence: percentage of kids involved
4. Point: prostitution, obligatory sex
   Evidence: percentage data
5. Point: substance abuse
   Evidence: percentage data
6. Point: panhandling, begging
   Evidence: difference in boys/girls
7. Point: victims of crime
   Evidence: percent assaulted
8. Point: violence among street kids
   Evidence: examples of weapons

- Save your draft argument outline file.
- For now, do not worry if some "arguments" only have a point but no evidence, or evidence and no point.

Revise Draft Arguments in Outline
Before you start to revise your draft argument outline, here is what you should do:

- Make a copy of your original draft argument outline.
- Save it as a separate file.

- Give it a new file name (e.g., "Revised outline v1"—you may want to keep earlier versions and make new versions as you revise).

Check the following in revising your draft argument outline:

- Make sure that one argument consists of a point and related evidence.
- Check to determine whether a point *is* a point (reason, idea) and your evidence is actually evidence (information, data, or example, not a continuation of your point).
- For points and evidence that cannot be made into arguments, decide if they can be used in your introduction.
- Check that each point and related evidence is a separate argument.
- Word any subordinate or related points and evidence as a separate argument.
- Check reference sources (within points and evidence as well as references section) to make sure that they are complete.
- You do not need to format the references section of your outline for now.

Example of revising draft arguments (condensed to save space):

Table 2.6 Revising Draft Arguments

Draft arguments	Revised arguments
1. Point: no point Evidence: info on runaway population	Use in introduction
2. Point: stealing, theft Evidence: percentage data	1. Keep
3. Point: dealing drugs Evidence: percentage of kids involved	2. Keep
4. Point: prostitution, obligatory sex Evidence: percentage data	3. Keep prostitution 4. Keep obligatory sex as a separate point
5. Point: substance abuse Evidence: percentage data	5. Keep
6. Point: panhandling, begging Evidence: difference in boys/girls	Use in introduction
7. Point: victims of crime Evidence: percentage assaulted	6. Keep
8. Point: violence among street kids Evidence: examples of weapons	Use in introduction

Your goal is to create good, solid arguments that fulfill the requirements of your social science term paper. Revising the draft arguments has reduced the number from a possible eight arguments to six for a five-argument term paper. Having one or two arguments beyond what is required is helpful in case you need to change or drop one as you create your aim.

Once you have settled on your arguments, then proceed to work on your aim.

2.4 How Do I Develop My Aim from My Arguments?

Now you should have a number of arguments that you can use to develop an aim. You will be using inductive reasoning to create your aim because you will be using specific arguments to create a general aim.

2.4.1 First, Create a Working Aim from Your Arguments

Recall that an aim in the social sciences must satisfy a number of conditions. One condition is that there must be at least two concepts. So far, only one concept for the aim has been decided on, and that is the phrase "street kids."

Because there is only one concept here, another concept and a view about these two concepts are still required to create a working aim. There are two steps that may help in creating a working aim:

- Start by wording your potential aim in everyday language.
- Translate the everyday wording of your working aim into the professional language and concepts of your course, discipline, or field of studies.

Use Everyday Wording for Your Working Aim
To create a working aim, begin by looking at what seems to be common to most of your arguments. Recall that you may have narrowed your arguments by grouping them. Use this to help you begin to word your aim.

Examples of possible everyday wording for working aims based on negative arguments of runaway teens living on the street or, simply, street kids:

- Street kids are involved in negative behaviours.
- Street kids get caught up in very serious problems.
- Street kids get caught up in negative activities to survive.

With this beginning, you should then word your aim more in the language of a social science. This will mean using an appropriate concept(s) from your course or field of studies.

Then Use Professional Wording for Your Working Aim
There are a number of possibilities here for changing the everyday wording of a working aim into the professional language of your discipline or field of studies. For example:

- Street kids develop their own culture.
- Street kids have to learn negative behaviours in order to survive.
- Street kids get involved in deviant behaviour.

What you are doing here is expressing everyday language in professional terms (and in turn stating what professional wording means in everyday language).

Also, you have to *judge* how well your aim expresses your arguments. In other words, the wording of your aim must be able to include all of your arguments. Note that it may take several attempts at wording before you decide on one working aim.

You must make a *decision* to select one working aim, for now. There may be further modifications to the wording of your working aim, but you need to decide which one to use. Here is an example of the *working aim* that was decided on:

> The aim of this paper is to show that street kids are very likely to be involved in deviant behaviour.

This is a working aim because there are two different concepts (*street kids* and *deviant behaviour*) that are part of the social sciences and because a relationship between the two is expressed. This relationship is expressed in the choice of concepts (*negative behaviour* now is *deviant behaviour*) and the wording between them (i.e., that street kids are *very likely to be involved in* deviant behaviour).

Following is an example of creating an aim from points in arguments.

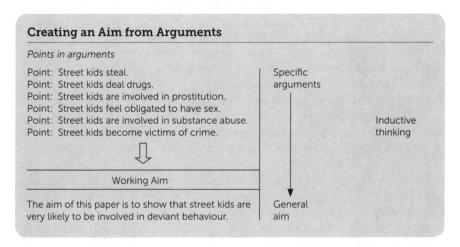

Creating an Aim from Arguments

Points in arguments

Point: Street kids steal. Point: Street kids deal drugs. Point: Street kids are involved in prostitution. Point: Street kids feel obligated to have sex. Point: Street kids are involved in substance abuse. Point: Street kids become victims of crime.	Specific arguments

Inductive thinking

Working Aim

The aim of this paper is to show that street kids are very likely to be involved in deviant behaviour.	General aim

2.4.2 Word Your Arguments to Include Your Aim

Once you have a working aim, work on the actual wording of the points of your arguments in your outline. Word each point to include the two main ideas of your working aim and write this point in a sentence. The wording of your points in proper sentences is important because these sentences will be the first sentence of your paragraph for the point that you are making in one argument.

For example, here is some preliminary wording of points in sentences about street kids and deviant behaviour:

1. Street kids are involved in the deviant behaviour of stealing.
2. Street kids are involved in the deviant behaviour of dealing drugs.
3. Street kids are involved in the deviant behaviour of prostitution.
4. Street kids are involved in the deviant behaviour of obligatory sex.
5. Street kids are involved in the deviant behaviour of substance abuse.
6. Street kids are involved in the deviant behaviour of victims of crime.

This first effort is clearly repetitive and will need to be improved upon. However, this repetition does start the process of putting together the ideas of the working aim with those of the points. From this beginning, these sentences will have to be reworded to show variety and interest in the different points. In revising these sentences, you will have to do the following:

- Judge how well your points relate to your aim.
- Determine if each sentence makes sense. For example, is being a victim of crime really deviant behaviour?
- Decide which sentences make the best case for the concepts that you are using.

Here are examples of revising the wording of the previous sentences:

1. Once you are a street kid, you are very likely to become involved in the deviant behaviour of stealing.
2. Dealing in drugs is a deviant activity of street kids.
3. Street kids become involved in the deviant behaviour of prostitution.
4. Another form of deviant behaviour related to prostitution is that street kids engage in obligatory sex.
5. One kind of deviant behaviour of street kids is their involvement in substance abuse.
6. Living on the street means that in all likelihood street kids will be victims of a crime. *(Does not really fit with aim, use in introduction?)*

Your revised sentences of points for arguments have to include your aim and make sense. If you are unsure about any points, keep them for now (e.g., point sentence number 6) until you finalize your arguments.

If you are having difficulty knowing and learning the difference between a topic, an aim, and arguments, Table 2.7 should help you. Note that the table uses concept, definition, and evidence/example to highlight the differences.

This completes Step 1. That is, you now have individual arguments that relate to your aim. This is where you would stop for a term paper consisting of a number of individual arguments and proceed to the remaining chapters.

For a term paper that requires headings/themes, proceed to Step 2. Here you will create your headings from Step 1 by grouping similar arguments or points by wording them with what they are about or what they have in common.

Table 2.8 helps to visualize this first priority process from the individual arguments of Step 1 to creating headings/themes of Step 2.

This example illustrates the following. The six points from the individual arguments that were considered to be related were grouped together. For example, points 2 and 5 are about street kids and drugs; points 3 and 4 are about street kids and sex. Point 1 did not relate to any other so it is by itself. Point 6 is omitted. The task now is to create possible wording or the name of a heading/theme for these related points.

Here is some possible wording for each of the examples.

Table 2.7 The Differences between a Topic, an Aim, and Arguments

Concept	Topic	Aim	Argument
Definition	General area of interest or question	The stance or position on the relationship between two different concepts of the topic	Consists of a *point* and the *evidence* to support that point for the aim
			Point: contains the two ideas from the aim plus one other idea
			Evidence: refers to the data (qualitative/quantitative) to support the point
Evidence/ Example	Teen runaways	Teen runaways will most likely be socialized into deviant behaviour.	*Point:* Teen runaways will likely become involved in deviant behaviour of dealing drugs.
	What happens to teens that run away from their home?	How do teens get socialized into a deviant behaviour?	*Evidence:* From 40 to 50 percent of kids sold, ran, or moved drugs (drug dealing) (Finkelstein, 2005, p. 79).

- Possible wording for a heading/theme about street kids and stealing:
  - Street kids' involvement in stealing
  - Street kids and stealing
  - Stealing
- Possible wording for a heading/theme about street kids and drugs:
  - Street kids get involved in drugs
  - Street kids and drugs
  - Street kids' deviant drug use
- Possible wording for a heading/theme about street kids and sex:
  - Street kids get involved in sex
  - Street kids and sex
  - The use of sex by street kids

Some criteria for deciding on the wording for headings/themes:

- The wording has to relate to the overall concepts in your aim (e.g., street kids and deviant behaviour).
- The wording must be able to include and convey convincingly all the points within a heading/theme.
- The wording is usually limited to a word or phrase. Avoid using a long sentence.
- Use appropriate professional wording and language.
- Variety in wording is generally more interesting than identical wording:
  - Identical wording (e.g., street kids and stealing, street kids and drugs, street kids and sex)
  - Variety in wording (e.g., street kids and stealing, street kids' deviant drug use, the use of sex by street kids)

Table 2.8 How to Group Individual Arguments/Points into Headings/Themes with Names

Step 1	Step 2	
Group and Name Related Individual Arguments	Decide on Wording of Heading/Theme *(not Points*	*organized yet)*
1. Street kids are involved in the deviant behaviour of stealing.	#1 stealing, no other point Possible wordings: • Street kids involvement in stealing • Street kids and stealing • Stealing	Street kids and stealing Point #1 only
2. Street kids are involved in the deviant behaviour of dealing drugs.	#2 and #5 have drugs in common Possible wordings: • Street kids get involved in drugs • Street kids' deviant drug use • Street kids and drugs	Street kids' deviant drug use For points #2 and #5
3. Street kids are involved in the deviant behaviour of prostitution.		
4. Street kids are involved in the deviant behaviour of obligatory sex.	#3 and #4 have sex in common Possible wordings: • Street kids use of sex • Using sex • The use of sex by street kids	The use of sex by street kids For points #3 and #4
5. Street kids are involved in the deviant behaviour of substance abuse.		
6. Street kids are involved in the deviant behaviour of victims of crime. (Does not relate to aim. Possible use in Introduction?)		

Here is a final revised version of what Step 2 might look like:

Step 2 Completed *(headings/themes and points are not organized)*

1. Heading/theme: Street kids and stealing

   Point #1 only: stealing

2. Heading/theme: Street kids' deviant drug use

   Point #2: dealing drugs
   Point #5: substance abuse

3. Heading/theme: The use of sex by street kids

   Point #3: prostitution
   Point #4: obligatory sex

Once you have completed Step 2, reorganize the *presentation of the headings/ themes* section of your outline according to the changes that you have made. This section should now contain the wording or names of your headings/themes plus their individual arguments (points and evidence). There is still time to revise the wording of the headings/themes when you undertake Step 3 in Chapter 4.

There are some benefits and drawbacks to having arguments presented individually compared to being grouped into headings/themes. These are presented in Table 2.9.

Table 2.9 Benefits and Drawbacks of Presenting Individual Arguments or Headings/Themes

	Individual Arguments	Headings/Themes
Benefits	Specific arguments can be made for specific evidence	Reduces long list of individual arguments
	Useful for short list of arguments	Keeps similar points together for greater understanding
Drawbacks	Long list is confusing especially if arguments are similar	Have to generalize each individual argument to fit name of heading/ theme
	May be unclear how all evidence of each argument relates to other arguments	May lose variations of specific evidence among different points for different heading/theme

Now, confer with your instructor about the aim, arguments or headings/themes, and references that you have in your outline.

2.4.3 Confer with Your Instructor

So far you have a working aim, individual arguments or headings/themes, and reference sources. Here are some things that you need to find out from your instructor:

- Does each argument relate to the aim?
- Are the ideas of the aim included in the arguments?
- Can the aim and arguments be reworded with a concept that will improve them?
- Are the grouped arguments related to each other, and are the headings/ themes worded to relate to the aim?
- Are there other possible sources to research?

Getting feedback from your instructor is very important. Instructors have different ways of providing feedback, according to the number of students in a class and the kind of class (such as correspondence or online courses). An instructor with smaller classes may be able to provide individual consultation, but an instructor with larger classes may not be able to do this. What is important for you is to get some feedback and comments on what you have done so far.

If you are able to see your instructor one-on-one, bring your outline and be prepared to write notes and suggestions as conveyed by your instructor. For other instructors (e.g., online), you might submit your social science outline to your instructor and ask for comments and suggestions. Remember to keep a copy of anything submitted to an instructor in case she or he loses it.

In addition, do not hesitate to follow up on any of your instructor's comments or suggestions that you do not understand. Make revisions based on your instructor's comments before proceeding to other parts of the outline.

2.4.4 Revise Your Aim and Arguments or Headings/Themes

Complete the revisions from your instructor and finalize your aim and arguments or headings/themes. Making revisions now is simply *more efficient* than completing everything else for the outline and then having to do those parts over again. If necessary, do the following:

- Research the references that your instructor recommended.
- Reword your aim and arguments or headings/themes as necessary.
- Regroup any arguments into differently worded headings/themes.
- Omit any arguments that do not relate to your aim or use them in your introduction. Make a final decision on which specific arguments to keep.

Your decisions should be based on keeping those arguments or headings/themes that

- match the clearest or are the best fit with your aim, and
- have the best evidence.

Chapter Summary

Start with a topic, subject area, or question:

- Know the meaning of *topic*—a subject area to be developed into a term paper.
- Be assigned a topic—it is already worded as part of your course.
- Choose your own topic—must be worded to fit in with your course or field of studies.

Learn how to create an aim:

- Learn the meaning of *aim*—a stance on two different ideas or concepts supported by convincing arguments.
- Follow the four principles to create an aim.
- Learn how to create your aim from your arguments. Create headings/themes from individual arguments.

- Start by creating arguments from reference sources. Use concept, definition, and evidence/example to assist you in looking for specific information.
- Develop a corresponding aim sentence or working aim from arguments.

Learn how to research to create arguments:

- Keep track of aim, arguments, and references by recording them in your outline.
- *Argument* means point and evidence to support that point.
- *Point* refers to idea or reason, and *evidence* means fact or results to support point.
- Look for quality research sources, peer reviewed, to create your working bibliography.

Use other information sources appropriately:

- You can do research to create arguments on the Internet or in your library.
- Learn basic Boolean operators to help you search.
- Know how to evaluate the quality of your Internet research sources by using Appendix D.
- For library research, search for arguments in relevant sources on your topic. If necessary, ask for assistance in searching and obtaining information.
- Record your arguments and references in your outline.
- Create a draft of your arguments in the outline by quoting, paraphrasing, and summarizing material from your reference sources. Be sure to include concept, definition, evidence/example in your arguments.
- If you don't have enough material, go to your second topic; if you have too much material, limit the arguments to one part or group of your topic.
- Save draft of arguments in outline; revise to create clear, separate arguments.
- Decide if unused portions of arguments can be used in introduction.
- Make sure you have enough arguments for your term paper as required (plus one or two more).

Develop your aim from your arguments:

- Start with Step 1 by creating a working aim from your individual arguments by what is common to them and by wording your aim in everyday language.
- Translate the everyday wording of your aim into the professional language of your field of studies or discipline.
- The wording of your working aim must fulfill the previous four principles required in the social sciences in order to be an acceptable aim.
- Word the points (in your arguments) in a sentence to include the ideas in your aim; record these in your outline.
- Ensure variety in each sentence and that each sentence makes sense; for now, keep arguments that you are unsure of.

If required, go on to Step 2, where you group arguments with similar and related points into headings or themes (an individual argument may be a heading/theme).

- Word the headings/themes to relate to your aim.
- Consult with your instructor about each item in your outline—aim, arguments, headings/themes, and reference sources.
- Revise items as directed by your instructor and finalize working aim and arguments.

✔ Checklist for Term Paper Research

Do you have a topic, subject area, or question?

☐ Do you have two to three topics that fit into your course or field of studies?

Do you know how to create an aim?

☐ Do you know how to create an aim and an aim sentence or question?
☐ Do you know how to create a working aim from your arguments?

Did you research to create arguments?

☐ Do you know how to evaluate the quality of your research sources?
☐ Can you use basic Boolean operators to search for sources?
☐ Did you check for sources in your library? Did you ask for assistance, online or in person, to find research sources for arguments?
☐ Do you have enough reference sources and material? If not, go to your second topic and repeat the process.
☐ If you have too much material, can you limit yourself to part of or one group of arguments of your topic?
☐ Did you save your draft argument outline and make a copy for your revision?
☐ Did you revise the draft of arguments to ensure each argument consists of a separate point and has at least one (no more than three) facts of evidence?
☐ Do you have enough required arguments (plus one or two more)?

Did you develop your aim from your arguments?

☐ Did you develop a working aim from what is common to your arguments as Step 1?
☐ Does your working aim fulfill the social science principles of an aim as required?
☐ Did you word each point to include the working aim, and did you write this point in a sentence?

☐ For Step 2, did you group individual arguments with similar and related points into headings or themes (individual arguments may be a heading/theme)?

☐ Does the name or wording of the headings/themes relate to your aim?

☐ Did you consult with your instructor and make revisions?

☐ Did you decide on your final aim and arguments or headings/themes?

Recommended Websites

California State University, Chico
Meriam Library on evaluating information by using the CRAPP test (a summary is in Appendix D):
http://www.csuchico.edu/lins/handouts/eval_websites.pdf

Meriam Library on distinguishing different kinds of scholarly articles:
http://www.csuchico.edu/lins/handouts/scholarly.pdf

Clark College (Vancouver, WA)
Cannell Library has free tutorials and useful information and research instruction suite (Iris), including research, deciding on a topic, and research notes:
http://www.clark.edu/Library/iris/index.shtml

Dartmouth College
Dartmouth Writing Program has some materials for students about topic, research, and argument:
http://www.dartmouth.edu/~writing/materials/student/ac_paper/research .shtml#cite/

The Writing Program also provides information on researching your topic, including working with sources:
http://writing-speech.dartmouth.edu/learning/materials/sources-and -citations-dartmouth

Mount Royal University
Library for help with a research topic and research strategy:
http://www.mtroyal.ca/Library/Research/index.htm

Purdue University
Online Writing Lab (OWL) includes numerous aspects about research and writing, starting with determining a topic:
http://owl.english.purdue.edu/owl/resource/658/03/

Simon Fraser University
SFU Library has a five-step research guide:
http://www.lib.sfu.ca/help/tutorials/start-research

Also check out the various subject research guides:
http://www.lib.sfu.ca/help/subject-guides/

Tidewater Community College
Learning Resource Centers includes information about choosing and developing a topic and citing sources:
http://www.tcc.edu/lrc/infolit/orieng/topic.htm

University of California
UC Libraries has a tutorial for research:
http://unitproj.library.ucla.edu/col/uc-research-tutorial/begin.html

University of Waterloo
Waterloo Library has online video tutorials starting with the basics of research:
http://www.lib.uwaterloo.ca/user_ed/basicsearching1.html

Western University
The library has video tutorials on searching for information on a topic:
http://www.lib.uwo.ca/tutorials

Recommended Readings

Alfano, C.L., & O'Brien, A.J. (2011). *Envision: Writing and researching arguments* (3rd ed.). Boston, MA: Longman.

Northey, M., & McKibbin, J. (2015). *Making sense: A student's guide to research and writing* (8th ed.). Don Mills, ON: Oxford University Press.

Chapter 3

Reference Your Sources

This chapter presents some of the common APA, Chicago (CMS), and ASA styles that many social science instructors require students to use in order to reference or document research resources. Specific items not addressed in this book can be obtained from the more comprehensive manuals of each style.

Some benefits of using one of the three common referencing styles for research sources include the following:

- A common style makes tracing ideas, sources, and original work easy.
- You do not have to rely on or trust someone else's interpretation or version of another work.
- Your instructor can easily check your sources.

In this chapter you will learn the following:

1. General referencing information
   - An understanding and use of the term *references*
   - The meaning of *in-text citation*
   - The two kinds of quotations
   - General referencing and formatting guidelines for online articles
2. How to cite sources for APA-style referencing
3. How to cite sources for Chicago (CMS)-style referencing using the author–date version
4. How to cite sources for ASA style referencing

Formatting instructions for the references page and in-text-citations in each referencing style are offered for the following types of sources:

- Books
- Articles in journals or periodicals
- Articles in newspapers and magazines
- Government publications
- Public lectures, conferences
- Websites and social media

You will save considerable time by recording all your reference information, the in-text citations and references list, in your research outline. If you do this for your outline, you will not have to go back and search for specific referencing information when you are writing your term paper. Also, include in your outline any library call numbers just in case you do need to find your source again. Use this chapter to help you to record all the information that you need for your required referencing style. There is no need to format your references list until you write your term paper. See an example of each formatted references page in Chapter 5.

Reminder

Record all your reference information in your outline to save yourself time and to help you avoid plagiarism.

Next, the terms *references* and *in-text citation* are clarified.

3.1 What General Referencing Information Do I Need to Know and Use?

3.1.1 References

We begin with the meaning of the term *references*, move to what to include in your references, and end with an example of a formatted book in each style.

First, Know the Meaning of References
The word *references* generally means to present the sources of your research, that is, a list of the books, articles, reports, documents, and so on, that you used for your research. The *references page* refers to the list of the full text of all your research sources. For your term paper (or book review or article critique), you must provide a complete and accurate list of your in-text citations in a required style, such as APA, CMS, or ASA.

Learn What to Include in Your References Page
Include in your references page only those books, articles, and materials that you *actually used*, which means that they are cited in the text of your term paper or book review (or article critique). In your research outline you may have a number of re-search sources that you examined but decided not to use in writing your term paper. The term *bibliography* may be used to refer to this list of research sources that you examined but did not use.

Use the Proper Format for the References Page
For your research outline, record all the necessary information about a research source, as outlined in your required referencing style, to ensure that your references are com-plete and accurate. Once you have all the information, then you can proceed to format this reference list. Unless your instructor states otherwise, you may not need to format your references page for your outline until you write your term paper.

Here is an example of how to format a book with one author for a references page; the format for each style is shown so that you can get a sense of their similarities and differences.

One Book, Single Author, for a References Page in Each Style

APA style:

> Smith, D. E. (2005). *Institutional ethnography: A sociology for people*. Lanham, MA: Altamira.

Chicago (CMS) style:

> Smith, Dorothy E. 2005. *Institutional Ethnography: A Sociology for People*. Lanham, MA: Altamira.

ASA style:

> Smith, Dorothy E. 2005. *Institutional Ethnography: A Sociology for People*. Lanham, MA: Altamira.

Note the differences in the following:
- First and middle names of author
- Use of parentheses for year
- Use of capital letters in the titles

3.1.2 In-Text Citations

This section introduces in-text citations. It begins by presenting the meaning and when to use in-text citations. The end of this section presents examples of each of the three styles of in-text citations for the same book.

Know the Meaning of Citation

In-text citations are references to sources that are presented in the text of your term paper or book review (as well as an article critique). When you write the name of an author(s) or a report from which information has been used in your term paper (or book review or article critique), that is called *citing* or a *citation*. The citation indicates the source of your quotation, information, or idea. Another term with a similar meaning as in-text citation is *parenthetical note*. That is, a parenthetical note is a source that is placed in parentheses. Citations or references in your term paper or book review are necessary. Most instructors prefer that you use a lot of citations to indicate some familiarity with the research sources of your aim and topic.

Know When to Use In-Text Citations

You *must* use in-text citations to give credit for an idea, point, example, direct quote, or anything from someone else. Otherwise, you are committing plagiarism.

There are, however, instances when no citation is required, such as for common knowledge. *Common knowledge* refers to ideas or information that is available or known generally to anyone. For instance, a definition from a general-use dictionary does not need to be cited because anyone can look up the meaning of that word. Similarly, you would not need to cite that Freud was a major figure in psychology because that is a well-known fact. On the other hand, when you use a definition from an author in your field of studies, you must cite that author because you are using that particular author's meaning for your purpose. As well, when you refer to specific ideas or information from Freud's theory of personality, you must cite that. If you are unsure about citing an idea or information, check with your instructor or provide a citation.

You will use in-text citations throughout your term paper (or book review). For example, you will use them in your definitions, throughout your arguments, or wherever you have used someone else's point or evidence. By citing research and writing sources, you learn how much work has been done before and how useful that work is to your aim or purpose.

Know How to Format In-Text Citations

You will need to know the format for in-text citations or parenthetical information from the start of your research. It is important that your in-text citations be consistent. If you know the format, you can include it in your outline and move parts of it to suit your eventual writing. To get started with in-text citations, here is how the previous author, year, and page number would appear in each of the three styles.

Two kinds of in-text citations are presented here:

- First, for an in-text citation that appears as *part* of a sentence
- Second, when it appears as an *addition* to a sentence

Note the similarities and differences in the styles for the *same* book that was presented as an example for the references page.

Example of a Book as an In-Text Citation in Each Style

APA style

Part of sentence: Smith (2005) maintains that . . . (p. 167).
Added to sentence: Texts are analyzed specifically as part of social activity (Smith, 2005, p. 167).

For two or more pages: (Smith, 2005, pp. 167–168).

Chicago (CMS) style

Part of sentence: Smith (2005) maintains that . . . (167).

Added to sentence: Texts are analyzed specifically as part of social activity (Smith 2005, 167).

For two or more pages: (Smith 2005, 167–168)

ASA style

Part of sentence: Smith (2005:167) maintains that. . . .

Added to sentence: Texts are analyzed specifically as part of social activity (Smith 2005:167).

For two or more pages: (Smith 2005:167–168).

Note the following in APA style:
- The use of the *p* (for *page*) and *pp* (for *pages*)
- The subtle differences in punctuation among all styles

The page number is given when you are quoting, paraphrasing, or referring to something specific as the previous examples point out.

3.1.3 Quotations

In general, use quotations sparingly. It is better to summarize or paraphrase a quote from an author than to give a quote. As well, avoid using long quotes and quotes that follow one another.

If you do need to use quotations, then follow the format of each referencing style. Each referencing style uses two ways to present quotations: a *short quotation* and a *long block quotation*.

Formatting Quotations in APA Style
Table 3.1 presents APA style and examples for each type of quotation.

Table 3.1 APA-Style Quotations

A short quotation:	A long block quotation:
• is under 40 words • is in quotation marks • is part of the text or sentence of your term paper • requires a page number(s) using p. or pp.	• is 40 words and over • does not use quotation marks • is single-spaced as a block of text • does not indent first line of paragraph; for two or more paragraphs indent the first line of the second and subsequent paragraphs five spaces or one-half inch [or 1.27 cm] • indents entire quotation one-half inch (or 1.27 cm) • requires a page number(s) using *p.* or *pp.*

- Short quotation as part of sentence:

  As Ritzer (2010) maintains, "The military has been pressed to offer fast food on both bases and ships" (p. 12).

The author, Ritzer, the year, 2010, and the page number (p. 12) are part of the sentence.

- Short quotation added to sentence:

  > . . . expresses that, "The military has been pressed to offer fast food on both bases and ships" (Ritzer, 2010, p. 12).

The author, year, and page number in parentheses (i.e., Ritzer, 2010, p. 12) are added to the sentence and are followed by a period.

- Long block quotation

  > Wilson and Pence (2006) describe the following difference between lived time and institutional time in a domestic dispute:

  >> The eruption of violence in lived time can be fast—within minutes something can escalate from verbal to putting a woman's life in danger. Once the police have arrived institutional time kicks in: the man is arrested; three days later he is out of jail; weeks later he is arraigned; seven months later the woman is subpoenaed; nine months later, the day his trial is to begin, he pleads guilty. Lived and institutional times intersect in some institutionally defined events; but once the institutional process begins, institutional "efficiency" takes priority over victims' needs. (p. 212)

The period at the end of the sentence is followed by a *p.* and the page number in parentheses.

Whenever you summarize or paraphrase another author within the text, you must cite the source, stating author and year. Follow the same referencing style as you would for a quote.

Formatting Quotations in CMS Style

Table 3.2 shows the CMS version of short and long quotations.

Table 3.2 CMS-Style Quotations

A short quotation:	A long block quotation:
• is up to and including four lines of text • is in quotation marks • is part of the text or sentence of your term paper • requires a page number(s) without using *p.* or *pp.*	• is five lines or more • does not use quotation marks • is single-spaced as a block of text • does not indent first line of paragraph; for two or more paragraphs indent the first line of second and subsequent paragraphs five spaces or one-half inch (or 1.27 cm) • indents entire quotation one-half inch (or 1.27 cm) • requires a page number(s) without using *p.* or *pp.*

- Short quotation as part of sentence:

  As Ritzer (2010) maintains, "The military has been pressed to offer fast food on both bases and ships" (12).

- Short quotation added to sentence:

  . . . expresses that "The military has been pressed to offer fast food on both bases and ships" (Ritzer 2010, 12).

The author, year and page number in parentheses (i.e., Ritzer 2010, 12) are added to the sentence and are followed by a period.

- Long block quotation:

  Wilson and Pence (2006) describe the following difference between

  lived time and institutional time in a domestic dispute:

  > The eruption of violence in lived time can be fast—within minutes something can escalate from verbal to putting a woman's life in danger. Once the police have arrived institutional time kicks in: the man is arrested; three days later he is out of jail; weeks later he is arraigned; seven months later the woman is subpoenaed; nine months later, the day his trial is to begin, he pleads guilty. Lived and institutional times intersect in some institutionally defined events; but once the institutional process begins, institutional "efficiency" takes priority over victims' needs. (212)

The period at the end of the sentence is followed by the page number only in parentheses.

Formatting Quotations in ASA Style

Finally, Table 3.3 presents ASA style for short and long quotations.

Table 3.3 ASA-Style Quotations

A short quotation:	A long block quotation:
• is under four lines of text • is in quotation marks • is part of the text or sentence of your term paper • requires a page number(s) using *p.* (or *pp.*) as part of sentence • omits *p.* or *pp.* if reference is added to the sentence	• is 50 words or more (about four lines or more) • does not use quotation marks • is single-spaced as a block of text • does not indent first line of paragraph; for two or more paragraphs indent the first line of second or subsequent paragraphs five spaces or one-half inch (or 1.27 cm) • indents entire quotation one-half inch (or 1.27 cm) • requires a page number(s) using *p.* (or *pp.*)

- Short quotation as part of sentence:

  As Ritzer (2010) maintains, "The military has been pressed to offer fast food on both bases and ships" (p. 12).

The author, Ritzer, the year (2010), and the page number (p. 12) are part of the sentence.

- Short quotation added to sentence:

  . . . expressed that "The military has been pressed to offer fast food on both bases and ships" (Ritzer 2010:12).

The author, year, and page number in parentheses (i.e., Ritzer 2010:12) are added to the sentence and are followed by a period.

- Long block quotation:

  Wilson and Pence (2006) describe the following difference between

  lived time and institutional time in a domestic dispute:

  > The eruption of violence in lived time can be fast—within minutes something can escalate from verbal to putting a woman's life in danger. Once the police have arrived institutional time kicks in: the man is arrested; three days later he is out of jail; weeks later he is arraigned; seven months later the woman is subpoenaed; nine months later, the day his trial is to begin, he pleads guilty. Lived and institutional times intersect in some institutionally defined events; but once the institutional process begins, institutional "efficiency" takes priority over victims' needs. (P. 212)

The period at the end of the sentence is followed by a *P.* and the page number in parentheses.

3.1.4 General Referencing and Formatting Guidelines for Online Articles with Digital Object Identifiers and URLs

As a student you can access articles in journals or periodicals through your library online. Online reference sources use the same in-text citation format as any other reference source. One main difference for online sources, however, concerns *page numbers*. The following in-text citations are suggested (whenever a style is suggested, it is stated as such under the respective heading) for DOI and URL.

The following are some common guidelines for online articles using the DOI and the URL.

- Use a digital object identifier (DOI) for an online source when there is one. Use lower case (doi).

- If there is no DOI, use the URL or the homepage URL if there is a subscription.
- To break up a URL or DOI at the end of a line, break it *before* punctuation. Do not add a hyphen to break it up or a period at the end. Always copy and paste the DOI.
- Include a retrieval date if the URL of a source is likely to change. See example in government publications.

3.2 How Do I Cite Sources According to APA Style?

The first style presented is that of the American Psychological Association (APA). The complete source for this style is in *The Publication Manual of the American Psychological Association* (2010, 6th edition). The following website provides more detailed referencing information, more current style changes, and a free tutorial on some of the basic APA styles: http://www.APAstyle.org.

3.2.1 Books

The complete reference for books with various numbers of authors is presented here followed by electronic or e-books. Their corresponding in-text citation follows each book reference.

The general pattern of referencing for a printed book is as follows:

- Start a book reference with the last name of the author followed by the initials of her or his first and middle names.
- Then, give the year the book was published in parentheses followed by a period.
- The title of the book, italicized, comes next. Capitalize only the first word in the title and subtitle, except for all proper nouns (for example, *Toronto, New York, London*), and end with a period.
- If the book is a second or subsequent edition, add the edition in parentheses (e.g., 5th ed.).
- The city and state or province of publication comes next (if there are multiple cities, choose the first one), followed by the name of the publishing company without the words *Publishing, Company*, or *Inc.*

Book with One Author

Smith, D.E. (2005). *Institutional ethnography: A sociology for people.* Lanham, MA: Altamira.

In-text citations:

Part of sentence: Smith (2005) maintains that . . .
Added to sentence: . . . texts are analyzed specifically as part of social activity (Smith, 2005, p. 167).
For two or more pages: (Smith, 2005, pp. 167–168).

Book with Two Authors

Kimmel, M.S., & Holler, J. (2010). *The gendered society* (Canadian ed.). Toronto, ON: Oxford University Press.

In-text citations:

- For two authors of a work, mention both last names when you cite them.

  Part of sentence: Kimmel and Holler (2010) suggest that . . .

- Note the use of the word *and*.

  Added to sentence: . . . significance of gender (Kimmel & Holler, 2010).

- Note the use of the ampersand (&).

Book with Three to Five Authors

Ferber, A., Holcomb, K., & Wentling, T. (2013). *Sex, gender and sexuality: The new basics* (2nd ed.). Toronto: Oxford University Press.

In-text citations:

Part of sentence: For first citation mention all the authors the first time that you cite them.

Ferber, Holcomb, and Wentling (2013) suggest . . .

For second and further citations: Use the last name of the first author, with the Latin abbreviation et al. (meaning "and others") following.

Ferber et al. (2013) suggest that . . .

Added to sentence for first citation: . . . the basics of sexuality (Ferber, Holcomb, & Wentling, 2013).
For second and further citations: . . . the further basics of sexuality (Ferber et al., 2013).

Book with an Editor

Gahagan, J. (Ed.). (2013). *Women and HIV prevention in Canada: Implications for research, practice and policy*. Toronto, ON: Women's Press.

In-text citations

- Same as for one author.

Book Chapter in an Edited Book

Archibald, C., & Halverson, J. (2013). The current state of women and HIV in Canada: An overview of HIV/AIDS epidemiology in Canada. In J. Gahagan (Ed.), *Women and HIV prevention in Canada: Implications for research, practice and policy* (pp. 5–14). Toronto, ON: Women's Press.

In-text citations:

Part of sentence: Archibald and Halverson (2013) present an overview . . .
Added to sentence: . . . highlight women and HIV/AIDS (Archibald & Halverson, 2013).

E-Book for a Printed Book

Henry, V.E. (2004). Death work: Police, trauma, and the psychology of survival. [MyiLibrary version]. Retrieved from http://www.myilibrary.com?id=50275

In-text citations:

- Same as for one author.

Book with a Group or Corporation as Author

Nishga Tribal Council. (1993). *Nisga'a: People of the Nass River.* Vancouver: Douglas & MacIntyre.

In-text citations:

Part of sentence: . . . as mentioned by Nishga Tribal Council (1993).
Added to sentence: . . . describing people's lives (Nishga Tribal Council, 1993).

Book with Publisher as Author

When the author and publisher of a book or e-book are the same, type the word *Author* where the name of the publisher would be:

National Crime Prevention Centre (Canada). (2012). A *statistical snapshot of youth at risk and youth offending in Canada*. Ottawa, ON: Author.

In-text citations:

- Same as preceding example.
  Part of sentence: . . . as stated by the National Crime Prevention Centre (2012).
  Added to sentence: . . . describing lives of youths (National Crime Prevention Centre, 2012).

Book with Group/Corporation Online
For the previous book online use:

National Crime Prevention Centre (Canada). (2012). *A statistical snapshot of youth at risk and youth offending in Canada*. Retrieved from http://www.publicsafety.gc.ca/res/cp/res/ssyr-eng.aspx

In-text citations

- Same as preceding example.

3.2.2 Articles in Journals or Periodicals

Article with One Author in Print
If the pages in an article are continuous, then no issue number need be provided. Provide the issue number in parentheses if the page numbers are not continuous. Below, issue number is omitted:

McKeen, W. (2012). The construction of "welfare mothers" in Canada's late 1960s/early 1970s "War on Poverty." *Canadian Woman Studies, 29*, 107–123.

With the issue number it would be: 29(3), 107–223. Note that the volume number (29) is italicized while the specific issue number (3) is not.

Article with One Author with DOI
Do not place a period at the end of a DOI or URL. See below.

Sullivan, T.P. (2013). Think outside: Advancing risk and protective factor research beyond the intimate-partner-violence box. *Psychology of Violence, 3*(2), 121–125. doi: 10.1037/a0032125

In-text citations:

- Same as one author for a book.

Article with One Author with URL

Atkins, P.J. (2003). Mother's milk and infant death in Britain, circa 1900–1940. *Anthropology of Food, 2* Retrieved from http://aof.revues.org/310?lang=fr

In-text citations:

* Same as one author.

Article with Two Authors

Moen, P., & Flood, S. (2013). Men's work/volunteer time in the encore life course stage. *Social Problems, 60*(2), 206–233. doi: 110.1525/sp.2013.11120

In-text citations:

Part of sentence for all citations: As Moen and Flood (2013) state . . .
Added to sentence for all citations: . . . life course stage (Moen & Flood, 2013).

Article with Three to Five Authors

List all the authors in the references page. Note the changes in the in-text citations.

Caron, A., Lafontaine, M-F., Bureau, J-F., Levesque, C., & Johnson, S.M. (2012). Comparisons of close relationships: An evaluation of relationship quality and patterns of attachment to parents, friends, and romantic partners in young adults. *Canadian Journal of Behavioural Science/Revue Canadienne des Sciences du Comportement, 44*(4), 245–256. doi: 10.1037/a0028013

In-text citations:

Part of sentence: . . . the attachments illustrated by Caron, Lafontaine, Bureau, Levesque, and Johnson (2012) include . . .
For second and further citations: . . . as presented by Caron et al. (2012) who suggest . . .
Added to sentence for first citation: . . . the significance of attachments by young adults (Caron, Lafontaine, Bureau, Levesque, & Johnson, 2012) requires that . . .
For second and further citations: . . . convincingly proposed (Caron et al., 2012) . . .

Six or More Authors

Nash, A., Dunn, M., Asztalos, E., Corey, M., Mulvihill-Jory, B., & O'Connor, D.L. (2011). Pattern of growth of very low birth weight preterm infants, assessed using the WHO Growth Standards, is associated with neuro-development. *Applied Physiology, Nutrition & Metabolism, 36*(4), 562–569. doi: 10.1139/h11-059

In-text citations:

For first and all citations as part of sentence: Nash et al. (2011) maintain . . .
Added to sentence for first and all citations: . . . preterm infants (Nash et al., 2011).

Article with a Group as Author
See online government documents and website.

3.2.3 Articles in Newspapers and Magazines

Article in Online Newspaper with Author

Daley, S. (2013, April 20). Danes rethink a welfare state ample to a fault. *The New York Times*. Retrieved from http://www.nytimes.com/2013/04/21/world/europe/danes-rethink-a-welfare-state-ample-to-a-fault.html?_r=0&adxnnl=1&ref=todayspaper&adxnnlx=1366585289-YmweA7y1W1iuQKoJrdrX9A

In-text citations:

* Same as for one author.

If there is no author, use the title of the article. Do not italicize the title. For on-line newspapers add the retrieved URL and page numbers. For consecutive page numbers use a hyphen (e.g., B1–B2), and, for non-consecutive page numbers use a comma (e.g., B1, B9).

Article in Newspaper with Group or Corporation as Author

The Nature Conservancy of Canada. (2004, May 28). Saving Canada's natural masterpieces. *The Globe and Mail,* pp. E1–E3.

In-text citations:

Part of sentence: . . . as stated by The Nature Conservancy of Canada (2004) . . .
Added to sentence: . . . preserving these masterpieces is vital (The Nature Conservancy of Canada, 2004).

Article in Printed Magazine

> Snider, M., & Borel, K. (2004, May 24). Stalked by a cyberbully. *Maclean's*,
> 17, 76–77.

In-text citations:

- Same as for two authors.
- Note that the different page number locations (17, 76–77) are separated by a comma.

3.2.4 Online Government Publications

> Human Resources and Skills Development Canada. (2013, April 6).
> *Funding: Employment assistance for older workers*. Retrieved from
> http://www.hrsdc.gc.ca/eng/jobs/older_workers/index.shtml

In-text citations:

> *Part of sentence*: . . . for older workers, Human Resources and Skills Development
> Canada (2013), has . . .
> *Added to sentence*: . . . federal government program (Human Resources and Skills
> Development Canada, 2013).

> The United States Census Bureau. (2012). *Poverty thresholds by size of
> family unit*. Retrieved from http://www.census.gov/compendia/
> statab/2012/tables/12s0710.PDF

In-text citations:

> *Part of sentence*: . . . as reported by The United States Census Bureau
> (2012) . . .
> *Added to sentence*: . . . as data suggest (The United States Census Bureau,
> 2012).

3.2.5 Public Lectures and Conferences

Add the month to the year.

> Werdal, T. (2013, May). *"When you're homeless, your friends are your
> home": Friendships among street youth in Victoria, Canada*. Paper
> presented at the annual meeting of the Canadian Anthropology
> Society/La Société Canadienne D'anthropologie, Victoria, Canada.

In-text citations:

- Same as for one author.

3.2.6 Websites and Social Media

The possible reference list entry for websites or their specific web pages and in-text citation are provided for the following. Note the following:

- If there is no date, use "n.d." without the quotation marks.
- Always keep a copy of any social media used for referencing.

Website

> National Institute of Mental Health. (2013, April 19). *Anxiety disorders.* Retrieved from http://www.nimh.nih.gov/index.shtml

In-text citations:

> *Part of sentence*: . . . as the website for the National Institute of Mental Health (NIMH) (2013) states . . .
> *For second and further citations*: . . . as NIMH (2013) states . . .
> Added to sentence: . . . widely known (National Institute of Mental Health [NIMH], 2013).
> *Added to sentence for second and further citations*: . . . widely known (NIMH, 2013).

Blog

> Moss, C., & Swan, A. (2013, March 11). Climate conversations—Gender analysis in forestry research: What policymakers should know, *Centre for International Forestry Research* (CIFOR) [Web log]. Retrieved from http://www.trust.org/alertnet/blogs/climate-conversations/gender-analysis-in-forestry-research-what-policymakers-should-know/

In-text citations:

> *Part of sentence*: . . . as Moss and Swan (2013) advance . . .
> *Added to sentence*: . . . must be included (Moss & Swan, 2013).

Video Blog

> Silk, E. (2012, April 23). Psychology and physiology of substance abuse Part 2 [Video file]. Retrieved from http://www.youtube.com/watch?v=w-cMvB9gC6s

In-text citations:

- Same as for one author.

Podcast

Anglin, M. (2012, July 2). *Gender and globalization in Appalachia* [Audio podcast]. Podcast retrieved from http://gws.as.uky.edu/podcasts/gender-and-globalization-appalachia-mary-anglin

In-text citations:

- Same as for one author.

Video Podcast

Basu, S. (2013, February 18). *Playing off courts: The spaces of adjudicating family and violence* [Video podcast]. Podcast retrieved from http://gws.as.uky.edu/video/playing-courts-spaces-adjudicating-family-and-violence

In-text citations:

- Same as for one author.

Twitter

[Obama, B.] BarackObama. (2013, April 22). Washington can't get away with ignoring 90% of the country on gun violence prevention. Say you'll keep fighting: http://OFA.BO/trSZWT [Tweet]. Retrieved from https://twitter.com/BarackObama/status/326433885791592448

In-text citations:

Part of sentence: . . . awareness by President Obama (Obama, 2013) on Twitter to encourage . . .
Added to sentence: . . . tweeting for more supporters by President Obama (Obama, 2013).

Facebook

Moyers, B. (2013, April 17). The toxic assault on our children is discussed with Sandra Steingraber. https://www.facebook.com/moyersandcompany?fref=ts[Facebook update]. Retrieved from https://www.facebook.com/photo.php?fbid=582580285093320&set=a.390979790920038.103036.114528955231791&type=1&theater

In-text citations:

> *Part of sentence*: . . . Bill Moyers (2013) uses Facebook to promote . . .
> *Added to sentence*: . . . public discussion of toxic assault on our children (Moyers, 2013).

3.3 How Do I Cite Sources According to Chicago Style (Author–Date)?

This reference section is based on *The Chicago Manual of Style* (CMS). The website for the Chicago Manual of Style is http://www.chicagomanualofstyle.org/home.html. There are two general formatting styles for CMS: a bibliography note style that is used mainly in the humanities, and an author–date style that is used most often in the social sciences. Here we present only the author–date style. Note that the word *references* is used and not *bibliography*, as opposed to the CMS note system, which uses *bibliography*. As well, there are no footnotes or endnotes in the author–date system since in-text citations or parenthetical notes are used.

3.3.1 Books

Book with One Author

> Smith, Dorothy E. 2005. *Institutional Ethnography: A Sociology for People.* Lanham, MA: Altamira.

In-text citations:

> *Part of sentence*: Smith (2005) maintains that . . .
> *Added to sentence*: . . . texts are analyzed specifically as part of social activity (Smith 2005, 167).
> *For two or more pages*: (Smith 2005, 167–168).

Book with Two or Three Authors

> Kimmel, Michael S., and Jacqueline Holler. 2010. *The Gendered Society.* Canadian ed. Toronto, ON: Oxford University Press.

In-text citations:

- For two authors of a work, mention both last names when you cite them.
  Part of sentence: Kimmel and Holler (2010) suggest that . . .

- Note the use of the word *and*.
  Added to sentence: . . . significance of gender (Kimmel and Holler 2010).

Ferber, Abby, Kimberly Holcomb, and Tre Wentling. 2013. *Sex, Gender and Sexuality: The New Basics*. 2nd ed. Toronto: Oxford University Press.

In-text citations:

- For three authors, mention all the authors when you cite them.

  Part of sentence: Ferber, Holcomb, and Wentling (2013) suggest . . .
  Added to sentence: . . . the basics of sexuality (Ferber, Holcomb, and Wentling 2013).

Book with Four or More Authors

Provide all the names of the authors and other information in the reference list in the same way as two or three authors.

For in-text citations:

- Use only the last name of the first author followed by *et al.* (meaning "and others").

  Part of sentence: Riley et al. (2007) maintain . . .
  Added to sentence: . . . for early childhood (Riley et al. 2007).

Book with an Editor

Gahagan, Jacqueline, ed. 2013. *Women and HIV Prevention in Canada: Implications for Research, Practice and Policy*. Toronto, ON: Women's Press.

In-text citations:

- Same as for one author.

Book Chapter in an Edited Book

Archibald, Chris, and Jessica Halverson. 2013. "The Current State of Women and HIV in Canada: An Overview of HIV/AIDS Epidemiology in Canada." In *Women and HIV Prevention in Canada: Implications for Research, Practice and Policy*, edited by Jacqueline Gahagan, 5–14. Toronto, ON: Women's Press.

In-text citations:

Part of sentence: Archibald and Halverson (2013) present an overview . . .
Added to sentence: . . . highlight women and HIV/AIDS (Archibald and Halverson 2013).

E-Book for a Printed Book

> Henry, Vincent E., and Robert Jay Lifton. 2004. *Death Work: Police, Trauma, and the Psychology of Survival*. New York, NY: Oxford University Press. MyiLibrary edition.

In-text citations:

- Same as for two authors.

Book with a Group or Corporation as Author

> Nishga Tribal Council. 1993. *Nisga'a: People of the Nass River*. Vancouver: Douglas & MacIntyre.

In-text citations:

> *Part of sentence*: . . . as mentioned by Nishga Tribal Council (1993) . . .
> *Added to sentence*: . . . describing people's lives (Nishga Tribal Council, 1993).

Book with Publisher as Author

When the author and publisher of a book or e-book are the same, repeat them:

> National Crime Prevention Centre (Canada). 2012. *A Statistical Snapshot of Youth at Risk and Youth Offending in Canada*. Ottawa, ON: National Crime Prevention Centre (Canada).

In-text citations:

- Same as preceding example.

Book with Group/Corporation Online

> Public Safety Canada. 2012. *A Statistical Snapshot of Youth at Risk and Youth Offending in Canada*. http://www.publicsafety.gc.ca/res/cp/res/ssyr-eng.aspx

In-text citations:

- Same as preceding example.

3.3.2 Articles in Journals or Periodicals

Article with One Author in Print

If pages in an article are continuous, then no issue number need be provided. Provide issue number in parentheses if page numbers are not continuous. Below, the issue number is omitted:

McKeen, Wendy. 2012. "The Construction of 'Welfare Mothers' in Canada's Late 1960s/Early 1970s 'War on Poverty.'" *Canadian Woman Studies* 29:107–123.

With the issue number it would be: 29(3):107–223. Note that the volume number, 29, is not italicized and that there is no space after the colon when the page numbers start.

In-text citations:

- Same as one author for a book.

Article with One Author with DOI

Sullivan, Tami P. 2013. "Think Outside: Advancing Risk and Protective Factor Research Beyond the Intimate-Partner-Violence Box." *Psychology of Violence* 3(2):121–125. doi:10.1037/a0032125.

In-text citations:

- Same as for one author for a book.
- Always use lower case for DOI (doi).

Article with One Author with URL

Atkins, P.J. 2003. "Mother's Milk and Infant Death in Britain, circa 1900–1940." *Anthropology of Food*. http://aof.revues.org/310.

In-text citations:

- Same as for one author.

Article with Two Authors

Moen, Phyllis, and Sarah Flood, S. 2013. "Men's Work/Volunteer Time in the Encore Life Course Stage." *Social Problems* 60(2):206–233. doi:110.1525/sp.2013.11120.

In-text citations:

Part of sentence for all citations: As Moen and Flood (2013) state . . .
Added to sentence for all citations: . . . life course stage (Moen and Flood 2013).

Article with Three Authors

> Kornrich, Sabino, Julie Brines, and Katrina Leupp. 2012. "Egalitarianism, Housework, and Sexual Frequency in Marriage." *American Sociological Review* 78(1):26–50. doi:10.1177/0003122412472340.

In-text citations:

> *Part of sentence for all citations*: Kornrich, Brines and Leupp (2012) maintain that . . .
> *Added to sentence for all citations*: . . . marriage (Kornrich, Brines, and Leupp 2012, 45–50).

Four or More Authors

> Caron, Angela, Marie-France Lafontaine, Jean-François Bureau, Christine Levesque, and Susan M. Johnson. 2012. "Comparisons of Close Relationships: An Evaluation of Relationship Quality and Patterns of Attachment to Parents, Friends, and Romantic Partners in Young Adults." *Canadian Journal of Behavioural Science/Revue Canadienne des Sciences du Comportement* 44(4):245–256. doi:10.1037/a0028013.

In-text citations:

> *Part of sentence for all citations*: . . . the attachments illustrated by Caron et al. (2012) include . . .
> *Added to sentence for all citations*: . . . by young adults (Caron et al. 2012).

Article with a Group as Author
See government documents and website.

3.3.3 Articles in Newspapers and Magazines

Article in Online Newspaper with Author
Use the same newspaper format for a magazine.

> Daley, Suzanne. 2013. "Danes Rethink a Welfare State Ample to a Fault." *New York Times*, April 20. http://www.nytimes.com/2013/04/21/world/europe/danes-rethink-a-welfare-state-ample-to-a-fault.html?_r=0&adxnnl=1&ref=todayspaper&adxnnlx=1366585289-YmweA7y1W1iuQKoJrdrX9A.

In-text citations:

- Same as for one author.

Article in Newspaper with a Group or Corporation as Author

> The Nature Conservancy of Canada. 2004. "Saving Canada's Natural Masterpieces." *Globe and Mail*, May 28: E1–E3.

In-text citations:

> *Part of sentence*: . . . as stated by The Nature Conservancy of Canada (2004) . . .
> *Added to sentence*: . . . preserving these masterpieces is vital (The Nature Conservancy of Canada 2004).

Article in Printed Magazine

> Snider, Michael, and Kathryn Borel. 2004. "Stalked by a Cyberbully." *Maclean's*, May 24:17, 76–77.

In-text citations:

- Same as for two authors.
- Note the different page number locations are separated by a comma (17, 76–77).

3.3.4 Online Government Publications

> Human Resources and Skills Development Canada. 2013. *Funding: Employment Assistance for Older Workers*. http://www.hrsdc.gc.ca/ eng/jobs/train ing_agreements/older_workers/in dex.shtml.

In-text citations:

> *Part of sentence*: . . . for older workers, Human Resources and Skills Development Canada (2013) has . . .
> *Added to sentence*: . . . federal government program (Human Resources and Skills Development Canada 2013).

> The United States Census Bureau. 2012. *Poverty Thresholds by Size of Family Unit*. http://www.census.gov/compendia/statab/2012/tables/ 12s0710.PDF.

In-text citations:

> *Part of sentence*: . . . as reported by The United States Census Bureau (2012) . . .
> *Added to sentence*: . . . as data suggest (The United States Census Bureau 2012).

3.3.5 Public Lectures and Conferences

Werdal, Thayne. 2013. "'When you're homeless, your friends are your home': Friendships among Street Youth in Victoria, Canada." Paper presented at the annual meeting of the Canadian Anthropology Society/La Société Canadienne D'anthropol ogie, Victoria, Canada, May 8–11.

In-text citations:

- Same as for one author.

3.3.6 Websites and Social Media

Reference list and in-text citation for websites, their specific web pages, and social media are provided for the examples. Note the following:

- If there is no date use "n.d." without the quotation marks.
- If your instructor requires an access date, add it before the URL.
- Always keep a copy of any social media used for referencing.

Website

National Institute of Mental Health (NIMH). 2013. *Anxiety Disorders*. April 19. http://www.nimh.nih.gov/index.shtml.

In-text citations:

Part of sentence: . . . as National Institute of Mental Health (NIMH) (2013) states . . .
For second and further citations: . . . as NIMH (2013) states . . .
Added to sentence: . . . anxiety disorders (National Institute of Mental Health [NIMH] 2013).
Added to sentence for second and further citations: . . . widely known (NIMH 2013).

Blog

Moss, Catriona, and Amelia Swan. 2013. "Climate Conversations—Gender Analysis in Forestry Research: What Policymakers Should Know." *Centre for International Forestry Research* (CIFOR), (web log), March 11. http://www.trust.org/alertnet/blogs/climate-conversations/gender -analysis-in-forestry-research-what-policymakers-should-know/.

In-text citations:

Part of sentence: . . . as Moss and Swan (2013) blog . . .
Added to sentence: . . . highlighted in their blog (Moss and Swan 2013).

Video Blog

Silk, Eric. 2012. "Psychology and Physiology of Substance Abuse Part 2." (Video blog), April 23. http://www.youtube.com/watch?v=w-c MvB9gC6s

In-text citations:

- Same as preceding for one author.

Podcast

Anglin, Mary. 2012. "Gender and Globalization in Appalachia." (Podcast), July 2. http://gws.as.uky.edu/podcasts/gender-and -globalization-appalachia-mary-anglin.

In-text citations:

- Same as preceding for one author.

Video Podcast

Basu, Srimati. 2013. "Playing Off Courts: The Spaces Of Adjudicating Family And Violence." (Video podcast), February 18. http://gws.as.uky. edu/video/playing-courts-spaces-adjudicating-family-and-violence.

In-text citations:

- Same as preceding for one author.

Twitter

Obama, Barack. 2013. "Washington Can't Get Away with Ignoring 90% of the Country on Gun Violence Prevention. Say You'll Keep Fighting." (Twitter post), April 22. https://twitter.com/BarackObama/ status/326433885791592448.

In-text citations:

Part of sentence: . . . on Twitter by the President (Obama 2013) to encourage . . .
Added to sentence: . . . president tweeting to seek more supporters (Obama 2013).

Facebook

> Moyers, Bill. 2013. "The Toxic Assault on Our Children Is Discussed with Sandra Steingraber." (Facebook update), April 17. https://www. facebook.com/photo.php?fbid=58258028509332 0&set=a.3909797 90920038.103036.1145289552317916&type=1&theater.

In-text citations:

> *Part of sentence*: . . . on Facebook, Bill Moyers (2013) promotes . . .
> *Added to sentence*: . . . public discussion of toxic assault on our children (Moyers 2013).

3.4 How Do I Cite Sources According to ASA Style?

This reference section and examples are based on *The American Sociological Association (ASA) Style Guide*. The website for the American Sociological Association is http://www.ASAnet.org/. Whenever there is little mention of how to format a given source in the ASA Style Guide, especially an electronic source, most instructors follow the CMS author-date style. This is also adopted here. In some instances, such as certain electronic publishing in social media, little guidance from either style is provided. Some instructors may require that all sources appear in your references section in order to check them. Suggested formats are presented for these styles.

3.4.1 Books

Book with One Author

> Smith, Dorothy E. 2005. *Institutional Ethnography: A Sociology for People.* Lanham, MA: Altamira.

In-text citations:

> *Part of sentence*: Smith (2005) maintains that . . .
> *Added to sentence*: . . . texts are analyzed specifically as part of social activity (Smith 2005:167).
> *For two or more pages*: (Smith 2005:167–168).

- Note that there is no space after the colon where the page numbers start.

Book with Two Authors

> Kimmel, Michael S. and Jacqueline Holler. 2010. *The Gendered Society.* Canadian ed. Toronto, ON: Oxford University Press.

In-text citations:

- For two authors of a work, mention both last names when you cite them.

  Part of sentence: Kimmel and Holler (2010) suggest that . . .
  Added to sentence: . . . significance of gender (Kimmel and Holler 2010).

Book with Three to Five Authors

Adapt the following three-author style below to four and five authors.

> Ferber, Abby, Kimberly Holcomb, and Tre Wentling. 2013. *Sex, Gender and Sexuality: The New Basics*. 2nd ed. Toronto: Oxford University Press.

In-text citations:

- For first citation, mention all the authors.

  Part of sentence: Ferber, Holcomb, and Wentling (2013) suggest . . .

- For the second and subsequent citations, use the last name of the first author, with the Latin abbreviation et al. (meaning "and others").

  For second and subsequent citations: Ferber et al. (2013) suggest that . . .
  Added to sentence for first citation: . . . the basics of sexuality (Ferber, Holcomb, and Wentling 2013).
  For second and subsequent citations: . . . the further basics of sexuality (Ferber et al. 2013).

Book with an Editor

> Gahagan, Jacqueline, ed. 2013. *Women and HIV Prevention in Canada: Implications for Research, Practice and Policy*. Toronto, ON: Women's Press.

In-text citations:

- Same as for one author.

Book Chapter in an Edited Book

> Archibald, Chris and Jessica Halverson. 2013. "The Current State Of Women and HIV in Canada: An Overview of HIV/AIDS Epidemiology in Canada." Pp. 5–14 in *Women and HIV Prevention in Canada: Implications for Research, Practice and Policy*, edited by Jacqueline Gahagan. Toronto, ON: Women's Press.

In-text citations:

> *Part of sentence*: Archibald and Halverson (2013) present an overview . . .
> *Added to sentence*: . . . highlight women and HIV/AIDS (Archibald and Halverson 2013:5–6).

E-Book for a Printed Book

> Henry, Vincent E. and Robert Jay Lifton. 2004. *Death Work: Police, Trauma, and the Psychology of Survival*. New York: Oxford University Press. (Also available at: http://www.amazon.co m/Death-Work-Psychology Survival-ebook/dp/B000W0UQPW/re f=sr_1_2_title_1_kin?s=boo ks &ie=UTF8&qid=1372185675&sr=1-2&keywords=death+work).

In-text citations:

- Same as for two authors.

Book with a Group or Corporation as Author

> Nishga Tribal Council. 1993. *Nisga'a: People of the Nass River*. Vancouver: Douglas & MacIntyre.

In-text citations:

> *Part of sentence*: . . . as mentioned by the Nishga Tribal Council (1993) . . .
> *Added to sentence*: . . . describing people's lives (Nishga Tribal Council 1993).

Book with Publisher as Author

When the author and publisher of a book or e-book are the same, repeat them:

> National Crime Prevention Centre (Canada). 2012. *A Statistical Snapshot of Youth at Risk and Youth Offending in Canada*. Ottawa, ON: National Crime Prevention Centre (Canada).

In-text citations:

- Same as for preceding example.

Book with Group/Corporation Online

> Public Safety Canada. 2012. *A Statistical Snapshot of Youth at Risk and Youth Offending in Canada*. Retrieved May 19, 2013 (http://www. publicsafety.gc.ca/res/cp/res/ssyr-eng.aspx).

In-text citations:

- Same as for preceding example.

3.4.2 Articles in Journals or Periodicals

Article with One Author in Print
Provide the issue number in parentheses after the volume number.

> McKeen, Wendy. 2012. "The Construction of 'Welfare Mothers' in Canada's
> Late 1960s/Early 1970s 'War On Poverty.'" *Canadian Woman Studies*
> 29(3):107–123.

Article with One Author with DOI

> Sullivan, Tami P. 2013. "Think Outside: Advancing Risk and Protective Factor
> Research Beyond the Intimate-Partner-Violence Box." *Psychology of*
> *Violence* 3(2):121–125. doi:10.1037/a0032125.

In-text citations:

- Same as for one author for a book.
- Reminder, always use lower case for DOI (doi).

Article with One Author with URL
The retrieval date refers to the most recent access date.

> Atkins, P.J. 2003. "Mother's Milk and Infant Death in Britain, Circa 1900–
> 1940." *Anthropology of Food*. Retrieved May 23, 2013 (http://aof.re-
> vues.org/310).

In-text citations:

- Same as for one author.

Article with Two Authors

> Moen, Phyllis and Sarah Flood. 2013. "Men's Work/Volunteer Time in
> the Encore Life Course Stage." *Social Problems* 60(2):206–233.
> doi:110.1525/sp.2013.11120.

In-text citations:

> *Part of sentence for all citations*: As Moen and Flood (2013) state . . .
> *Added to sentence for all citations*: . . . life course stage (Moen and Flood 2013).

Article with Three Authors

>Duffy, Mignon, Randy Albelda, and Clare Hammonds. 2013. "Counting
>Care Work: The Empirical and Policy Applications of Care Theory."
>*Social Problems* 60(20):145–167. doi:10.1525/sp.2013.60.2.145

In-text citations:

>*Part of sentence:* . . . Duffy, Albelda, and Hammonds (2013) present care
>theory . . .
>*For second and further citations as part of sentence:* . . . Duffy et al. (2013) suggest
>that . . .
>*Added to sentence for first citation:* . . . present a theory of care (Duffy, Albelda,
>and Hammonds 2013).
>*Added to sentence for second and further citation:* . . . present a theory of care
>(Duffy et al. 2013).

Four or More Authors

>Caron, Angela, Marie-France Lafontaine, Jean-François Bureau, Christine
>Levesque, and Susan M. Johnson. 2012. "Comparisons of Close
>Relationships: An Evaluation of Relationship Quality and Patterns
>of Attachment to Parents, Friends, and Romantic Partners in Young
>Adults." *Canadian Journal of Behavioural Science/Revue Canadienne
>des Sciences du Comportement.* 44(4):245–256. doi:10.1037/
>a0028013

In-text citations:

- Use "et al." starting with first citation.
  Part of sentence for all citations: . . . the attachments illustrated by Caron et
  al. (2012) include . . .
  Added to sentence for all citations . . . the significance of attachments by
  young adults (Caron et al. 2012) requires that . . .

Article with a Group as Author
See government documents and website.

3.4.3 Articles in Newspapers and Magazines

Article in Online Newspaper with Author

>Daley, Suzanne. 2013. "Danes Rethink a Welfare State Ample to a Fault,"
>*The New York Times*, April 20. Retrieved May 23, 2013 (http://
>www.nytimes.com/2013/04/21/world/europe/danes-rethink-a

-welfare-state-ample-to-a   fault.html?_r=0&adxnnl=1&ref=todays
paper &adxnnlx=1366585289YmweA7y1W1iuQKoJrdrX9A).

In-text citations:

- Same as for one author.

Article in Newspaper with a Group or Corporation as Author

The Nature Conservancy of Canada. 2004. "Saving Canada's Natural
Masterpieces," *The Globe and Mail*, May 28, pp. E1–E3.

In-text citations:

Part of sentence: . . . as stated by The Nature Conservancy of Canada
(2004) . . .
Added to sentence: . . . preserving these masterpieces is vital (The Nature
Conservancy of Canada 2004).

Article in Printed Magazine

Snider, Michael and Kathryn Borel. 2004. "Stalked by a Cyberbully,"
Maclean's, May 24, pp. 17, 76–77.

In-text citations:

- Same as for two authors.
- Note that the different page number locations are separated by a comma
  (17, 76–77).

3.4.4 Online Government Publications

Human Resources and Skills Development Canada. 2013. *Funding:*
Employment Assistance for Older Workers, April 6. Retrieved May 24,
2013 (http://www.hrsdc.gc.ca/eng/jobs/older_wor kers/index.shtml).

In-text citations:

Part of sentence: . . . for older workers, Human Resources and Skills Development
Canada (2013) has . . .
Added to sentence: . . . federal government program (Human Resources and Skills
Development Canada 2013).

The United States Census Bureau. 2012. *Poverty Thresholds by Size of*
Family Unit. Retrieved May 25 (http://www.census.gov/compendia/
statab/2012/tables/12s0710.PDF).

In-text citations:

> *Part of sentence*: . . . as reported by The United States Census Bureau
>   (2012) . . .
> *Added to sentence*: . . . as data suggest (The United States Census Bureau 2012).

3.4.5 Public Lectures and Conferences

> Werdal, Thayne. 2013. "'When you're homeless, your friends are your home':
>   Friendships Among Street Youth in Victoria, Canada." Presented at the
>   annual meeting of the Canadian Anthropology Society/La Société Ca
>   nadienne D'anthropologie, May 8–11, Victoria, Canada.

In-text citations:

- Same as for one author.

3.4.6 Websites and Social Media

Not all parts of social media are covered in the ASA style guide. Consequently, some styles are suggested for the reference list.

- In general, include the source in the text and in the references list. It is helpful to the reader to indicate the kind of electronic source being referred to, such as a blog, on Facebook, on Twitter, and so on.
- If there is no date use "N.d." without the quotation marks.
- Add the retrieval date, generally before the URL.
- Always keep a copy of any social media used for referencing.

Website

> National Institute of Mental Health. 2013. "Anxiety Disorders." Bethesda,
>   MD: National Institute of Mental Health. Retrieved May 21, 2013
>   (http://www.nimh.nih.gov/health/topics/anxiety-disorders/index.
>   shtml).

In-text citations:

> *Part of sentence*: . . . as the website of the National Institute of Mental Health
>   (NIMH) (2013) states . . .
> *For second and subsequent citations*: . . . as NIMH (2013) states . . .
> *Added to sentence*: . . . widely known website (National Institute of Mental Health
>   [NIMH] 2013).
> *Added to sentence for second and subsequent citations*: . . . widely known (NIMH
>   2013).

Blog

Moss, Catriona and Amelia Swan. 2013. "Climate Conversations—
Gender Analysis in Forestry Research: What Policymakers Should
Know," *Centre for International Forestry Research* (CIFOR). Blog.
Retrieved May 24, 2013 (http://www.trust.org/alertnet/blogs/climate
-conversations/gender-analysis-in-forestry-research-what-policy
makers-should-know/).

In-text citations:

Part of sentence: . . . as Moss and Swan blog (2013) gender . . .
Added to sentence: . . . blog analyzes gender for policy makers (Moss and Swan
2013).

Video Blog

Silk, Eric. 2012. "Psychology and Physiology of Substance Abuse Part
2." Video Blog. Retrieved April 9, 2013 (http://www.youtube.com/
watch?v=w-cMvB9gC6s).

In-text citations:

• Same as for one author.

Podcast

Anglin, Mary. 2012. "Gender and Globalization in Appalachia." Audio
Podcast. Retrieved April 4, 2013 (http://gws.as.uky.edu/podcasts/
gender-and-globalization-appalachia-mary-anglin).

In-text citations:

• Same as for one author.

Video Podcast

Basu, Srimati. 2013. "Playing Off Courts: The Spaces of Adjudicating Family and Violence." Video Podcast. Retrieved May 25, 2013
(http://gws.as.uky.edu/video/playing-courts-spaces-adjudicating
-family-and-violence).

In-text citations:

• Same as for one author.

Twitter

Suggested for reference list:

> Obama, Barack. 2013 "Washington Can't Get Away with Ignoring 90% of the Country on Gun Violence Prevention. Say You'll Keep Fighting." Twitter. Retrieved May 24, 2013 (https://twitter.com/BarackObama/status/326433885791592448).

In-text citations:

> *Part of sentence*: . . . on Twitter by the President (Obama 2013) to encourage . . .
> *Added to sentence*: . . . president using Twitter to seek more supporters (Obama 2013).

Facebook

> Moyers, Bill. 2013. "The Toxic Assault on Our Children Is Discussed with Sandra Steingraber." Facebook. Retrieved April 24, 2013 (https://www.facebook.com/moyersandcompany?fref=ts). Facebook Update. Retrieved from (https://www.facebook.com/photo.php?fbid=5825 802850 93320&set=a.390979790920038.103036.114528955231791 &type=1&theater).

In-text citations:

> *Part of sentence*: . . . on his Facebook, Moyers (2013) discusses . . .
> *Added to sentence*: . . . public discussion of toxic assault on our children on Facebook (Moyers 2013).

Chapter Summary

- *References* means a separate page with the full text of your research sources used in your term paper or book review.
- *In-text citation* refers to those sources used in your term paper or book review and formatted according to one of the three styles.
- Each referencing style has its own meaning and formatting for short and long quotations.
- All three referencing styles share similar online referencing for the use of DOIs and URLs.
- To format a book or an article in a journal or periodical (and other sources), follow either the APA, CMS, or ASA styles. An example of a reference and its corresponding in-text citations are provided for each style.

✓ **Checklist for**
Referencing Sources

☐ Did you document all information from all your sources to avoid plagiarism?

☐ Did you record all the relevant information for your reference sources according to the style that you are required to use?

☐ Do you know what additional formatting you will have to do once you write your paper, including in-text citations, short and long quotations, and the references page?

Recommended Websites

Monash University (Australia)
Monash University Library—Demystifying citing and referencing; contains tutorials on citing and referencing:
http://www.lib.monash.edu.au/tutorials/citing/

University of Wisconsin at Madison
The Writing Center—The writer's handbook: documentation styles for citing references in your paper:
http://www.wisc.edu/writing/Handbook/Documentation.html

Recommended Readings

Gibaldi, J. (2009). *MLA handbook for writers of research papers* (7th ed.). New York, NY: The Modern Language Association of America.

Szuchman, L.T. (2013). *Writing with style: APA style made easy* (6th ed.). Scarborough, ON: Wadsworth/Cengage.

Trimmer, J.F. (2012). *A guide to MLA documentation* (9th ed.). Scarborough, ON: Nelson/Cengage.

Turabian, K.L. (2010). *Student's guide to writing college papers* (4th ed.). (Revised by Colomb, G.G., Williams, J.M., & University of Chicago Press Editorial Staff). Chicago, IL: University of Chicago Press.

Chapter 4

Research to Define Concepts in the Aim, Organize Arguments, and Draft a Conclusion

Once you have completed the first-priority items, focus on defining the concepts in the aim sentence, organizing the individual arguments or headings/themes, and drafting the conclusion to the term paper. You should add any research sources used in this process to your reference list in your outline.

In this chapter, you will learn to

1. define the concepts in the aim sentence,
2. organize arguments or headings/themes, and
3. draft a conclusion.

At the end of this chapter, you will find a sample first social science outline for up to five individual arguments to support an aim. This is followed by a sample second social science outline at Step 3 (the final step) for headings/themes. The second sample outline builds on the individual arguments created in the first outline to show how they can be grouped into headings/themes with their corresponding points.

4.1 How Do I Define the Concepts in the Aim Sentence?

Certain words in your aim sentence will require clarification. Recall that to define a concept means clarifying the meaning of the words that present the key ideas in the aim. To assist you in providing definitions for your aim or question, follow this general process, starting with knowing which keywords or concepts to define.

4.1.1 Know Which Concepts or Keywords to Define

Not every word in the aim sentence needs to be defined. Only those words, concepts, or terms that are the *main* ideas in your aim must be defined.

Following are examples of aim sentences, followed by the concepts to be defined:

> The aim of this paper is to demonstrate that street youth will become involved in deviant behaviour.

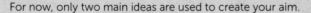

Reminder

For now, only two main ideas are used to create your aim.

The concepts to be defined here are *street youth* and *deviant behaviour.*

> This paper will show that street kids come from dysfunctional families.

The concepts to be defined are *street kids* and *dysfunctional families.*
Here is an example of a more complicated aim:

> This paper will focus on the coping skills that street kids develop in order to survive.

The concepts or keywords to be defined are the following: *coping skills, street kids, develop,* and *survive.*

The wording of your aim is very important because you will have to define the general concepts that you decide to use. You are expected to *know* which words are the concepts in your aim sentence that need to be defined.

Here is where you use your knowledge of *concept* and *definition* from the building blocks. The aim consists of two concepts (and sometimes more) that you define. The concepts in the aim and their corresponding definitions are referred to generally as the *main argument* with all the other individual arguments or those in headings/themes providing the "evidence" to support it. No particular evidence or examples are provided here because the emphasis is on making sure that the aim will be understood with the clearly expressed definitions of the concepts in your aim.

The next section presents how to go about defining the concepts in the aim sentence.

4.1.2 Define the Concepts in Sequence

You must define the concepts in the order that they appear in the aim sentence. The first concept in the aim sentence will, therefore, be the first concept defined. The next concept in the aim sentence is defined after that. You must adhere to this order for the definitions to be consistent with the aim. Here is an example of the order in which concepts must be defined for an aim sentence:

> The aim of this paper is to demonstrate that street youth will become involved in deviant behaviour.

The concept that must be defined first is *street youth* because it appears first in the aim sentence. The concept that must be defined second is *deviant behaviour* because it appears second in the aim sentence. Record this order of your definitions in your outline.

4.1.3 Know That You Must Use Defined Concepts in Only One Way

A concept or keyword that you define in your aim sentence will be used in only that way. By defining a word or concept, you are restricting or limiting the meaning of that word or term (Davis et al., 2013, p. 25). That meaning applies to your entire term paper. That is, you must use the meaning of your concepts in the aim sentence consistently in the way that you have defined them.

To illustrate:

- Assume that your aim uses the concept *street kid* and that you define *street kid* as a homeless adolescent between the ages of 13 and 19.
- Defining the concept of *street kid* this way means that the words *street kid* can be used only that way throughout your paper.
- If you use the words *street kid* in any other way in your term paper (for example, to include information on someone over 19 years of age), you are using these keywords or this concept inconsistently.

TIPS When your instructor reads your term paper, she or he will use your definitions to read your term paper. Your definitions, then, are adopted or shared by the instructor reading your term paper (L. Barkley, personal communication, May 19, 2005). Your instructor will use the definitions of your concepts to determine how consistent you are in your use of them for your entire term paper.

You will run into problems if your use is inconsistent:

- If you do not use your overall concepts in the way that you have defined them, then your use of them is not consistent or logical. This will weaken your term paper by making it less convincing in the inconsistent parts.
- The specific argument in which your concept is used incorrectly may, in turn, weaken the understanding of your term paper's aim. Your inconsistent use may create ambiguity or doubt about your aim for your instructor.

In sum, the definitions of your concepts that you decide to use must make sense and must be applicable to your entire term paper.

4.1.4 Know That Definitions Must Come from the Course, Discipline, or Field of Studies

Your definitions of concepts or keywords must come from the course you are taking or from its field of studies. Each of these areas of study has a literature. The word *literature* is used here to mean all the writings that are part of these areas of study, including everything that has been published in books, journal articles, research reports, etc. Concepts are a part of the discourse of your field of studies. So, the definitions of your concepts must come from the particular literature in which you are writing your term paper:

- For an anthropology course, you must use the anthropology literature.
- For a gender studies course, you must use the gender studies literature
- For a political science course, you must use the political science literature
- For a psychology course, you must use the psychology literature.
- For a sociology course, you must use the sociology literature.

There are a number of places for you to research to find definitions for the literature that you need.

4.1.5 Know Where to Research for Definitions of Concepts

Your goal in undertaking research for definitions of concepts is to record the following in your outline:

- The exact quote and reference source for the definitions
- Any additional definitions of words in your first definition

For example:

> Deviance is defined as "the recognized violation of cultural norms" (Macionis & Gerber, 2011, p. 198).

An additional concept in the preceding is *norm*, which is defined as the "rules and expectations by which a society guides the behaviour of its members" (Macionis & Gerber, 2011, p. 65).

Record both the first and additional definitions in your outline. There are a number of general areas to research for definitions of concepts, starting with textbooks.

In Textbooks
One good place to start looking for definitions is in the textbook(s) for your course. The definitions in your course textbook already fulfill the requirement that they are part of the literature.

One word of caution concerning the use of textbooks: Do not use a definition from one course for a course of a different subject area. That is, do not use a definition from a sociology course in an economics course. A similar concept, like *socialization*, will have one definition and meaning in sociology and another definition and meaning in economics.

In Books and Articles
Another source of finding definitions of concepts in your aim is the books and articles of the relevant literature:

- The definitions of concepts in your aim will probably come from some of the books or articles that you used as the reference sources of your arguments.
- If you are unable to find definitions of concepts in these materials, then you should research other books and articles in the discipline or in the specific field of studies.
- If none of the preceding is useful, your best resource is to confer with your instructor.

In Dictionaries and Encyclopedias

Recall that there are various kinds of dictionaries and encyclopedias:

- The general community college- or university-level dictionaries (for example, *Merriam Webster Dictionary* or *Canadian Oxford Dictionary*)
- Specialized encyclopedias (for example, *Encyclopedia of Anthropology*)
- Dictionaries specializing in a discipline or field of studies (for example, dictionary of psychology or sociology)

Here are some guidelines about using the above for defining concepts:

- Use all of the above in order to understand the meaning of concepts or words.
- Do not use the general dictionaries for definitions of concepts because they present the meaning of words in everyday language and not in the professional language of the social sciences.
- Avoid using the specialized encyclopedias and dictionaries for definitions, or confer with your instructor about using them. Many instructors discourage you from using these definitions in your term paper because they want you to be more familiar with authors and their research in a particular area and to encourage you to work with the relevant literature of your studies.

4.2 How Do I Organize the Arguments?

Recall that to organize the arguments or headings/themes refers to the sequence or the order in which they will be made in your term paper. That is, you will state the first argument or heading/theme, then the second, and the third, etc. The goal here is to determine the best way to organize your arguments or headings/themes in support of your aim in your outline.

Individual arguments or headings/themes are usually arranged based on a reason. Provide a reason at the outset in this part of your outline for the sequence of your arrangement. Providing a reason for the way you decided to organize your arguments or headings/themes is helpful to the reader, your instructor, in understanding how you are going to demonstrate your aim. Your instructor will read your arguments or headings/themes with this reason in mind. Make sure the rest of your outline is consistent with this reason and with the sequence of your arguments or headings/themes.

Only two ways are presented here on how to organize your individual arguments or headings/themes. You will have to decide which one suits your outline.

4.2.1 Organize Arguments or Headings/Themes in One of Two Ways

You can start to arrange your arguments or headings/themes in two general ways:

- In a time sequence (historically or developmentally)
- In varying orders of importance

In a Time Sequence

One way to arrange individual arguments or headings/themes is in a time sequence. The term *time sequence* means that there is a chosen starting point in time and an end period. The more common terms that are used here are *historical* time period or stages of *development*. These versions have arguments or headings/themes that start at one point in time, such as a given time in history or the start of a process of development, and end with the last argument or headings/theme pertaining to that part of history or development being considered. There are various reasons for arranging arguments this way: to show a general pattern or trend of activities, or to highlight the increasing seriousness of a situation, problem, or issue.

For instance, you might arrange the *arguments* in your term paper so that they start with the first problem that street kids encounter, move on to the next one, and so on:

- Start with the first kind of deviant behaviour that street youth become involved in.
- End with the last kind of deviant behaviour that they are likely to become involved in.

The individual arguments would thus be in the following possible sequence:

Individual Arguments Organized in a Time Sequence

1. One kind of deviant behaviour of street kids is their involvement in substance abuse.
2. Once you are a street kid, you are very likely to become involved in the deviant behaviour of stealing.
3. Dealing in drugs is another deviant activity of street kids.
4. Another form of deviant behaviour that street kids engage in is obligatory sex.
5. Street kids also become involved in the deviant behaviour of prostitution.

The arrangement of these individual arguments then becomes *your guide for reorganizing the rest of your outline.* Now is the time to do this.

Arranging the *headings/themes* in a time sequence is done in a similar way based on the same reason: to show that street kids tend to become more involved in deviant behaviour. There are two steps involved: (1) arranging the headings/themes in a time sequence (or historically or developmentally) to show the increasing development of deviant behaviour, and (2) organizing the individual arguments within each, again, to show increasing involvement in a particular behaviour. From Step 2 (of Chapter 2), the headings/themes and their individual points can be organized into the possible time sequence shown in Table 4.1.

Table 4.1 Step 2 and Step 3 in Creating Headings/Themes

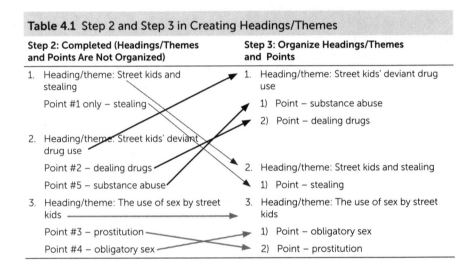

Step 2: Completed (Headings/Themes and Points Are Not Organized)	Step 3: Organize Headings/Themes and Points
1. Heading/theme: Street kids and stealing	1. Heading/theme: Street kids' deviant drug use
Point #1 only – stealing	1) Point – substance abuse
	2) Point – dealing drugs
2. Heading/theme: Street kids' deviant drug use	
Point #2 – dealing drugs	2. Heading/theme: Street kids and stealing
Point #5 – substance abuse	1) Point – stealing
3. Heading/theme: The use of sex by street kids	3. Heading/theme: The use of sex by street kids
Point #3 – prostitution	1) Point – obligatory sex
Point #4 – obligatory sex	2) Point – prostitution

This type of sequence of headings/themes can be written in your outline in the following ways. The first way states the headings/themes and the points to be made for each. The second way presents a shortened version of this by stating only the headings/themes in the organization of headings. Table 4.2 shows this.

Table 4.2 Organization of Headings/Themes in Time Sequence

Step 3: Organize Headings/Themes (with Points)	Organization of Headings/Themes (Condensed Version—No Mention of Points)
1. Heading/theme: Street kids' deviant drug use	1. Heading/theme: Street kids' deviant drug use
1) Point – substance abuse 2) Point – dealing drugs	
2. Heading/theme: Street kids and stealing	2. Heading/theme: Street kids and stealing
1) Point – stealing	
3. Heading/theme: The use of sex by street kids	3. Heading/theme: The use of sex by street kids
1) Point – obligatory sex 2) Point – prostitution	

The organization of headings/themes with points is useful because *it serves as a guide for you to rearrange your headings/themes and points within each.* You can keep the longer version in your outline until such time as you write this part of your term paper. Then, you can decide which version is more appropriate. In general, the shorter version without the points should be used in writing the organization of headings/themes.

In Order of Importance

Individual arguments or headings/themes can also be arranged according to their importance to the aim. That is, the sequence of arguments or headings/themes is used to show their significance or prominence in supporting the aim. The strength of the evidence in relation to the aim is used to make the decision on the significance of each argument or heading/theme. There are various ways to do this: arrange them from the most prominent to the least, from the least prominent to the most important, and variations of this.

For example, following is a general way of presenting individual *arguments* that starts with the second highest involvement in deviant behaviour by street youth, then presents the rest in decreasing order, and ends with the kind of deviant behaviour that has their highest involvement. The box that follows shows what this way of organizing arguments might look like using the street youth example:

Individual Arguments Organized in Order of Importance

1. Once you are a street youth, you are very likely to become involved in the deviant behaviour of stealing.
2. Dealing in drugs is a deviant activity of street youth.
3. Street youth become involved in the deviant behaviour of prostitution.
4. Another form of deviant behaviour related to prostitution is that street youth engage in obligatory sex.
5. One kind of deviant behaviour of street youth is their involvement in substance abuse.

This box shows that stealing would be the second highest deviant behaviour; dealing in drugs, the third highest; and so on. The most widespread deviant behaviour would be the last one, substance abuse. This arrangement emphasizes the seriousness of the deviant behaviour in which street kids become involved.

The arrangement of these individual arguments then becomes *your guide for re-organizing the rest of your outline.* Again, now is the time to do this.

The *headings/themes* can also be arranged based on their importance to the aim and the seriousness of the deviant behaviour in which street kids become involved. The two steps that are involved here are arranging (1) the headings/themes and (2) the arguments within each. The headings/themes are organized starting with the second most serious deviant behaviour, to the next one, and ending with the most serious kind. As well, the arguments within each heading/theme have been reorganized from the first to the second.

Table 4.3 shows how the previous headings/themes correspond to the final organization of headings/themes; only the individual arguments within them have been renumbered.

Table 4.3 Renumbering Points in Headings/Themes

Step 2: Completed (Headings/Themes and Points Are Not Organized)	Step 3: Organize Headings/Themes and Points
1. Heading/theme: Street kids and stealing	1. Heading/theme: Street kids and stealing
Point #1 only – stealing	1) Point – stealing
2. Heading/theme: Street kids' deviant drug use	2. Heading/theme: Street kids' deviant drug use
Point #2 – dealing drugs Point #5 – substance abuse	1) Point – dealing drugs 2) Point – substance abuse
3. Heading/theme: The use of sex by street kids	3. Heading/theme: The use of sex by street kids
Point #3 – prostitution Point #4 – obligatory sex	1) Point – obligatory sex 2) Point – prostitution

Table 4.3 indicates the following about the headings/themes for this term paper: stealing would be the second most serious problem followed by drug use; the most serious problem for street kids would be the use of sex; in general, street kids become involved in some significant deviant behaviours, as stated in the aim.

This type of sequence of headings/themes can be written in your outline in the following ways: (1) state the headings/themes and the points to be made for each; (2) state only the headings/themes in the organization of headings. Table 4.4 shows both of these options.

Table 4.4 Organization of Headings/Themes in Order of Importance

Step 3: Organize Headings/Themes and Points	Organization of Headings/Themes (Condensed Version – No Mention of Points)
1. Heading/theme: Street kids and stealing	1. Heading/theme: Street kids and stealing
1) Point – stealing	
2. Heading/theme: Street kids' deviant drug use	2. Heading/theme: Street kids' deviant drug use
1) Point – dealing drugs 2) Point – substance abuse	
3. Heading/theme: The use of sex by street kids	3. Heading/theme: The use of sex by street kids
1) Point – obligatory sex 2) Point – prostitution	

Similar to organizing headings/themes in a general way, the organization of headings/themes with points is useful because *it serves as a guide for you to rearrange your points within each heading/theme.*

Remember to provide a general reason for your arrangement and use your arrangement to reorganize your term paper, the presentation of arguments, or headings/themes. Once again, now is the time to do this.

4.3 How Do I Draft a Conclusion?

Recall that the word *conclusion* means the closing and end of your term paper. Although it is the end of your term paper, your conclusion is very important, especially to your aim. In your conclusion, you can remind the reader, your instructor, of all the arguments that you presented to demonstrate your aim. Think of the conclusion as the final opportunity to make a convincing case for your aim sentence or question.

4.3.1 Know What to Include

Your conclusion should include the following:

- A restating of your aim sentence
- A summary of each argument or headings/themes, and a reason why each argument or heading/theme supported the aim
- Recommendations for further research

Restate Your Aim Sentence
Restate your aim sentence in the past tense because you are now looking back at it. Here is an example:

> The aim of this paper was to demonstrate that street youth are very likely to be involved in deviant behaviour.

The past tense in this example is indicated by the word *was*. Using the past tense will indicate to your instructor that you are now looking back at what you have done, including summarizing your arguments or headings/themes.

Summarize Each Argument or Heading/Theme to Show How Each Supported the Aim
There are two general parts involved in your summary:

- Summarize each argument or heading/theme. Follow the same sequence of arguments or headings/themes that you used in organizing them to provide consistency and logic in your writing.
- Then, in a sentence or two, state how each argument or heading/theme supported your aim. Your goal is to present a clear link between each argument or heading/theme and your aim in order to make your case as convincing as possible.

Here are two examples that can be used for individual arguments or headings/themes (more examples are presented in the sample outlines):

1. One kind of deviant behaviour of street youth is their involvement in substance abuse.

Supported aim—substance abuse violates laws, especially when involving street youth who are under the required age for consuming alcohol; drug usage violates laws.

2. Once you are a street youth, you are very likely to become involved in the deviant behaviour of stealing.

Supported aim—stealing violates law of private property; unacceptable behaviour in order to acquire money and property; driven to steal to support habit of substance abuse.

Make Recommendations for Further Research

It is quite acceptable to include in the conclusion any recommendations or suggestions for further research. However, keep this part short—no more than a paragraph.

Here are examples of possible ideas for further research:

- How do street youth cope by engaging in deviant behaviour?
- What happens to street youth as they transition from youth into adulthood?
- What kinds of policies and services might help them?

4.3.2 Consult with Your Instructor

You should now have a completed outline. There are still, however, some final additional questions that you should ask your instructor based on your previous consultation:

- Are the definitions of concepts appropriate?
- Does the organization of arguments or headings/themes make sense?
- Is the conclusion fitting for the aim?
- Is the outline complete?

Again, incorporate your instructor's comments into revising your outline before you proceed to write your term paper.

Following are two examples of outlines. The first sample outline is for a starting social science term paper that has five arguments to support an aim. The second outline is for a social science term paper that has three headings/themes. Only Step 3 (the final step) of this second outline is presented. Please note the following about these outlines:

- A title page has been omitted.
- Some extra information and formatting has been added to help clarify the decisions made in the development of the outlines.
- Some additional evidence beyond the suggested two or three has been included. This additional evidence allows you to see patterns or trends for each point. You can always decide to omit weaker evidence for your point.

- The references page and the individual references will need to be formatted using APA, CMS, or ASA style once the term paper is written. At present, all information that is necessary for each research source is included.

Sample Outline 1
The First Social Science Outline: Individual Arguments

General Topic: street kids; teen runaways; street youth, homeless youth (alcohol abuse; FASD—these extra topics were not required because there was enough available information on teenage runaways and street kids)

For Introduction to Aim Sentence *(From Unused Portions of Arguments)*

Some possible sources on the significance and importance of research on street kids, teenage runaways, street youth, and homeless youth.

"What You Should Know about Homelessness" is an Appendix in Gillard's (2012) edited book called *Homelessness*. The following information from Covenant House is taken from this Appendix:
- Up to 40% of US homeless population is under 18 years old (p. 96).
- Half of teens too old to stay in foster care or juvenile justice systems become homeless in six months (p. 96).

The National Alliance to End Homelessness (NAEH) is the source for the following information in this Appendix:
- An estimated 50 000 US youth experience homelessness (p. 96).
- In 2008 and 2009 about 29 500 youth aged out of foster care (p. 96).

The following information is taken from the Appendix in the American Psychological Association report:
- Homeless children in US are estimated to be 1 in 50 or 1.5 million with 650 000 below six years of age (p. 97).

The Canadian Centre for Child Protection website, Missingkids.ca, states that "Every year, more than 50,000 reports of missing children are made to police in Canada." Retrieved 19 June, 2013 (http://missingkids.ca/app/en/about_us).

Shalev (2010) states that in her research on missing children (primarily living on the streets), "86% had been arrested at least once" though the conviction rate was much lower if there was a lack of prior convictions (p. 33).

Glassman (2012) cites a report that "20 to 40 percent of homeless youth nationally identify themselves as LGBT [lesbian, gay, bisexual, and transgender], at least two to four times the average of the general population" (p. 79).

continued

Ferguson et al. (2011), in their study of homeless young people, refer to prostitution, selling blood or plasma, dealing drugs, stealing and panhandling as survival behaviour.

A significant aspect to investigating teenage runaways, street kids, homeless youth, street youth was that there was no consensus on the use of these words and their meaning.

A decision was made to use street youth in the aim for the reason given in the section on define concepts.

Aim Sentence

The aim of this paper is to demonstrate that street youth are very likely to be involved in deviant behaviour.

Aim Sentence Worded as a Question

In what kinds of deviant behaviour are street youth likely to be involved?

Define Concepts (Concepts from the Aim That Will Be Defined and Their Sources)

The two main concepts from the aim that need to be defined are street youth and deviant behaviour.

Define the First Concept of Street Youth in the Aim

Here is why the concept *street youth* (or homeless youth) was chosen instead of *teenage runaways* or street kids for the aim.

The following definitions were examined.

1. *Street kids*

Finkelstein (2005) defines street kids "(and the alternative terms, homeless adolescents or homeless youth) as young people under the age of 21 who have separated themselves from their families (whether by parental consent or not) and now live entirely on the streets (i.e., not in shelters)" (p. 3).

2. *Street youth*

Gibson (2011) defines street youth as "young people, twelve to twenty four years old, who are living without family support or a stable residence, both on and off the actual streets and in the public spaces of cities and towns. They may live intermittently in shelters, with friends or relatives (couch surfing), or on the streets" (p. 7).

Roy et al. (2011) define a street youth as someone in the last year who had been without a place to sleep more than once or who regularly used the services of street youth agencies (such as drop-in centres, shelters, or outreach vans), was 14 to 23 years of age, and who spoke French or English (p. 121).

Hadland et al. (2011) distinguish between younger street youth, those below 20 years, and those that are older, 21 and over (p. 1487). Most youth were older in their study (60.3%) and the rest were younger (30.7%) (p. 1488). About 75% of all their participants reported that they were homeless (p. 1488). The majority were white (71%) males (68%) (p. 1488). A significant number of the remaining youth were Aboriginal (p. 1488).

From the preceding definitions (*street kids, street youth*):

There is overlap in comparing all definitions and hence it is difficult to separate homeless kids, and youth living on the street.

The word *street* is used to refer to being homeless or of no fixed address. *Street* and *homeless* are used interchangeably.

The age range from the definitions is from 12 to 24 and older.

The time away from home or residence, being absent, ranged from overnight to three or more days.

Here is the wording of the definition of *street youth* or *homeless youth* and the reason for this decision:

For this term paper, a street youth is defined as a homeless person under 24 years of age who is absent without permission from overnight to three or more days.

The reason for choosing *street youth* or *homeless youth* was so that all research data from the reference sources that are used as evidence in the arguments could be included.

This decision resulted in a change of wording in the aim sentence from *street kids* to *street youth* (or *homeless youth*).

Define the Second Concept of Deviant Behaviour in the Aim

Deviance is defined as "the recognized violation of cultural norms" (Macionis & Gerber, 2011, p. 198).

The word *norm* in this definition refers to the "rules and expectations by which a society guides the behaviour of its members" (Macionis & Gerber, 2011, p. 65).

Specifically, the emphasis of the aim is on "proscriptive norms," which is defined as "what we should not do" (Macionis & Gerber, 2011, p. 65).

Restate the Definition of Deviance

Deviance refers to the kind of behaviour that defies what members of a society consider acceptable and what should not be done.

continued

Restate the Aim Using the Definitions of Street Youth *and* Deviant Behaviour
Here are examples of stating the aim by using the meanings of the preceding definitions:

Homeless youth will become involved in behaviour that defies the rules and expectations of their society.

Street youth will behave in ways that members of their society consider unacceptable.

Organize Arguments (The Sequence of Five Individual Arguments)

The arguments have been organized according to street youths' greatest to least involvement in deviant behaviour:

1. One kind of deviant behaviour of street youth is their involvement in substance abuse.
2. Once you are a street youth, you are very likely to become involved in the deviant behaviour of stealing.
3. Dealing in drugs is a deviant activity of street youth.
4. Street youth become involved in the deviant behaviour of sex trade.
5. Another form of deviant behaviour related to prostitution is that street youth engage in obligatory sex.

Presentation of Arguments (The Points and Evidence to Support Each Point)

1. Point (or Point 1): One kind of deviant behaviour of street youth is their involvement in substance abuse.
Basically, *substance abuse* refers to the overindulgence in or dependence on an addictive material. Substance abuse and use includes alcohol and illegal drugs.

Evidence:
Hadland et al. (2011) found that younger street youth were more likely to have binged on alcohol abuse (95%) while older street youth were more involved with drug use (95%) (p. 1488).

Roy et al. (2011) report on 352 participants (72% males) with an average of 20 years. Of these, 37 (7 girls, 30 boys) initiated drug injection.

The first substance injected was cocaine (54%), followed by heroin (40%), or something else (6%) (p. 126).

They conclude that daily alcohol consumption, heroin and cocaine use are independent predictors of transition to injection among young participants (p. 129).

Paquette et al. (2010) report, that in their initial analysis, a high incidence of crack use was prevalent among street youth.

Hadland et al. (2010) state that drug use tends to lead to injection: nearly half of all females became regular injectors within one week of their first injection, while less than one-third of males ultimately became regular injectors (p. 94). The main difference is in marijuana use: "youth engaging in daily use of marijuana were significantly less likely to have a history of injection" (p. 94).

2. Point or (Point 2): *Once you are a street youth you are very likely to become involved in the deviant behaviour of stealing.*
Generally, stealing means taking something that does not belong to you.

    Stealing or theft includes shoplifting, boosting (stealing merchandise from one store and selling it to another), and scams (conning people) (Finkelstein, 2005, p. 81).

Evidence:
Shalev (2010) found that missing children living on the streets committed shoplifting and theft and constituted 22% of the arrests. She refers to these as "survival" crimes since these children may have no other means to support themselves (p. 34).

Finkelstein's (2005) research showed that 60% admitted to petty crimes, for example, stealing in hospitals (Finkelstein, 2005, p. 81); scams, for example, fake drug deals—just take money and never return with the drugs (pp. 82–83).

From Baron and Kennedy (2001), the less certain that street youth were of punishment and the lower the severity of the punishment, the more houses and cars they broke into (p. 167).

3. Point or (Point 3): *Dealing in drugs is a deviant activity of street youth.*
Finkelstein's (2005) definition of dealing drugs refers to selling illegal drugs in order to make money, primarily to support their habit (p. 79).

Evidence:
Hadland et al. (2011) found that it was primarily older street youth (21 and older) who dealt drugs and spent an average of more than $50 daily on drugs (p. 1488).

Finkelstein (2005) states that from 40 to 50% of kids sold, ran, or moved drugs (drug dealing) (p. 79). Street youth can make over five times their investment from acid, for example, buy for $100 a sheet and sell up to $500 a sheet (p. 80).

4. Point or (Point 4): *Street youth become involved in the deviant behaviour of the sex trade.*
The term *sex trade* is used by Kidd and Liborio (2011) instead of *prostitution* and includes children and youth. It refers not only to sex for money but also to survival sex, which Mayers (2001) defines as "sex in exchange for money, food, or shelter" (p. 152).

continued

Similar to survival sex is Public Health Agency of Canada's (PHAC) definition of *sex trade*, which is the "exchange of sexual activities to meet subsistence needs such as food, shelter and protection" (PHAC, 2006, p. 19).

Evidence:
Marshall et al. (2010) found that sexual minority (lesbian, gay, bisexual, or transgender/transsexual) street youth, whose median age was 22, were involved in survival sex work. Engagement in survival sex work was reported by 11.3%. Of these, 23.8% were heterosexual males, 34.9% were heterosexual females, 14.3% were sexual minority females, and 27.0% were sexual minority males (p. 662). The authors conclude that they found a high prevalence of survival sex work among sexual minority street-involved youth (p. 663).

Finkelstein's (2005) research indicated that 18% admitted to prostitution (under-reported) (p. 76), and 35% engaged in some type of sexual favours in exchange for either money or shelter (p. 75).

The average was 21.2 per cent of street youth who were involved in sex trade (PHAC, 2006, p. 19).

5. Point or (Point 5): *Final form of deviant behaviour related to sex trade is that street youth engage in obligatory sex.*
The meaning of *obligatory sex* is "having sex when obligated to do so after having received money, gifts, drugs, or a place to sleep" (PHAC, 2006, p. 20).

May also include *unwanted sex*, meaning "having sex but not wanting to do so with someone in a position of authority" (PHAC, 2006, p. 19).

Evidence:
The obligatory sex average was 18.5%. Street youth reported feeling obligated to have sex at some time; females more likely than males—25.5% vs. 14.3% (PHAC, 2006, p. 20).

Kinds of obligatory sex included shelter (38%), cigarettes, drugs and/or alcohol (33.2%), and money (25.9%) (PHAC, 2006, p. 20).

From 1999 to 2002, around 18% of street youth had unwanted sex (PHAC, 2006, p. 19).

Percentage of female youth experiencing unwanted sex was more than double that of males. The difference was significant: between 1999 and 2002, the average was 27.5% (females) vs. 12% (males) (PHAC, 2006, p. 19).

Conclusion (Restate Aim and How Each Argument Supported the Aim)

(Aim sentence in past tense):

The aim of this paper was to demonstrate that street youth are very likely to be involved in deviant behaviour.
1. *Argument:* One kind of deviant behaviour of street youth is their involvement in substance abuse.
   Supported aim—substance abuse violates laws, especially for those street youth who are under the required age for consuming alcohol.

2. *Argument*: Once you are a street youth, you are very likely to become involved in the deviant behaviour of stealing.
   Supported aim—stealing is a property crime and is a criminal offence, possibly driven to steal to survive, and to support habit of substance abuse.
3. *Argument*: Dealing in drugs is a deviant activity of street youth.
   Supported aim—selling illegal drugs violates laws; possible prison sentence.
4. *Argument*: Street youth became involved in the deviant behaviour of sex trade.
   Supported aim—prostitution by youth is sexual exploitation; for youth under a certain age it violates criminal laws.
5. *Argument*: Another form of deviant behaviour related to prostitution is that street youth engage in obligatory sex.
   Supported aim—obligatory sex violates the expectation that a favour is done out of kindness; now there is an expectation of payment or reward involved, and that is sex.

Possible further research:
- How do street youth cope by engaging in deviant behaviour?
- What happens to street youth as they transition from youth into adulthood?
- What kinds of policies and services might help them?

References (APA, CMS, or ASA Style: List All Books, Periodicals, and Other References)

Note the following:
- References have been organized by the last name of the first author to make finding them easier; *only a few sources are provided here in order to save space.* These sources have *not* been formatted according to one of the styles in this sample outline. (If your instructor requires you to format your reference sources in your outline then you must do so.)
- The library call numbers have been added in case the books are needed after they have been returned.
- Possibly, not all sources will be used in writing the term paper.
- The references page will need to be formatted, as per one style, after the term paper is written (see Chapter 5).

Baron, Stephen W., & Kennedy, Leslie W. (2001). Deterrence and homeless male street youths. In Fleming et al., pp. 151–184.

Ferguson, Kristin M., Kimberly Bender, Sanna Thompson, Bin Xie, and David Pollio. (2011). Correlates of street-survival behaviors in homeless young adults in four U.S. cities. *American Journal of Orthopsychiatry* 81(3):401–9. doi:10.1111/j.1939-0025.2011.01108.x.

continued

Finkelstein, Marni (2005). *With no direction home: Homeless youth on the road and in the streets.* Belmont, CA: Thomson Wadsworth. [HV 1437 N5 F56 2005]

Fleming, Thomas, Patricia O'Reily, and Barry Clark. (Eds.) (2001). *Youth injustice: Canadian perspectives* (2nd ed.). Toronto, ON: Canadian Scholars' Press. [KE 9445 Y69 2001]

Gibson, Kristina E. (2011). *Street Kids: Homeless youth, outreach, and policing New York's streets.* [Kindle version]. Retrieved from http://www .amazon.com/Street-Kids-Homeless-Outreach-ebook/dp/B005C9GOF4/ ref=sr_1_1_title_1_kin?s=books&ie=UTF8&qid=1372097802&sr=1-1& keywords=kristina+gibson

Glassman, Anthony. (2012). Lesbian, gay, bisexual, and transgender homeless youth face special challenges. In Arthur Gillard (Ed.), *Homelessness* (pp. 78–83). Farmington Hills, MI: Greenhaven Press. [HV 4505 H65 2012]

Sample Outline 2
The Second Social Science Outline: Headings/ Themes (Step 3: Completes the Outline)

General Topic: the deviant behaviours of kids or youth who are homeless and living primarily on the streets

For Introduction to Aim Sentence (From Unused Portions of Arguments)

The information here is the same as the first outline.

Aim Sentence

The aim is the same as in the first outline.

Aim Sentence Worded as a Question:

This is the same as in the first outline.

Define Concepts (Concepts from the Aim That Will Be Defined and Their Sources)

This part is the same as the first outline and is omitted to save space.

Organize Headings/Themes (The Sequence of the Headings/Themes)

The headings/themes are organized according to the increasing involvement of street youth in deviant behaviour.

1. Heading/theme: Street youths' deviant drug use
2. Heading/theme: Street youth and stealing
3. Heading/theme: The use of sex by street youth

Presentation of Headings/Themes

1. Heading/Theme: Street youths' deviant drug use

Introduction
Two points concerning street youths' deviant drug use here are substance abuse and dealing in drugs.

1. Point or (Point 1): One kind of deviant behaviour of street youth is their involvement in substance abuse.
Basically, substance abuse refers to the overindulgence in or dependence on an addictive material. Substance abuse and use includes alcohol and illegal drugs.

Evidence:
The evidence is the same as the previous outline for this point.

2. Point or (Point 2): Dealing in drugs is a deviant activity of street youth.
Finkelstein (2005) definition of dealing drugs refers to selling illegal drugs in order to make money, primarily to support their habit (p. 79).

Evidence:
The evidence is the same as in the previous outline for this point.

Summary
Significant evidence to support the theme that street youth engage in deviant behavior of drug use. Includes substance abuse and dealing in drugs.

2. Heading/Theme: Street youth and stealing

Introduction
Only concerned with street youth involved in the deviant behaviour of stealing.

1. Point or (Point 1): Once you are a street youth, you are very likely to become involved in the deviant behaviour of stealing.
Generally, stealing means taking something that does not belong to you.

Stealing or theft includes shoplifting, boosting (stealing merchandise from one store and selling it to another), and scams (conning people) (Finkelstein, 2005, p. 81).

Evidence:
The evidence is the same as in the first outline for this point.

continued

Summary
Street youth are involved in various kinds of stealing. Some were arrested for these crimes. The likelihood of being punished may determine the degree of theft.

3. Heading/Theme: Street youths' use of sex

Introduction
There are two general ways presented about street youths' deviant use of sex. The first is about obligatory sex. This is followed by street youth becoming involved in the sex trade.

1. Point or (Point 1): Final form of deviant behaviour related to sex trade is that street youth engage in obligatory sex.
The information here is the same for this point as the first outline.

Evidence:
The evidence is the same here as in the first outline.

2. Point or (Point 2): Street youth become involved in the deviant behaviour of the sex trade.
The information here is the same as in the first outline.

Evidence:
The evidence here is the same for this point as in the first outline.

Summary
Evidence does suggest support for the theme that street youth become involved in the deviant behaviour of using sex. They feel obligated to do so in return for a favour, especially females. They may also become involved in the sex-trade in order to survive.

Conclusion (Restate Aim and How Each Heading/Theme Supported the Aim):

Restate Aim Sentence in Past Tense:
The aim of this paper was to demonstrate that street youth are very likely to be involved in deviant behaviour.

The themes were organized in the way that street youth would become increasingly involved in deviant behaviour. The arguments started with deviant drug use. This was followed by stealing. The last theme highlighted street youths' deviant use of sex.

1. Heading/Theme: Street Youths' Deviant Drug Use
This theme included substance abuse and then dealing in drugs.

Supported aim

Substance abuse was a way for street youth to start getting involved in deviant behaviour, such as under the required age for consuming alcohol or start using illegal substances.

Dealing in drugs, selling illegal drugs, violates laws; possible prison sentence.

2. Heading/Theme: Street Youth and Stealing

Only one argument presented here concerning street youth and deviant behaviour of stealing.

Supported aim

Stealing is a property crime and is a criminal offence, possibly driven to steal to survive, support habit of substance abuse.

3. Heading/Theme: The Use of Sex by Street Youth

There were two arguments presented here to demonstrate street youths' involvement in deviant behaviour of using sex. These were obligatory sex and the sex trade.

Supported aim

Previous behaviour can lead to increase in deviant behaviour by using sex. Obligatory sex violates the expectation that a favour is done out of kindness; now there is an expectation of payment or reward involved, and that is sex.

Sex trade, such as prostitution, is sexual exploitation of youth; for youth under a certain age it violates criminal laws.

Possible further research:
Same as the first outline.

References

They are the same as the first outline, condensed to save space.

Chapter Summary

Define the concepts in the aim sentence:

- Define concepts in the same order as the aim sentence and use them only in that way.
- Use definitions from the course, discipline, or field of studies.
- Locate research definitions of concepts in textbooks, books, and articles.

Organize the arguments or headings/themes:

- Provide a reason for your organization of individual arguments or headings/theme.
- Arrange them in a time sequence or in order of importance.
- Reorganize your outline based on the organization of your arguments or headings/themes.

Draft a conclusion:

Include the following in your conclusion:

- A restating of your aim sentence
- A summary of each argument or theme/heading in the same sequence as the organization of your arguments or headings/themes
- A reason why each argument or heading/theme supported the aim
- Some recommendations for further research

Consult with your instructor about your completed outline.

☑ Checklist for Term Paper Research

Define the concepts in the aim sentence:

- ☐ Did you define the concepts in the same order as the aim sentence?
- ☐ Did your definitions come from the course, discipline, or field of studies?
- ☐ Did you do research for definitions of concepts in textbooks, books, and articles and record them in your outline?

Organize the arguments or headings/themes:

- ☐ What reason did you use to organize your individual arguments or headings/themes?
- ☐ Did you organize the arguments or headings/themes in your outline?
- ☐ Is your organization consistent with the way that the individual arguments or headings/themes will be presented?

Draft a conclusion:

- ☐ Did you restate your aim sentence?
- ☐ Did you summarize each argument or heading/theme in the same sequence as you organized them?
- ☐ Did you give a reason why each argument or heading/theme supported the aim?
- ☐ What kinds of recommendations for further research did you make?
- ☐ Did you consult with your instructor about your completed outline—what comments were made—and did you revise your completed outline?

Recommended Websites

Purdue University
Purdue OWL on organizing an argument following the Toulmin method of logic:
http://owl.english.purdue.edu/owl/resource/588/03/#resourcenav/

University of North Carolina at Chapel Hill
The Writing Center Handouts: click on your writing interest:
http://writingcenter.unc.edu/handouts

Recommended Readings

Kirszner, L.G., & Mandell, S.R. (2012). *Patterns for college writing: A rhetorical reader and guide* (12th ed.). Boston, MA: Bedford/St. Martin's.

Stewart, K.L., Allen, M., & Galliah, S. (2009). *Forms of writing: A rhetoric, handbook, and reader* (5th ed.). Toronto, ON: Pearson.

Chapter 5

Writing the First Social Science Term Paper

Once you have completed your research outline on your digital device, you should do the following:

- Make sure that you have made a full backup copy of your completed research outline on a separate storage device.
- For an online submission of your research outline, make sure you submit the correct file and request confirmation from your instructor that he or she received it.
- If you need to hand in a printed copy of your research outline, print two copies: one for you and one for your instructor.

You have completed your research outline, where you used *inductive* thinking. Now, you need to write a coherent term paper where you will use *deductive* reasoning to present your research. You will use deductive thinking to write your term paper because you will convey your general aim before you present your specific arguments in support of your aim or headings/themes. You use your aim to think through and write your entire term paper, from introduction to conclusion, to make it as convincing and coherent as possible.

This chapter will show you how write your term paper in order to produce it for your instructor. Here is what you will learn:

1. How to write a term paper draft.
2. How to revise the draft.
3. How to format the term paper.
4. How to write the abstract (if required).
5. What to do to create a title page.
6. How to produce the final copy.

5.1 How Do I Write a Term Paper Draft?

You should prepare to write the draft of your term paper by doing the following:

- Make a copy of your research outline to create a new file that you will now use to write your term paper draft.

- Make a backup copy of your new term paper draft file on a separate storage device (for example, USB drive), and update your backup copy regularly as you write.

This section will help you write a better term paper draft by presenting some introductory writing skills. Follow these recommendations or confer with your instructor on items not mentioned here.

5.1.1 Use Required Writing Skills

The Introduction to this book presented some required writing skills for a social science term paper. This section adds to the list of skills and encourages you to *double-check* for any of the following errors.

Spelling
All of the words in your term paper must be spelled correctly. Use a dictionary to assist you in your writing.

There are some aspects of spelling that cause problems for students. They include abbreviations, acronyms, capitalization, and numbers. Following are some brief suggestions on how deal with each.

An *abbreviation* is a shorter version of a word, phrase, or term that contains periods.

For example:

Before the common era (BCE)

In general, you should avoid using abbreviations. Instead, write your intended abbreviations out in full. The reason for this is that your writing will be clearer and you are more likely to use the full words correctly:

- Do not use *e.g.* Write out *for example.*
- Do not abbreviate days, months, and holidays. (Do not use *Xmas;* write out *Christmas.*)

There are, however, some generally accepted abbreviations that you do not necessarily have to write out first:

- Some large institutions

  Examples:

  SFU, MIT

- Commonly referred to organizations

  Examples:

  CIA, UN

- Large corporations

  Examples:

  MSN, RIM

- Some countries

  Examples:

  U.S.A. (USA) or U.S. (US)

If you are unsure about using a common abbreviation, use the following guideline: write out the full words or terms that you are abbreviating the first time that they are used, and put their abbreviations in parentheses after the term.

Example:

fetal alcohol syndrome (F.A.S.)

An *acronym* is an abbreviation that spells a pronounceable word that does not contain periods. Acronyms are used so often that you do not have to write out what they stand for.

Examples:

WHO

NATO

NASA

Again, if you are unsure about any of the preceding, then follow the previous guideline of writing out the words followed by their abbreviation or acronym in parentheses.

For a word-processing program, you will need to learn to work with your AutoCorrect function. For uppercase letters, you may want to turn off this function so that it does not capitalize words unnecessarily. In general, it is a good idea to turn off any automatic style or formatting function. If you are unsure about capitalizing a certain word, look up the word in a recent dictionary.

As well, there are different ways to write numbers for your term paper. Two general ways are to write out the numbers or to use the figure for the number:

1. Write the word for the number when it is part of the general use for your term paper.

    Example:

    My first argument is . . .

2. Use the numeral for the number, unless it begins a sentence (in which case you would write the word).

Example:

There were 23 runaway teens last year.

In some instances, either numbers or words are acceptable.
Example:

From 2011 to 2015 [or 2011–2015] . . .

The court awarded damages of one million dollars. [or The court awarded damages of $1,000,000.]

Finally, *avoid* using verbal contractions in your writing such as *didn't* instead of *did not*. Writing out these negations will help you avoid the potential use of double negatives.

All of the preceding should help you to write a term paper with correct spelling and usage.

Grammar

You must write your term paper using correct grammar. As you are writing, make sure that your sentences adhere to the following grammar basics presented in the Introduction to this book:

- Singular and plural agreement
- Correct group use
- Correct verb tense
- Clear pronoun reference
- Grammatically parallel sentences

One general area of grammar to note here is the correct use of verb tense in your draft:

- For the organization of arguments or headings/themes portion, use the future verb tense.

  Why? Because in this section you refer to arguments or headings/themes that you *will* present in a certain order.
- For the conclusion, use the past verb tense.

  Why? Because in this section you are writing about what you *have* presented.

Punctuation

The punctuation in your term paper must be exact. When writing your draft, keep in mind the following: keep your sentences simple, which will simplify your use of correct punctuation.

One particular area of concern for punctuation is where to put quotation marks.

Standard North American practice is to put all punctuation inside the quotation marks (see Appendix B, p. 208). An alternative practice follows these guidelines:

- If the end punctuation is part of a quote, then put the *quotation marks after* it.

  Example:

  The runaway teen said, "Where will I live?"

- If the end punctuation is *not* part of the quote, then put the *quotation marks before* it.

  Example:

  The researcher was not sure what caused the runaway teen to say, "I knew exactly where I would go".

- When a *quotation occurs within a quotation*, use *single quotation marks* (' ').

  Example:

  The researcher said, "I heard you say, 'I will never go home again.'"

Whichever practice you adopt, be sure to follow it consistently throughout your paper.

Quotations

This section will offer some brief suggestions on the use of quoting in your research paper.

It is better to integrate a quote into your sentence:

Example of original quote:

"Psychologists have made great strides in understanding the addictive personality," maintains Smith.

Example of original quote integrated into your sentence:

Smith argues that significant advances have been made by psychologists in "understanding the addictive personality."

Reminder

All quotes from an author must be referenced properly (see Chapter 3 for details).

Once you have presented your quote, then *clarify* what the quote means and *elaborate* on how these words relate to what you are writing about. This process will make your use of a quote clear and relevant to what you are writing about.

In addition, here are two things to avoid in quoting: long quotes and stringing quotes.

Limit the length of quotes in your term paper.
Avoid long quotes such as those that fill an entire page. Your term paper should make sense when a lengthy quote is omitted. Your quote should support your argument instead of making it for you!

Instead of using a long quote, *paraphrase* the author's idea. Paraphrasing demonstrates to your instructor than you can competently summarize and use the idea or point from an author's work to support your argument.

Do not string one quote after another.
Stringing quotations means that one quote follows another with no clarification of each one. Having one quote after another makes it difficult to understand what you are saying. Instead, present the first quote and how it supports your argument, then present your second quote and what it means for your argument, and so on. Remember, each quote requires that you state its source or author, year, and page number.

Appropriate Language
In addition to using these required writing skills, avoid words and language that are sexist or bigoted. Instead, use non-sexist, non-racist, and non-derogatory words. As well, avoid using local phrasing, slang, or swear words as well as metaphors. Remember that this is a *formal* social science term paper.

Reminder

Remember to write in a *neutral tone* even though you are writing an argumentative term paper. To write in a neutral tone means to use words, phrases, and evidence that present your view(s) in a factual and reasonable manner. Avoid writing in a highly emotional or arrogant style.

5.1.2 Write the Draft of Your Term Paper: Use Proper Sentences, Paragraphs, and Transitions

This section will help you write a draft of your term paper. To do this, you must write your term paper draft as follows:

- In the same order as the headings of your basic social science argumentative format and process
- By including all parts of your research outline

- By adding to your research outline (such as adding an introduction to your aim sentence)

It is worth repeating that all parts of your social science term paper must be written in complete sentences and proper paragraphs. Connecting the ideas from one sentence to the next or from one paragraph to the next is referred to as a *transition*. You can use a word, phrase, or sentence to connect sentences, and to connect paragraphs. The goal of your writing is to create a *coherent* and *unified* term paper.

Here, we temporarily use the headings of the basic social science argumentative format and process so that you will know where to use the suggestions for sentences, paragraphs, and transitions. You must delete these headings in your draft, except the heading "References," unless your instructor directs you to do otherwise.

TIPS   Delete the headings of the basic social science argumentative format and process as you work on each one throughout your term paper. Deleting these headings should remind you to use transitions in your writing to connect each part.

Introduction to Aim

The introduction to your aim should generally consist of one to two paragraphs. These paragraphs might include the following:

- Important background or historical information leading up to your aim sentence
- The significance and importance of your aim
- The current relevance of your aim

Writing the first sentence for your introduction may be intimidating. Here are some possibilities for first sentences:

One of the main areas of interest within the topic of [*fill in general area of aim*] is this.

The [*insert your topic*] did not develop suddenly. It developed in the following general way.

What makes [*fill in general area of aim*] important is this.

This term paper is about [*fill in general area of aim*]. It is significant because ...

Your introductory sentences and paragraphs should lead naturally to your aim sentence.

Transition to aim sentence.

Here are some suggestions for the transition to your aim sentence:

> The preceding discussion has highlighted the importance of [*fill in general area of aim*]. [*Present your aim.*]
>
> The significance of this [*topic/aim/issue*] suggests the following. The aim of this paper is . . .
>
> The controversy of this debate continues, and the term paper will present the following aim.

Aim Sentence

You should keep your aim to one brief sentence or question that should appear toward the end of your introduction. Here are some suggestions for wording your aim sentence:

> The aim of this paper is to demonstrate . . .
>
> The thesis of this paper is . . .
>
> The question that this term paper addresses is this: . . .

Notice that these sentences clearly state that this is your aim sentence or question. There should be no doubt what the aim of your paper is. Do not write an aim sentence or question that contains only one concept instead of the required two. Also, avoid having three or more concepts in your aim for now so that your task is more manageable.

Transition from aim to definitions.

Here are some possible transitions that you might use to connect the aim sentence to the definitions of the general concepts in your aim:

> In order to clarify the aim of this paper, the following definitions are presented.
>
> The concepts in the aim sentence are defined as follows.
>
> The aim sentence is going to be elaborated on by defining these concepts.

Definition of Concepts in Aim

You can usually write the definitions of the concepts in your aim sentence in one or two paragraphs. The order of the definitions is generally as follows:

- The concept that is defined first is the one that appears first in your aim sentence or question.
- The second concept will be the second one in your aim sentence or question, and so on.

Here is the general pattern that you should use in writing a definition for a concept in your aim:

- State that you are presenting the first concept from your aim.

  Example:

  The concept is . . .

- Present the definition of the concept, usually another author's, place it in quotation marks, and cite it appropriately.
- Then state what the words of the definition mean in your own words.
- Now, state how the definition relates to your aim.

After you present the first definition in this way, you will need a transition to your next definition:

Example:

The next concept in the aim is . . .

Then repeat the previous pattern, starting by giving the definition of the second concept. It is vital that you use references for your definitions from your research. These reference citations are important to your instructor because it shows that you are using the language or discourse of the discipline or field of studies in your term paper. It also shows that you are aware of other authors and their research, and are able to use their work to support your writing.

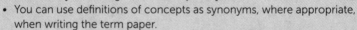
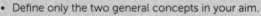

Reminder
- Define only the two general concepts in your aim.
- You can use definitions of concepts as synonyms, where appropriate, when writing the term paper.
- Presenting definitions is part of the building block of writing with you as the author.
- Do not define any additional words that are not used in the aim sentence. Define them where they are used in the text of your term paper.

Restate your aim sentence using the definitions of your concepts. This will help to clarify what your aim means.

Transition from definitions to organization of arguments or headings/themes.
Use a transition after you have finished defining the concepts in your aim to indicate that you are now going to write about the order in which you will present your arguments or headings/themes.

Examples:

> Having defined the concepts of the aim, the next section will present the order of the arguments or headings/themes.

> The concepts of the aim and how they will be used have been clarified. The next aspect of this term paper presents the sequence of arguments or headings/themes that will be made in support of the aim.

Organization of Arguments or Headings/Themes

Do not merely list your arguments or headings/themes. That is what you did in your outline but doing so is not acceptable in a term paper. Write this part of your first term paper in a paragraph. Writing this section clearly will help guide your instructor to which argument or heading/theme leads off and which one is last—just like a table of contents or a menu.

Start by giving a reason for the sequence of your individual arguments or headings/themes. Present your arguments or headings/themes in general terms here because you will be going into more detail for each later. In general, you should do the following:

• For individual arguments, provide the two main concepts or terms of your aim in the point of each argument.
• For headings/themes, provide at least one concept from the aim and the idea that is common to all arguments in a heading/theme.
• Use the future tense because you are referring to what you *will* present.

Here are some suggestions for the wording of your arguments or headings/themes, concerning their sequence:

> The first argument (or heading/theme) will be . . .

> The next argument (or heading/theme) will be . . .

> This is followed by . . .

> A further argument (or heading/theme) that will be made is . . .

> The final argument (or heading/theme) that will be presented is . . .

Note the use of *variety* in the wording of transitions here. Do *not* simply state "The first argument (or heading/theme) will be," "The second argument (or heading/theme) will be," "The third argument (or heading/theme) will be," and so on. Such writing would clearly lack interest.

In future papers, as the number of your arguments (or headings/themes) increases, you will be able to write proper sentences about them.

Transition from organization to presentation of arguments or headings/themes.

> **TIPS**
> Here, do not refer to an example, clarify a point, or define a term that will be used in an argument. Provide this kind of information in the presentation of arguments (or headings/themes) section later in your term paper.

You need a transition to indicate that you are now changing from the organization of individual arguments or headings/ themes to their presentation. Suggestions for transitions here include the following:

> Having presented the sequence of arguments or headings/themes, the next part of this term paper will present the actual arguments or headings/themes.

> This part of the term paper stated how the arguments or headings/themes in support of the aim have been organized. The next aspect will present these arguments or headings/themes in their pre-arranged order.

Presentation of Arguments or Headings/Themes

This section begins by showing how individual arguments may be presented and then goes on to add headings/themes. If you are required to write a term paper with headings/themes, then you will need to know the information on presenting individual arguments.

Begin by stating that the individual arguments or headings/themes to support the aim will be presented next. Some examples include the following:

> The first argument or heading/theme is . . .

> The first argument or heading/theme demonstrating the aim is . . .

> To begin, the first argument or heading/theme is . . .

For headings/themes, you start with the sequence of the individual arguments to be presented. That is, you write a short introductory version of each argument in the order that it will be presented. This can be done in various ways. For example:

> There is only one argument presented here and it is about . . .

There are two [*or three, and so on*] arguments presented here that relate to [*insert heading or theme*]. They are concerned with . . .

A number of arguments deal with [*insert heading or theme*]. They begin with [*insert brief wording of argument*], move to [*insert brief wording of argument*], and end with [*insert brief wording of argument*].

Then, present each argument, the point, and its evidence

The following presents the point of an argument, whether it is for individual arguments or in headings/themes. For a term paper with individual arguments, you would have jumped over the previous headings/themes portion and gone on to the information below.

Presentation of the point of an argument.

State one point and clarify it in a paragraph. You can clarify your point in a number of ways:

- Define a particular concept in your point, and write the definition in your own words.
- You can also include synonyms for certain words.
- Restate your point in the other terminology that you have introduced.

Here is a much more detailed version of the preceding. It is a general pattern of what should be included in presenting your point.

A Condensed General Pattern of What to Include to Present a Point

- Transition to presenting a point.
- Present the point with its new concept(s).
- Transition to define or clarify the new concept/idea in the point.
- Present the definition (or clarification) of the concept/idea.
- Transition to relate definition or clarification to the point.
- Present how the definition or clarification relates to the point.

If more ideas or concepts need to be defined or clarified in your point (such as another point or a *sub-point*) then do the following:
- Transition to present sub-point.
- Present sub-point.
- Transition to definition or clarification of sub-point.
- Present definition (or clarification) of sub-point.
- Transition to relate definition or clarification to previous point.
- Restate point using clarification of sub-point.
- Present transition to evidence.

The elaboration of your point should be absolutely clear. The order that you clarify words in the point should follow the order that they appear in your point. (This is the same pattern that you used in defining the concepts in the aim sentence.) The first word clarified is the word that is used first in your point sentence, then the second, etc.

Summarize your clarifications and write what they mean for the point that you are presenting. Elaborating on your point like this will give more meaning to your evidence.

Reminder

- *A one-sentence point without any clarification is unacceptable.* Clarifying the words of your point will help to make your point clear. It will also help your instructor understand the point that you are writing about.
- Do not present more than one point for each argument because each point will require evidence or proof.

 If you are concerned about what to do with *history* or background information on a topic, include it in your introduction or make it into an argument. If neither of these options works for you, omit history or background from your term paper.

Transition from point to evidence.

It is important to have a transition to indicate that you are presenting evidence in support of your point.

Example:

> The evidence to support [*restate your point*] is . . .

> One example of [*restate your point*] is the following.

Presentation of evidence in support of your point.

You should provide the evidence for a point in a separate paragraph because you are presenting something different. A different paragraph helps keep the tasks of presenting a point and its evidence separate for now. Separating the evidence in another paragraph from the point also makes it easier for the instructor to follow what you are writing.

Here is a more detailed version of presenting evidence for your point. It is a general pattern of what should be included in presenting your evidence.

A Condensed General Pattern of What to Include to Present Evidence

- Transition to evidence/example (if required)
- Present evidence/example
- Transition to clarify any part of evidence/example
- Present clarification of evidence/example
- Transition to relate evidence/example to point
- Present relation of evidence/example to point
- Transition to next point

Some examples of presenting evidence after your transition might start as follows:

> The example here is by [*insert author's last name and year*]. The(se) author(s) describe(s) . . .

> [*Insert author(s) last name(s) and year*] present the following statistic . . .

> The research by [*insert author's last name and year*] indicates . . .

> The information gathered by [*insert author's last name and year*] . . .

Reminder

You need to present only one clear finding or evidence/example of your point. Remember, do not present more than two or three pieces of evidence for a point for now, nor provide long, detailed descriptions and thus fail to specify the point with the evidence that you are providing. Shorten descriptions that are more than one paragraph. Always state how your evidence relates to your point.

Transition from one argument to another argument or heading/theme to another heading/theme.

Once you have completed an argument for an individual argument paper, you will need a transition to the next argument. Some examples of transition sentences for you to use are as follows:

> In addition to the preceding argument, . . .

> An additional argument is that . . .

> Furthermore, there is the point . . .
>
> The final argument addressing the aim of this term paper is that . . .

The transition between individual arguments is also used in headings/themes that contain more than one argument.

Once the first heading or theme and its supporting points and evidence have been presented, end this heading or theme with a brief summary. For example:

> These arguments have shown that [insert heading or theme] involves [insert a few words about each argument]. They play an important role in contributing to [insert heading or theme].
>
> This completes the arguments about [insert heading or theme]. They indicated that . . .
>
> [Insert wording of heading or theme] was supported with the arguments pertaining to [insert brief words about each argument].

Here are some more suggestions on what to include at the end of each heading or theme:

> The significance of the order of the arguments is . . .
>
> The sequence of the arguments suggests the following about [insert heading or theme] . . .
>
> The reason for having the first argument start the arrangement of arguments and end with the last one is . . .

Remember that the wording that you use must be logical and must make sense.

After completing the preceding, you will need a transition from one heading or theme to another. Here are some suggestions on how to do that:

> This completes the [insert heading or theme]. The next group of arguments are about [insert next heading or theme] . . .
>
> From arguments about [insert heading or theme], we shift to [insert heading or theme].
>
> The final heading or theme after [insert preceding heading or theme] is the following. It is . . .

If your headings or themes do not have such transitions, then the term paper loses some of its coherence. Always use transitions whenever you change from one heading or theme to another.

Transition from argument or heading/theme to conclusion.
Once your arguments or headings/themes have ended, you will need a transition to indicate that you are ending your term paper.

Here are some examples of possible transitions:

> The preceding argument or heading/theme was the last one offered in support of the aim. Here is how all the arguments or headings/themes supported the aim.

> This was the last argument or heading/theme. The term paper will end by summarizing how the previous arguments or headings/themes supported the aim.

Conclusion

The conclusion includes suggestions for individual arguments and headings/themes. Write a couple of paragraphs to end your term paper for each. The format for your conclusion should generally be as follows:

- Begin the conclusion by restating your aim in the past tense.
- Then briefly summarize each argument (or group of arguments, headings/themes) in the past tense and state how each supported your aim.

One way to start is to introduce your conclusion with a sentence such as the following:

> In conclusion, this paper has demonstrated that [*restate your aim here*].

> In summary, the aim of this paper was [*restate your aim here*].

This sentence signals to your instructor that what follows is the conclusion of your term paper. Present the same sequence of individual arguments or headings/themes in summary form as you did in your term paper:

- Start with a summary of each argument or heading/theme in a sentence or two.
- Then present a sentence or two of how each argument or heading/theme supported the aim. Do not omit any one of these.
- Avoid presenting a summary argument or heading/theme and how it supported the aim in one sentence. Use separate sentences for now until you gain some experience in writing a summary.
- Provide an overview of all arguments or headings/themes and how they supported the aim. That is, you might include something like this:

> The arguments or headings/themes suggest support for the aim, . . .

Do not include any new points, definitions, or examples in your conclusion. Your term paper is essentially finished, with the exception of the references. As you gain experience in writing, your conclusions will include restating the aim and summarizing how various groups of arguments (headings, subheadings, or themes) supported the aim. You may also wish to suggest, in a paragraph, further work in the area that you are writing about.

Once you are done writing your draft, make sure that you have *deleted the headings of the basic social science argumentative format and process* (unless directed otherwise by your instructor).

References

Follow and use APA, CMS, or ASA style (see Chapter 3). Avoid making errors in their use, such as leaving out the city of a published book. You must provide the complete reference. Include only those references that you *actually used* in writing your term paper.

> **Reminder**
> - Do not number your references.
> - Always include sources in your term paper. Otherwise, you do not really have a research paper.
> - Avoid having too few references, i.e., fewer than your instructor requires. Using too few sources indicates to your instructor that you did not do enough research on the topic. Your term paper then does not have enough research supporting your aim and arguments.

5.1.3 Consult Your Instructor

Once you have completed the previous portion and any other directions from your instructor, you will have a draft of your social science term paper. Before revising your draft term paper, you should confer with your instructor one final time about your draft. Your instructor's suggestions or recommendations must be included when revising your draft term paper.

5.2 How Do I Revise My Draft?

Before you revise the draft copy of your term paper, it is a good idea to do the following:

- Set aside the draft for a day or two.
- Read your work aloud.
- Find someone with more writing experience and familiarity with the subject to read and check your work before you hand it in.
- Keep in mind how your term paper might be evaluated (see Table 5.1), and fulfill these requirements in your revision.

Then, proofread your draft. To *proofread* means to read your paper again, checking for any errors. When proofreading, you should check for the following:

Table 5.1 Two Ways Your Term Paper May Be Evaluated

Completeness: Do You Have All the Required Parts?	Individual Criteria: How Well Did You Do on Each Part and on Overall Coherence?
• Abstract (if required) • Introduction and aim sentence • Definition of concepts • Organization of arguments or headings/themes • Presentation of arguments or headings/themes • Conclusion • In-text citations • References	• Writing skills • Abstract (if required) • Introduction and aim sentence • Definition of concepts • Organization of arguments or headings/themes • Presentation of arguments or headings/themes • Conclusion • In-text citations • References

Note: Your instructor may change, delete, or add to these minimum criteria.

- Clear use of words and basic writing skills—replace redundant words and use variety for overused words
- Neutral tone in your writing
- That all required parts are included—there are no missing parts, from introduction to references page
- Coherent and consistent writing—your writing is logical and deals with each idea or thought in its proper sequence, using transitions
- Clear and effective arguments—each point and supporting evidence relates to each other and is convincing
- Unified term paper—your writing relates clearly every idea, paragraph, or part of the term paper

Remember that virtually all instructors will evaluate basic writing abilities as part of the term paper. Proofreading your work is essential. As well, you should make sure that you have formatted your term paper properly.

5.3 How Do I Format My Term Paper?

To format your term paper refers to its appearance. There are certain APA, CMS, or ASA styles about what your term paper should look like. As a reminder, *if your instructor requires any changes to formatting presented here you must follow those directions*.

The following items are general standards for formatting your term paper (some are repeated briefly for your convenience):

- Use standard letter-size paper.
- Use one side of the page only.

- Use one-inch or 2.54-centimetre margins.
- Use 12-point font size.
- Use Times New Roman font.
- Indent all paragraphs one-half inch or 1.27 centimetres. (The default tab key is usually set for this.)
- Double-space the rest of term paper, including the abstract and the references pages.
- For the abstract (if required), follow the style guidelines in Section 5.4 of this chapter for APA, CMS, or ASA style.

For the formatting of short and long quotations for each style, see Chapter 3, section 3.1.3.

5.3.1 References Page(s)

A general format that each style requires for its references pages is provided below, starting with the APA style.

In APA Style

- Include the running head, capitalized on the left side of the page and the page number on the right side in the header.
- Centre the word *References* below the header at the top of a separate page.
- Provide two line spaces before starting the reference list.
- Place all references in correct alphabetical sequence based on the last name of the first author.
- Indent second and any additional lines a half-inch, or 1.27 centimetres.

STREET YOUTHS   (page number)

References

Baron, S.W., & Kennedy, L.W. (2001). Deterrence and homeless male

    street youths. In T. Fleming, P. O'Reilly, & B. Clark (Eds.),

    Youth Injustice: Canadian perspectives (2nd ed.) (pp. 151–184).

    Toronto, ON: Canadian Scholars' Press.

Figure 5.1 Brief APA-Style Sample References Page

In CMS Style

- The page number is in the header on the right side.
- If you are required to provide your name in the header place it to the left of the page number.
- Centre the word *References* on a separate page below the line of the header.
- Provide two line spaces before starting your reference list.
- Place all references in correct alphabetical sequence based on the last name of the first author.
- Indent second and any additional lines a half-inch, or 1.27 centimetres.

(your name, if required) (page number)

References

Baron, Stephen W., and Leslie W. Kennedy. 2001. "Deterrence and

homeless male street youths." In *Youth Injustice: Canadian*

Perspectives (2nd ed.), edited by Thomas Fleming, Patricia

O'Reilly, and Barry Clark, 151–184. Toronto, ON: Canadian

Scholars' Press.

Figure 5.2 Brief CMS-Style Sample References Page

In ASA Style

- The page number is in the header on the right side.
- Centre the word *References* on a separate page below the header.
- (Your instructor may require the word *References* capitalized and centred on the page after your term paper ends or placed on the left side of the page.)
- Provide two line spaces before starting your reference list.
- Place all references in correct alphabetical sequence based on the last name of the first author.
- Indent second and any additional lines half-inch, or 1.27 centimetres.

(page number)

References

Baron, Stephen W., and Leslie W. Kennedy. 2001. "Deterrence and

Homeless Male Street Youths." Pp. 151–184 in *Youth Injustice:*

Canadian Perspectives, 2nd ed., edited by Thomas Fleming,

Patricia O'Reilly and Barry Clark. Toronto, ON: Canadian

Scholars' Press.

Figure 5.3 Brief ASA-Style Sample References Page

Reminder
If your instructor requires changes to any of the previous formatting,
you must follow those directions.

5.4 How Do I Write an Abstract?

If required, this section will help you write an *abstract*, which is a brief summary of your term paper on a separate page following the title page. Some instructors may require you to write an abstract of your term paper, while others may not.

Follow this order for your abstract:

- State the importance or significance of your aim sentence.
- State the aim or purpose of your term paper.
- End with a summary of your arguments or headings/themes as conclusions in support of your aim. That is, state what some of your conclusions are with respect to your aim that a reader would find significant.

Consult journals or periodicals in your specific discipline or field of studies for examples of abstracts.

Each referencing style has its own requirements for an abstract.

5.4.1 APA Style

The abstract must include the running head, such as STREET YOUTHS, on the left side of the header and the page number on the right side of the header. Depending on your instructor's requirements, the page number might be 2 or ii because the title page would be i. For example:

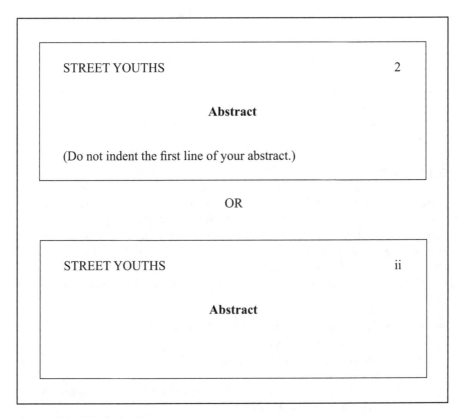

Figure 5.4 APA-Style Abstracts

Follow these guidelines for this separate page:

- Capitalize the first letter of the word *abstract* (Abstract) and place it at the top of the page and centred below the header.
- Provide two lines before starting your abstract.
- Make sure the abstract does not exceed 120 words.
- Type the abstract as one paragraph with no indention for the first line.
- Double-space the abstract.

5.4.2 CMS Style

There is usually no page number in the header here since the term paper text does not start until after the abstract. Some instructors may require you to number this page, in which case it would be Roman numeral ii, placed usually at the bottom of the page and centred. The title page would be Roman numeral i. The page numbering starts with the first page of the text, which would be page one.

Follow these guidelines for your abstract, which should appear on a separate page after the title page:

- Capitalize the word *abstract* (Abstract) and centre it at the top of the page.
- Provide two lines before starting the abstract.
- Indent the first line of the abstract with a half-inch, or 1.27 centimetres. It is best to use the default Tab key.
- Ensure that the abstract is no more than 200 words.
- Double-space the abstract.

5.4.3 ASA Style

As with CMS style, ASA style does not number the title page and the abstract page since the term paper text does not start until after the abstract. Page one of the term paper starts when the text starts. Some instructors may require you to number the abstract page, which would be Roman numeral ii, placed usually at the bottom of the page and centred. The title page would be Roman numeral i.

Follow these guidelines for an abstract, which should appear on a separate page after the title page:

- Capitalize the word *abstract* (Abstract), and centre it or insert it at the left side at the top of the page.
- Provide two lines before presenting the title of the term paper as the heading, with no author.
- Indent the first line of the abstract with a half- inch, or 1.27 centimetres. It is best to use the default Tab key.
- Ensure the abstract is no more than 200 words.
- Double-space the abstract.

5.5 What Should the Title Page Look Like?

You have already recorded your instructor's requirements for a title page at the outset of this assignment (see Introduction). You should now create your title page. The title page is a separate page with margins that are set at one inch, or 2.54 centimetres.

Instructors adapt the styles of APA, CMS, and ASA for the student information that they require on the title page. There is common student information required by all styles on the title page, including that it be centred and double-spaced:

- Title
- Student name
- Course name and number (section number if necessary)
- Instructor or professor
- Community college or university
- Date due or submitted

The title of the term paper should be worded according to your aim. For example, if the aim of the term paper is to demonstrate that street youths are likely to become involved in deviant behaviour, then the title of your term paper might be "Street Youths' Involvement in Deviant Behaviour." A title such as "Street Youths Go Bad" would be inappropriate.

Always submit the original copy of your term paper. As a general rule, do not colour, underline, paste, or draw anything on the title page unless directed by your instructor.

5.5.1 APA Style

APA style has a manuscript page header on *every page* of the term paper, including your title page, abstract, and references page. Follow these guidelines for the manuscript page header:

- On the left side of the header, include the words "Running head," a colon, and the paper's title, which may be abbreviated (the title should include no more than 50 spaces including blank spaces) and must be capitalized. Use key concepts from your title.
- Insert the page number on the right side of the header. (Remember to close your header after this is done.)
- Start the title of your term paper about 2 inches below the header by pressing the Enter key. The number of times to press the Enter key will vary depending on whether or not you have already set your line spacing from single to double spacing.

For example, your term paper would have the following *manuscript page header* for a term paper that is entitled "Street Youths' Involvement in Deviant Behaviour" as "STREET YOUTHS."

Figure 5.5 is an example of an APA style title page and the first page (without an abstract):

Note that the words *Running head* are omitted on the first page. The title is repeated and centred. (If the title and subtitle are more than one line they are double-spaced just like your entire term paper.)

Title Page   **First Page**

| Running Head: Street YOUTHS 1 | STREET YOUTHS   2 |

Street Youths' Involvement in Deviant Behaviour

by

A. Smith

Sociology 101, Section 135

A. Jones

Rainforest University

November 30, 2015

Street Youths' Involvement in Deviant Behaiour

Start the text of your term paper here. Remember to indent the first line of a paragraph by one-half inch (or 1.27 centimetres). Use the Tab key since it is usually set to this spacing.

Figure 5.5 APA-Style Title Page and First Page

TIPS If you require some assistance setting up your word processor for APA style running heads, a helpful video is presented on You Tube by the Daytona State College Writing Center. Here is the most recent link: https://www.youtube.com/watch?v=A_sy4LxaNwo

5.5.2 CMS Style and ASA Style

The general requirements for each of these styles are similar, so they are combined here. There are two ways to put titles on a term paper. The first way, and most common, is for a title page of a term paper that is *five or more pages*. The CMS style title page does not have a running head and does not include a page number on the title page. Start your title about a third of the way down the page. Capitalize the title. (See Figure 5.6.)

The ASA style title page is similar to the CMS style except that the title is not entirely in uppercase. (A separate title page may not be required for a term paper of fewer than five pages. Check with your instructor.) (See Figure 5.6.)

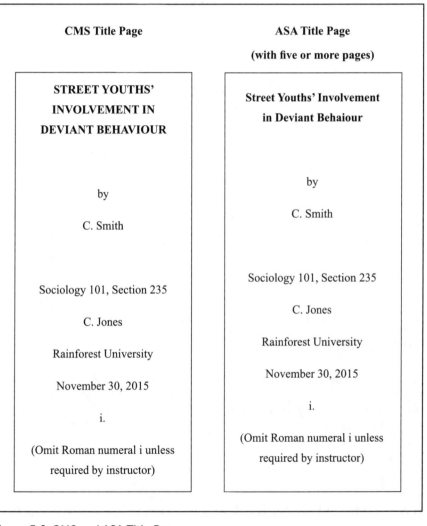

CMS Title Page

ASA Title Page

(with five or more pages)

STREET YOUTHS'
INVOLVEMENT IN
DEVIANT BEHAVIOUR

Street Youths' Involvement
in Deviant Behaiour

by

C. Smith

by

C. Smith

Sociology 101, Section 235

C. Jones

Rainforest University

November 30, 2015

i.

(Omit Roman numeral i unless required by instructor)

Sociology 101, Section 235

C. Jones

Rainforest University

November 30, 2015

i.

(Omit Roman numeral i unless required by instructor)

Figure 5.6 CMS and ASA Title Pages

The page after the title page, without an abstract, would be the first page of your term paper. Figure 5.7 is an example of this:

1

Steet Youths' Involvement

in Deviant Behaviour

Start the text of your term paper here. Remember to indent the first line of a paragraph by one-half inch (or 1.27 centimetres). Use the Tab key since it is usually set to this spacing.

Figure 5.7 CMS- and ASA-Style Next Page

A separate title page may not be required in ASA style if the term paper is four pages or fewer (you will need to check with your instructor about this). Rather, place the title page information on the first page where you start your term paper. On the first page, put the title of your term paper at the top. Leave four lines blank and then present the same information, in the same order that would go on a title page. Leave four more blank lines and then start your term paper.

(See Figure 5.8.)

5.6 What Do I Need to Do to Produce My Final Copy?

If you have just written a five-argument term paper, check to see how many words or pages the paper is (omit the title, abstract, and references page). For

1

Steet Youths' Involvement in

Deviant Behaviour

C. Smith

Sociology 101, Section 235

Rainforest University

November 30, 2015

Start the text of your term paper here.
Remember to indent the first line of a paragraph by one-
half inch (or 1.27 centimetres). Use the Tab key since it
is usually set to this spacing.

Figure 5.8 ASA-Style Title Page with Four or Fewer Pages

now, it is worthwhile to remember the word or page count for your second term
paper.

Before you submit your term paper, you should do the following:

- Check it over one final time to make sure it is error-free and complete.
- Make a full backup copy of your completed term paper in your separate
  storage device.
- For a *printed* term paper submission:
  - Print two copies: one for your instructor and one for you.
  - Make sure you do not attach any material unless directed to do so by
    your instructor.
  - Check that the pages are in proper sequence.
  - Staple the pages together at the top left-hand corner.
  - Hand in the paper on the due date, at the start of your class.

- For an *online* term paper submission:
  - Remember to attach your term paper file if your software requires it.
  - Submit the online paper before the stated time deadline.
  - Request that your instructor confirm that your term paper was indeed received online.

This chapter has been an introduction to the basic social science argumentative term paper, which is the most prevalent kind of research and writing in the social sciences. Another form of writing that is receiving growing interest in the social sciences is based on the work of Dorothy Smith (2005, 2006). Smith calls her form of research and writing *institutional ethnography*. The institutional ethnography form of writing takes the author into account by requiring a standpoint from which her or his research and writing takes place. Your term paper would thus include the standpoint that you are taking in writing your term paper as you describe a particular process of work. Your standpoint and involvement in carrying out your research become part of writing your term paper. Adding the institutional ethnography form of writing to what you already know and have learned in this book will enhance your knowledge and ability to write different kinds of term papers.

Chapter Summary

Write a term paper draft:

- Use required writing skills: spelling, grammar, punctuation, quotations, appropriate language.
- Write your draft: Use sentences, paragraphs, and transitions. Include all aspects of the basic social science argumentative format to write a term paper with individual arguments or headings/themes.
- Use transitions throughout writing your term paper (from introduction to aim to conclusion).
- Confer with your instructor about your draft.

Revise your draft:

- Proofread your draft, and correct basic writing errors to ensure a coherent, unified paper.

Format your term paper:

- Follow APA, CMS, or ASA style rules for appearance, from title page to references page.
- Write abstract (if required) following the APA, CMS, or ASA style format.

Create a title page:

- Follow APA, CMS, or ASA style.

Produce final copy:

- Check it one final time before making a backup copy. For print submission, submit on the due date. For online submission, send before the deadline and ask your instructor to confirm receipt of your term paper.

☑ Checklist for Writing Term Paper

Write a term paper draft:

☐ Did you make a copy of your outline to create a draft term paper file?
☐ Did you follow the basic social science argumentative format and use proper sentences and transitions throughout the writing of your draft?
☐ Did you confer with your instructor about your draft term paper and make any necessary revisions?

Revise your term paper:

☐ Did you proofread it for errors in writing, transitions, and consistency?
☐ Is your paper written as a coherent and unified whole?

Format your term paper:

☐ Is your entire paper double-spaced, except for APA long quotes over 40 words and CMS and ASA over 100 words (which are single-spaced)?
☐ Are your references in correct alphabetical sequence and formatted according to APA, CMS, or ASA style?

Write an abstract (if required):

☐ Does your abstract contain the importance of your aim, your aim, and some major arguments as conclusions to your aim?
☐ Is your abstract on a separate page after the title page and formatted according to one of the styles?

Create a title page:

☐ Did you create a proper title page by following APA, CMS, or ASA style requirements?

continued

Produce final copy:

☐ Did you make a backup copy of your term paper file in a separate storage device before printing?

For print submissions:
☐ Did you print two copies—one to hand in to your instructor and the second one to keep?
☐ Did you staple the top left corner of your term paper and submit it at the start of class?

For online submissions:
☐ Did you attach your term paper file (if necessary) and send it before the deadline?
☐ Did you request the instructor to confirm receiving it?

Recommended Websites

Purdue University
The OWL at Purdue University—on academic writing in general:
https://owl.english.purdue.edu/owl/section/1/

The OWL at Purdue University—on transitions and transitional devices:
http://OWL.english.purdue.edu/OWL/resource/574/01/

Recommended Readings

Dunn, S.D. (2004). *A short guide to writing about psychology*. New York, NY: Pearson.

Kirszner, L.G., & Mandell, S.R. (2012). *Patterns for college writing: A rhetorical reader and guide* (12th ed.). Boston, MA: Bedford/St. Martin's.

Northey, M., & Timney, B. (2015). *Making sense in psychology: A student's guide to research and writing* (2nd ed.). Toronto, ON: Oxford University Press.

Norton, S., & Green, B. (2011). *Essay essentials with readings* (5th ed.). Scarborough, ON: Nelson.

Reinking, J.A., von der Osten, R., Cairns, S.A., & Fleming, R. (2010). *Strategies for successful writing: A rhetoric, research guide, reader, and handbook*. Toronto, ON: Pearson.

Chapter 6

Writing the First Social Science Book Review or Article Critique

In addition to a term paper, you may be required to write a book review or an article critique. Writing a review in the social sciences generally means that you will be required to evaluate or critique another author's work. A *critique* means that you must make positive, neutral, and negative evaluations or comments about someone's research and writing.

Learning to do a book review or article critique has many benefits, including the following:

- You will learn in some detail about another author's work.
- You will discover how a work has been organized and presented.
- You will be prepared to analyze texts or documents.
- You will gain practice for further reviews.

This chapter will show you how to use the basic social science argumentative format and process to help you write a social science book review. You can also apply this to writing a review of an article. You will need to undertake the following to prepare for a review:

- Have a competent, working knowledge of the previous chapters. This is important because some of the material and requirements for writing a social science review are similar to those for writing a term paper.
- Know that a book review requires you to use the basic social science argumentative format and process to evaluate another author's work (and any additional items).
- Read this entire chapter before you start your review. You should recognize some material from previous chapters that is presented here in condensed form to assist you in writing your book review or article critique.

You will learn the following from this chapter:

1. The requirements of a book review (or article critique)
2. How to create and use an outline for a book review or article critique
3. How to write your first social science book review or article critique

4. How to format a book review or article critique
5. How to format the title page of a book review or article critique
6. How to submit your final copy
7. Suggestions for writing an article critique

6.1 What Are the Requirements for My Book Review (or Article Critique)?

As with a term paper, your instructor will inform you of the requirements for your book review (or article critique). Record and follow your instructor's directions. This is your responsibility. (Note that we will refer to book reviews in this section, but you can also apply what you learn here to writing an article critique.)

6.1.1 Know What Kind of Book Review Is Required

There are two general requirements involved in undertaking a book review:

1. It must be a critical review or an evaluation of a book. Your evaluation must make positive or negative comments about an author's work—in other words, you must form an opinion about the work. You do this by reading the book and making comments.
2. Your book review will have its own particular requirements, outlined below. Change anything as required by your instructor.

Specific Requirements
Title Page (APA, CMS, or ASA Style)

*   Check to see what is required on your title page.
*   Check to see if a manuscript page header is required. Most instructors do *not* require this for a book review. This chapter assumes that none is required.

Page Numbers

*   First page number starts with the text of the book review.

Title of Book Being Reviewed

*   Place title on first page where book review starts.
*   Give complete APA, CMS, or ASA style reference.

Due Date

*   You must record when the book review is due to be submitted, including the day and, if online, the time.

Outline

- Most instructors do not require an outline for a book review.
- If your instructor does require an outline, use the First Social Science Outline in Appendix E to record your arguments about the work (adjust for more or fewer words, pages, or arguments for length).
- Make any changes to the outline to suit instructor requirements for a book review.
- *Record the due date and time for outline*, if you are required to submit it.

Length

- Book reviews are usually shorter than term papers, so brevity in writing is very important.
- Length is generally stated in minimum to maximum number of words (for example, 1200–1500 words). (Your instructor may also state the minimum and maximum length in page numbers or in number of arguments: 6–8 pages or 5–8 arguments. *Record and follow this requirement.*)
- Book review length is taken *very seriously*, and your instructor may impose *penalties* for violating the minimum and maximum length.

Margins, Font Size, and Type

- You must use one-inch margins, or 2.54 centimetres, and the size of the required font, such as 12 point, and the required font type, such as Times New Roman.

References (APA, CMS, or ASA Style)

- You may or may not be asked to use references in your book review.
- Using more references (books and articles) will mean a more informative book review.
- Check with your instructor to see if any additional references are required and what kinds are acceptable.

6.2 How Do I Work on My Book Review Outline?

The basic social science argumentative format and process can be used as a guideline to help you evaluate another author's work. If you have not done so, we highly recommend that you read about the use of the building blocks (concept, definition, and evidence/example) in the Introduction to this book and how it relates to the basic format and process.

Begin your book review outline by doing the following:

- Create a computer file of a complete book review outline (use Appendix E: The First Social Science Outline as a guide).

- Make any other changes to your outline as directed by your instructor.
- Make a backup copy of your outline in a separate storage device (for example, USB drive). Regularly make backup copies of your original file.

Your social science book review outline is thus similar to the term paper outline. You may, however, have to increase the arguments section to allow for more arguments.

Now, work on the *first-priority* items of the basic social science argumentative format and process for your book review.

6.2.1 Work on First-Priority Items in Outline

Recall the first-priority items in the basic social science argumentative format and process for individual arguments only (*aim, arguments, in-text citations,* and *references*).

Here is how these first-priority items are used for your book review:

- Your opinion of the author's book will become your *aim* sentence.
- Your opinion will be based on the kinds of *arguments* that you will make about the work: generally positive, undecided, or negative.
- The *in-text citations* will be the actual references from the book that you will use to substantiate your points and evidence.
- Any additional *references* that you use in your book review should also be recorded in your outline.

The *inductive process* for developing your aim or opinion about the work is as follows:

- Either start with a working aim or stay neutral about the work being reviewed.
- Develop individual arguments first, and then categorize all your arguments as positive, undecided, or negative.
- Create your book review aim inductively based on the general categorization of your arguments.

The first-priority items are now presented in more detail, starting with the aim.

Aim

The aim sentence for your book review will present your opinion about the author's work. You may have formed an early opinion of the book by skimming through it. Treat your opinion as a *working aim* since you have no arguments yet to support your evaluation.

Here are some guidelines about using a working aim for a book review:

- Keep your working aim under control, and remember that it may be revised.

- Do *not* use your working aim to look for arguments to fulfill it because this is unfair to the author—just as it would be unfair to you if someone evaluated your work this way.
- Stay *neutral* at the outset so that you can look at the positive and negative arguments of a work before you create and finalize your aim.

Arguments

An argument for a book review consists of the following:

- The point you wish to make
- The evidence to support the point or missing evidence from the book

Taken together, the point and evidence make an argument. Note the following about arguments:

- Where you are making a point and are unable to find evidence in the book, then this may be a negative argument.
- Record your individual points and evidence about the work in your book review outline.

Follow these guidelines about presenting a point and evidence:

- Do not present more than one point per argument; each point will require evidence or proof from the author's work. Many reviewers in popular magazines present many points without providing evidence for some of them. Your review will be more convincing if you state only one point with supporting evidence.
- In general, present only one clear example for each point. Avoid long, detailed descriptions from the author's work that fail to state an exact point with the evidence provided. Paraphrase or summarize descriptions to a few sentences.

Start your review by *reading* the work in its entirety, preferably twice. You are reading this book in order to

- find and recognize the features of the basic social science argumentative format and process in the book;
- see what other items have been added and used in the book;
- familiarize yourself with and determine the sequence of the book's contents; and
- prepare yourself to make arguments about all of the preceding.

Here is a very general and brief list of some *contents of a book* that you are reviewing, about which you might create arguments:

- Aim, which may be stated as purpose, focus, or a research question
- Theory or theoretical perspectives

- Definition of the concepts in the purpose of the book, which may refer to theory
- Research methods, which may include various aspects, such as design of research
- Organization of arguments, which will most likely refer to the sequence of the various headings or themes of the book
- Presentation of arguments, usually separated and presented in various parts, such as data, analysis, discussion
- Conclusion
- References (there may be a glossary of terms and an index)

Note that this list of what an author's book might contain includes the basic social science argumentative format and process, plus theory and research methods. However, an author might use words that differ from those used in the basic social science argumentative format and process. For example, the aim may be called *the purpose* or it may be stated as a question to be addressed in the research. An answer to the question may also be given.

As well, most books will have more content than the basic social science argumentative format and process. A book will generally include theory and research methods. The word *theory* (or *theories*), in the social sciences, means to provide an *explanation* of the arguments, points, or evidence. The various disciplines or fields of study have different theories or theoretical perspectives to explain research. *Research method* (or *methods*) refers to the different kinds of systematic and planned investigations that are carried out to obtain evidence or information about a problem or question. Each discipline or field of studies has acceptable research methods that create the evidence for its arguments and theories. The theory (or theories) of the book are used to explain the evidence (or findings, results) in order to draw conclusions about the book's aim.

In evaluating a book, *make notes*, write comments, or ask questions about its contents. Remember to write each one of your comments separately as a point in your outline, making sure to add the page reference. Start your comments by *following the content sequence of the book*. In other words, your remarks should start where the book starts and end where the book ends. Much thought and planning has gone into organizing a book before it is published, so it makes sense to follow that organization.

By following the sequence of the book's contents, you will learn how the book has been coherently and logically organized and the reasons for that organization. In reading the sequence of the book, make notes about points (or specific concepts and their definitions) and evidence on the following:

- What you liked or were positive about
- What you were unsure about or questioned
- What you disliked or were negative about

Some examples of the kinds of positive or negative comments (meaning your points and evidence from the book) that you might make are as follows:

- The author's *aim* is either clearly expressed *or* difficult to determine. Parts of the aim may be assumed.
- The key *concepts* are either clearly defined and explained *or* are assumed.
- The author's work is both well organized and logical, *or* the author is vague about how some parts relate to each other.
- The *arguments* may be either very convincing, with reliable and valid evidence, *or* very general and weak and lacking proof.
- The *conclusion* may outline solid support for the aim and the arguments, *or* it may be vague and unclear. What research might be helpful?
- Add comments on contributions to the relevant theory, as well as on the appropriateness of the author's research methods.

TIPS Check out the questions at the end of this chapter (pp. 188–190) on writing an article critique for more evaluative comments.

Record your points (or concepts and definitions) and evidence about any of the preceding in the arguments section of your outline (include the page reference). Attempt to create as many arguments as possible so that you can omit the weaker ones later. Your arguments should include some or all of the following:

- The book's purpose, usually related to a theory or theories
- The research method or methods used
- The evidence (quantitative and/or qualitative data) presented
- The theoretical explanation of the evidence
- The degree to which the purpose was met and any advancements made in concluding the book

Take any of the preceding into account as you complete your outline of the arguments about the book. These arguments are vital for good, quality research. Once you have completed your arguments, *determine the aim* of your book review in the following general way. *Group the arguments* in your outline into one of three categories as follows:

1. The arguments about the book are generally positive.
2. There appears to be a balance of positive and negative arguments.
3. The arguments about the book are generally negative.

In short, the quality of arguments and the category containing the majority of arguments will indicate what your aim should be. *It is the actual arguments that you have created that determine the aim of your book review.* For instance:

- If your arguments about the work are favourable, your aim will have a positive view of the author's work. Your favourable arguments about the author's work will support your positive aim.

- Considerable negative arguments will suggest a negative aim.
- If you have a similar number of positive and negative arguments, you are uncertain about a clear direction for an aim.

The wording of your aim will usually include some or all of the general concepts concerning the book's purpose. The aim for your book review will be worded to say that you are positive, undecided, or negative about the overall concepts in the purpose of the book. Record the wording of your aim in the outline.

TIPS In wording the aim sentence of your review, avoid merely stating that you liked or disliked the author's work. Such a statement only emphasizes your emotional response to research material, which is not the main objective of a social science review. Instead, state that you agree or disagree with the purpose of the author's work by including that purpose in your aim sentence.

In-Text Citations

Chapter 3 presented the meaning and use of in-text citations. For any information taken from the book you are reviewing, be sure to include the page number. You do not need to record the author's last name as part of your in-text citations because it is assumed that the page number refers to that author. Be sure to include all reference sources in your outline for other authors according to APA, CMS, or ASA style.

References

If you do not have any references other than to the work you are reviewing, do some research to find references to other works in the specific area or topic of your review. Read other reviews (positive or negative) as well to improve your critical analysis of another work. For any additional references, record the complete reference in your outline, according to the required style.

Now that you have an aim, and arguments to support that aim, you should *consult with your instructor* about your book review outline. Obtaining feedback from your instructor may

- provide insight on your aim and arguments that you had not considered for the book; and
- challenge you to think about or rethink what you were planning to write.

Although three general kinds of reviews that you might write about an author's work have been covered in this chapter, your instructor might require a different type of a review. *Follow your instructor's directions*, which should include some of the aspects of writing a review covered in this chapter.

In addition, your instructor might encourage you to write a *positive review* of another author's work. You will thereby learn how to do the following:

- Evaluate another author's work based on certain criteria rather than just on your own personal likes or dislikes.
- Recognize the various parts of someone else's work and the language that is used for making evaluative comments on these different aspects of a work.
- Describe the specific contributions that another author makes.

A positive review is, therefore, a good starting point for a student in order to learn some of the basic aspects involved in writing a review.

Your instructor might also point out that the other two kinds of reviews (balanced and negative) are more difficult to write:

- The *balanced review* is more difficult to write because it requires you to be more familiar with the subject matter and field of studies. You have to be able to present both sides convincingly and then make a recommendation.
- A good, convincing *negative review* will require knowledge of the field of studies that you will probably not yet have. You may not be aware of gaps in theoretical assumptions and omissions of research methods. These comments are not meant to discourage you from writing this type of review. Just understand the challenge of writing such a review as pointed out by your instructor.

Treat these comments about your review as excellent learning opportunities because your instructor has more knowledge about and experience with the subject matter, discipline, or field of studies.

6.2.2 Work on Second-Priority Items in Outline

After consulting with your instructor and making any changes to your review outline, work on the remaining parts (definition of concepts in aim, organization of arguments, conclusion, and references (if any).

Definition of Concepts in the Aim
You do not need to define every word in your book review's aim sentence. Instead, *define only the key ideas or general concepts*. In a book review, the main concepts usually come from the author's work. Therefore, list those concepts (in the same order as they appear in the aim) in your book review outline.

You may want to present a quotation for the work's overall concepts. Be forewarned, however, that you will need to paraphrase any long definitions. Brevity in a book review is considered crucial; anything more than a few words is considered long. You must learn and be able to condense long definitions while remaining true to their original meaning.

Organization of Arguments
Many book reviews do not have a separate part that highlights how the arguments have been organized. At best, there may be a sentence or two to suggest *the general*

sequence of arguments that will be made. This part of the outline is included to help you order the arguments that you will make and thus assist you in the general wording of those arguments:

- For a positive aim, list your positive arguments first, followed by one or two minor negative arguments.
- For a balanced review, separate your positive and negative arguments, starting with the positive ones. However, a better way is for you to alternate the positive and negative arguments so that you make a positive argument, then a negative one, or vice versa. If you do this, make a list of the sequence you will follow.
- For a negative review, list your negative arguments first, then one or two minor positive arguments.

Conclusion

In the conclusion of your outline, restate your aim and summarize the arguments. Book reviews usually state whether or not to recommend the book. Given that there were three general kinds of reviews presented, there are three possible types of recommendations:

- For a positive aim, you will enthusiastically recommend the work.
- For a balanced or neutral aim, you will have a mixed opinion about the work. At best, you can recommend that the reader of the review (your instructor) read the work and decide for her- or himself.
- For a negative aim, you will recommend against reading the work.

References (APA, CMS, or ASA Style)

Make sure that you list any additional *references* in your outline that you used or were required to use for your review. List these reference sources alphabetically according to the last name of the author (see Chapter 3).

Once you have completed your outline, you should *confer with your instructor* again to verify any revisions that you were asked to rethink to see if your outline is complete and to see if any further changes might be required.

6.3 How Do I Write My First Social Science Book Review?

Once you have completed your book review outline, you should do the following:

- Make a full backup copy of your book review outline on a separate storage device.
- Print or send a copy of your outline to your instructor (if required).

You should now proceed to write your review, keeping in mind the following required writing skills.

6.3.1 Use the Required Writing Skills

You must have good basic writing skills to write a clear and understandable book review, including the following: spelling, grammar, punctuation, quoting, appropriate language, proper sentences, paragraphs, and transitions.

Reminder

See the Introduction and Chapter 5 for more details on writing skills.

Here are some more suggestions to help you write your first book review:

- Maintain an *impartial tone* in writing your evaluations. Even though you are making critical comments about a book, your writing style must be neutral.
- Use appropriate *variety* in what you are presenting, especially in your choice of words, phrases, language, and transitions.
- *Clarify* what you are writing about. This means elaborating on what the words or phrases mean that you are using. *Rephrasing* your writing helps to clarify what you are presenting.
- Explain how you are going to present what you are writing. In other words, tell the reader, your instructor, what you are going to write about next. Pointing out what you are doing in your writing will help make your book review more *coherent*.

Improving these writing skills will help you create a clearer and more understandable book review.

6.3.2 Write Your Draft

Use your outline to help you write a draft of your book review. You will be writing the draft of your book review *deductively* by following your outline. Once you have written a draft of your book review, revise it to improve it (see also Chapter 5).

This section will present the three types of book review drafts that were mentioned previously in working on your outline:

- A positive review of a book
- A balanced review of a book
- A negative review of a book

We will present each one of the preceding in turn. Remember to do the following:

- Add transitions to your writing as you switch from one idea, sentence, or paragraph to the next.

- Delete the headings of the basic social science argumentative format and process, which are to be used as a guide only.
- Write your book review as a *coherent, unified* whole (and not as unrelated parts).

A Positive Review

If you have a positive aim or your instructor suggests that a certain book has made a significant contribution to an area of study, your review will probably be positive. In a positive review, most of the arguments will praise the work while a few will point out weaknesses.

Introduction and Aim

Write an interesting, favourable introduction for a positive review, suggesting that the work is important and well researched. You should include an aim sentence stating that your review of the author's work will be positive.

For example:

> This review will show that the author has clearly demonstrated how family dysfunction produces teen runaways.

> That fetal alcohol syndrome can be prevented is convincingly and clearly presented by this author.

Definition of Concepts in the Aim

In writing your review, clarify any general concepts or terms in your aim, but do not give formal definitions. You will probably draw on the author's work for clarification of these overall concepts, but you will paraphrase them, thereby indicating that you agree with the way the author uses the concepts. Use this understanding of the definitions to reword or clarify your aim in this positive review.

If you are familiar with the work's general field of studies, state the significance of the field. Then, put the author's work in its analytical and theoretical context, showing your instructor that you understand the overall context of the work you are reviewing. You can then mention the positive contributions the work has made to the field of studies.

Organization of Arguments

You can sometimes omit a paragraph outlining the sequence of arguments that your review will follow because published reviews have stricter space limitations than a published paper. Experienced reviewers are able to suggest the sequence of their arguments through their excellent use of language and knowledge of the specific area. However, as a student you can briefly state in very general terms what your positive arguments will be, followed by some minor problems with the work.

Do not merely list the arguments you will make in your review. Instead, in several sentences, state how your arguments are organized. Also, do not refer to an example or clarify a point. This is not the place to go into detail. Present this information later in your review.

Presentation of Arguments

Write arguments, with points and specific examples, that show that the work is valuable. Your examples might consist of a quote or paraphrased or condensed material from the author's work.

Below are examples of some general arguments for a review. Notice that the arguments here follow the items of the basic social science argumentative format and process with the addition of theory and research methods. The words are italicized to show you this. Do *not*, however, italicize words like this in your review.

Suggested positive arguments and what information to add:

The author has a clear and concise statement of the *aim* of the work.

Add what the aim or hypothesis of the work is.

The author's aim falls clearly within a *theory's* framework and will certainly advance part of the theoretical framework being studied.

Add specifically what will be revealed from the aim of this study and how the theoretical knowledge of the field in question will be advanced. You might also say that the theory chosen to explain the study is appropriate and understandable. Give an example from the author's work, showing how the theory explains the study's aim.

The concepts of the aim are *defined* clearly and are easy to understand. The definitions are used consistently throughout the work and provide a solid foundation for the work. Some definitions of the concepts may be appropriate extensions of current usage.

Add examples from the work whenever a separate argument is introduced.

The author's *research methods* yield the kind of information that is required for this work.

Present the positive and negative aspects of the author's research methods.

The research methods yield the relevant kind of data that is necessary to support the arguments of the hypothesis or aim.

Add examples from the work to substantiate any arguments.

The author's work is *organized* logically and is coherent. The sequence that the arguments are presented in assists in understanding the work.

Justify presenting the arguments in this order or give a general observation on how the work is organized.

The *arguments* in the work are convincing; the points are clear and understandable.

Add one impressive example from the work by paraphrasing the point or using minimal quotes.

There is solid evidence to substantiate most of the author's points.

Give an example of evidence that clearly supports a point. Put it in your own words by paraphrasing the author.

continued

The *conclusion* reflects how convincing arguments supported the author's aim. The theory convincingly explains and interprets what the aim and arguments mean in the larger theoretical context.

Add an example for each point.

Once you have given positive arguments, present the one or two negative arguments and their minimal detraction from the work. A negative argument might highlight that a certain point is either missing or vague, and then present evidence of this from the reading. (You might suggest that the author could clarify this in a future work.) A negative comment might also suggest that there is a lack of evidence for a particular point from the reading but that this could be corrected with further research. (Note the pattern of following each negative comment with a statement that it does not detract significantly from the author's work.)

Conclusion

In a paragraph or two, end your review by restating your positive and favourable opinion of the author's work. Include comments to the effect that the author's position is clear, with sound arguments. Do not include any new points or examples. You can also state the significance of this specific work and how it contributed to the field of studies. Consider including an overall recommendation that other readers would greatly benefit from reading this book.

A Balanced Review

A review that is balanced will present convincing arguments that both praise the work and point out significant problems with it. The aim of the review is to provide a similar number of positive and negative arguments. A good balanced review will require you to be more familiar with the work, its theory, its research, and the subject area.

There are variations in writing a balanced review. One way is to begin your review by being undecided or neutral in the introduction and aim, presenting balanced positive and negative arguments, and concluding by favouring one side of the arguments over the other. The arguments in the review thereby justify your decision. The reader of your review can then see how you arrived at the positive or negative opinion.

A less common way to write a balanced review is to start the review again by being undecided or neutral in the introduction and aim, presenting balanced positive and negative arguments about the work, but concluding by remaining neutral or undecided and recommending that readers of the work decide for themselves. The review does not recommend either reading the book or not. The neutral conclusion is that the reader should consider reading the work to make up her or his own mind. However, your instructor might require you to take a position, with either a positive or negative recommendation.

Confer with your instructor for direction if you want to conclude by being undecided about the work.

Introduction and Aim

Write an introduction that convincingly expresses your indecision or neutrality about the work. For example, you might mention both the favourable and detrimental aspects of the work, which makes the author's work of limited value. Another way is to state that the work is interesting but that its value is not easily understood. Include an aim sentence in your introduction that states that this will be a neutral or balanced review of another author's work.

Examples:

> This review will demonstrate that the author was unclear in showing that teen runaways stem from working-class families.

> It is doubtful that habitual alcohol abuse has an impact on mortality rates as advanced in this work.

Write your review's aim sentence so it suggests that a balance of positive and negative arguments will be put forward in reviewing the work. If you plan to conclude the review with a positive or negative recommendation of the work, include a sentence to that effect. This sentence might state that after presenting positive and negative arguments, you will then be able to offer a tentative recommendation to either read the work or not.

The aim sentence then sets the direction and focus for the rest of the review. Its wording reflects how the other parts of the review will be worded to give a neutral or balanced view.

Definition of Concepts in the Aim

Your comments about definitions of the general concepts in the aim should likewise be neutral or undecided. You might agree with parts of the author's definitions of overall concepts, and disagree with other parts.

For example, you might say something to the effect that the author's definition of *teen runaways* is adequate, but there is some confusion with the concept of *working class*. You might also indicate that there are some problems with the definitions in the work on habitual alcohol abuse.

Quoting or paraphrasing parts of the definition will indicate that you understand their use. Follow up this understanding by rewording or clarifying the aim of your balanced review to indicate where you agree and disagree with the definitions.

Organization of Arguments

As mentioned, this paragraph is usually omitted. However, in your first review there is no harm in giving a brief overview of your arguments. It will demonstrate to your instructor that you have given some thought to the organization of your arguments. There are two general ways to organize the arguments of the review:

- Keep the positive and negative arguments separate and state that either all the positive or all the negative arguments will be presented first. (This is the block method, Davis et al., 2013, p. 107.)
- Integrate the positive and negative arguments. That is, follow a positive argument with a negative argument, or vice versa. (This is the point-by-point method, Davis et al., 2013, p. 107.)

Presentation of Arguments

Present both the arguments that are in support of the work and those that are negative about the work. Integrate them, with a negative argument following a positive one. For favourable arguments, include a specific example from the work, using short quotes, paraphrases, and condensed material. For negative arguments, indicate where crucial points and evidence in the work are either lacking or are not addressed.

Below are brief examples and suggestions for neutral arguments used in each item of the basic argumentative format and process. The same recommendations apply here as in the positive review.

Suggested balanced arguments and what information to add:

The author's *aim* is neither clear nor easy to understand.

Add what the purpose of the work is and what is not clear about it.

It is unclear how the author's aim falls within the general *theoretical* framework of the field of studies and it is doubtful that the aim will contribute to that framework.

Add specifically what both supports and detracts from the aim of the work, and how it is unclear that the field of studies will benefit from this work. You might also say that the theory chosen to explain the study is not appropriate or clear. Give an example from the author's work that shows how the theory fails to explain the aim of the study.

There are problems with the way the author *defined* the concepts of the aim.

Provide clear examples of problems with any definitions.

The author's research *methods* yield only partially useful information in the work. Other research strategies would have yielded more relevant data for the arguments and aim.

Provide examples from the work to substantiate any problems with it.

There are problems with the way the work is *organized*. Parts of the work are well organized while others do not flow smoothly.

Provide an example of how the author's work lacks coherence.

Some of the *arguments* are convincing whereas others are incomplete and difficult to follow. Some points are clear and easy to understand while others are confusing.

Provide examples by quoting or paraphrasing from the work.

Some of the points have evidence to support them while others do not have any evidence or data to substantiate them.

Present evidence of this by paraphrasing and condensing material from the work.

The *conclusion* does not clearly show that all the arguments convincingly support the author's aim. The author makes a number of assumptions to show how the arguments relate to the aim of the work. The theory the author used to interpret the aim and arguments is questionable.

Give an example for each point you make.

Conclusion

In a paragraph or two, restate the aim of your balanced review, highlighting both the favourable and negative arguments about the author's work. Include any possible statements about the work's strengths and the weaknesses and its relation to the field of studies.

End your review with a possible recommendation, to the effect that after having presented both the positive and negative arguments about the work, you would either recommend or not recommend reading this work. Provide a reason for your decision:

- Some possible reasons *for* recommending the work include that the favourable arguments arouse more curiosity about the field of studies. The work is worth reading because it gives some valuable insights for future research.
- Recommendations *against* reading this work might include that there are too many problems with the work to recommend it. Another possible way of wording this might be that the difficulties with the work significantly detract from it.

If you remain neutral (with your instructor's approval), you might make no recommendation either way but might instead urge the reader to use her or his own judgment. You might recommend reading the book, letting readers draw their own conclusions about the work. However, *confer with your instructor before reaching this conclusion.*

A Negative Review

In a negative review, a majority of the arguments will find the work seriously flawed while a minority, usually just one or two, will mention some positive contributions. A well-written negative review of a work assumes considerable familiarity with the subject and with related theory and research.

Introduction and Aim

Write an introduction stating that there are significant problems with the work that detract considerably from its potential importance. Include an aim sentence stating that this will be a negative review of another author's work.

Examples:

> This review will show that this work does not demonstrate convincingly that working-class teenagers have a higher rate of running away from home than middle- or upper-class adolescents have.

> The author has not shown a relationship between increased advertising of alcohol in the media and an increased rate of alcoholism.

Definition of Concepts in the Aim

If your review has a negative aim, there are probably significant problems with the definitions of the general concepts. Indicate how you disagree with these definitions in the author's work. Your disagreement might be over deviations from generally accepted definitions of concepts in the field, or over invalid or contradictory assumptions, or over serious omissions of part or all of the definitions from current research.

You will have to give an example for each point made here. Your examples will come from both the author's work (omissions, assumptions, or contradictions) and from the works of other authors in the field (what those authors include in their works, and their reasons and logic for doing so). Your examples will show your instructor that you understand the problems with the definitions and how they relate to the field of studies.

Organization of Arguments

As mentioned with the other kinds of reviews, this paragraph is sometimes omitted for the sake of brevity. However, compose a few sentences anyway if you have never written a social science review. State very briefly the negative arguments that you will present, followed by the minor contributions. This sets the stage for the specific arguments that you will make.

Presentation of Arguments

Write arguments that show that the work is negative. Below are suggestions and examples of arguments worded negatively for the same criteria as in the previous reviews. The previous recommendations apply here as well.

Suggested negative arguments and what information to add:

The author does not have a clear and concise *aim*. The aim is convoluted and difficult to understand.

For example, you might add that there are too many concepts to give this work a clear, definite focus.

Another problem is that the aim does not advance anything new and is merely a summary of a selected part of the field.

State what the serious problem(s) is with the aim of the work.

The author's aim or purpose does not fall within the *theoretical* framework of the work. The theoretical framework of the work is difficult to understand. Also, a different theoretical framework is better at explaining or interpreting the author's work.

Add an example for each point, including the different theoretical framework and how it is better at explaining the author's work than the one the author used.

The concepts of the aim are not *defined* clearly. Parts of the definition are missing, misleading, or vaguely worded. The concepts and definitions are used inconsistently or inappropriately. There is no attempt to build on current knowledge or to use definitions as they currently exist in the literature.

Each point means you need to provide a convincing example.

The author's *research methods* used to support the work's focus do not yield the kind of information that is required for this work. There are other research methods, quantitative or qualitative, that would yield more relevant data needed to support the hypothesis's arguments.

Provide examples to substantiate any arguments.

The work is not *organized* coherently. The sequence of arguments is haphazard and makes the work confusing.

Present an example from the work of each problem that you point out.

The majority of *arguments* in the work are not convincing. Most of the points in the work are unclear. These points need considerable elaboration in order to be understood.

Present an example of this from the work.

Many points also have no evidence or data to support them and are only opinions.

As an example, present a point that has no evidence to support it.

Overall, the arguments in the work are weak and seriously flawed.

The *conclusion* of the work does not hold up because of the weak arguments made to support the aim. There is no attempt to show how arguments support the aim of the author's work. The theory does not interpret convincingly what the aim and arguments mean in the larger theoretical context.

Give an example for each point.

Once you have presented the negative arguments, then put your one or two positive arguments forward. Your positive arguments might highlight that a certain point is valid and then you might give evidence from the reading. Another positive comment might be that there is important evidence for a particular point from the reading. Offer these positive comments in the context of the overwhelming negative arguments. The usual opinion will be that these positive comments do not make a significant contribution to the field. In short, the problems with the work outweigh its minor contributions.

Conclusion

In a paragraph or two, state why the reading was negative and that no significant contribution was made to the field. You will usually conclude that other readers will not benefit from reading the book or article. In short, you cannot recommend the author's work.

6.3.3 Confer with Your Instructor

Now that you have a draft of your book review, consult with your instructor one final time. Make sure that you have included your instructor's suggestions from previous discussions.

6.3.4 Revise Your Draft Book Review

Before you revise the draft copy of your book review, you should do the following:

- Set it aside for a day or two.

- Read your work aloud.
- Find someone with more writing experience and familiarity with the subject to read and check your work before handing it in.

Table 6.1 Two Ways Your Book Review May Be Evaluated

Completeness: Do You Have All the Required Parts?	Individual Criteria: How Well Did You Do on Each Part and on Overall Coherence?
• Introduction and aim sentence • Definition of concepts • Organization of arguments • Presentation of arguments • Conclusion • In-text citations • References	• Writing skills • Introduction and aim sentence • Definition of concepts • Organization of arguments • Presentation of arguments • Conclusion • In-text citations • References

Note: Your instructor may change, delete, or add to these minimum criteria.

Now proofread your draft. To *proofread* means to read your review again, checking for any errors. When proofreading, you should check for the following:

- Clear use of words and basic writing skills—replace redundant words and use variety for overused words
- Neutral tone is used in your writing
- That all required parts are included—there are no missing parts, from introduction to references
- Coherent and consistent writing—your writing is logical and deals with each idea or thought in its proper sequence
- Clear and effective arguments—each point and supporting evidence relates to each other and is convincing
- Unified book review—your writing relates clearly every idea, paragraph, or part of the review.

Remember that virtually all instructors will evaluate basic writing abilities as part of a book review. Proofreading your work is essential. As well, you should make sure that your book review is formatted properly.

6.4 How Do I Format My Book Review?

Formatting a book review is the same as for a term paper (see Chapter 3 for quotations; and Chapter 5, section 5.3, for margins, font size, and type; and Chapter 5, section 5.3.1, for APA, CMS, and ASA style references pages.

6.5 How Do I Create the Title Page for a Book Review (and Article Critique)?

The title page is a separate page with all items centred and double-spaced. Your instructor may require the following on your title page:

- The words *Book Review* (or *Article Critique*) and the complete title of the book (or journal article) written as a complete reference in one of the styles (APA, CMS, or ASA)
- Your name (and, if required, your student number)
- The course name, number, and section number
- Your instructor's name
- The name of your college or university
- The due date (the date by which the review must be submitted) and time deadline

Many instructors use a format for a book review and article critique title page that is similar to that of a term paper. This is suggested here. The title of the book or article being reviewed is presented below in the respective APA, CMS, or ASA referencing style.

Book Review	**Article Critique**
of	of
Smith, D.E. (2005). *Institutional ethnography: A sociology for people.* Lanham, MA: Altamira.	Moen, P., & Flood, S. (2013). Men's work/volunteer time in the encore life course stage. *Social Problems, 60*(2), 206–233. doi: 110.1525/sp.2013.11120
by	by
Jane Smith, #212345678	Jane Smith, #212345678
(The rest of the page is the same as a term paper. Chapter 5, section 5.5)	(The rest of the page is the same as a term paper. Chapter 5, section 5.5)

Figure 6.1 Example APA-Style Title Page for Book Review and Article Critique

Book Review	Article Critique
of	of
Smith, Dorothy E. 2005. *Institutional Ethnography: A Sociology for People.* Lanham, MA: Altamira.	Moen, Phyllis, and Sarah Flood,. 2013. "Men's Work/Volunteer Time in the Encore Life Course Stage. *Social Problems,* 60 (2): 206–233. doi: 110.1525/ sp.2013.11120
by	by
Jane Smith, #212345678	Jane Smith, #212345678
(The rest of the page is the same as a term paper. Chapter 5, section 5.5)	(The rest of the page is the same as a term paper. Chapter 5, section 5.5)

Figure 6.2 Example CMS- and ASA-Style Title Page for Book Review and Article Critique

Some instructors using the ASA-style title page for a short book review may require the student information at the top of the page where the book review starts (see also Chapter 5 title page for term paper, section 5.5.2). Check with your instructor for her or his specific requirements.

As a general rule, do not colour, underline, paste, or draw anything on the title page unless directed to do so by your instructor. As well, you should do the following:

- Put the full reference of the book at the top of the page where the text of your book review starts.
- Make sure that the text of your book review starts your page numbering with the number on the right side (as a header with no added text).

6.6 What Do I Need to Do to Produce My Final Copy?

If you have just written a five-argument book review, check to see how many words or pages you used (omit the title and references pages). For now, it is worthwhile to remember the word and page count for your next book review. Before you submit your book review, you should do the following:

- Check your book review over one final time to make sure it is error-free and complete.
- Make a full backup copy of your completed book review in your separate storage device.
- Make sure you do not attach any material unless directed to do so by your instructor.
- For print submissions:
  - Staple the top left-hand corner: make sure that the pages are in order.
  - Print two copies: one for your instructor and one for you, and submit at start of class.
- For online submissions:
  - Submit before deadline time and request instructor acknowledgement of receipt.

6.7 How Do I Write an Article Critique?

You can use the previous material on writing a book review to write a review of an article, which is commonly referred to as an *article critique*. If you have not done so, you should read this entire chapter to get an overview of doing a review. This overview will help you to understand the adaptations and further suggestions that are presented here.

Reminder

- Adapt the book review outline to *create an article critique outline*.
- Consult with your instructor as you progress through the steps of completing your article critique outline and *revise* it as necessary.
- For your outline and eventual writing, focus on the author(s) and what she or he says. For example, state what the author's aim is, *not* the article's aim.

Writing an article critique involves summarizing and evaluating what an author has written. Your instructor may require you to summarize and evaluate an article in a periodical in one of two ways (or possibly a variation of these):

- A separate summary and evaluation of an article
- An integrated summary and evaluation of an article

6.7.1 Write a Separate Summary and Evaluation

Your instructor may require that you keep the summary and evaluation of an article separate. Your article critique would then start with a summary of an author's work followed by your evaluation or opinion of it.

There are a number of good reasons for you to learn how to summarize or condense an author's work:

- To recognize the various significant organizational parts of an article
- To understand what the author has presented
- To determine the most significant features of an author's work
- To write your understanding of the main arguments of an author's work in a condensed way
- To write your summary in a neutral and unbiased tone or manner

Summarizing an author's work may include the following significant parts or a variation of them (the keywords used in doing a book review are also highlighted here):

1. *Introduction, background, aim*, and the author's important *concepts*
2. *Methods* and how they were *designed* to investigate the *aim*
3. *Arguments* presented based on *evidence* and *analysis* of the results
4. *Conclusions* concerning the relation between the *aim* and the *analysis* of the *findings*

TIPS If your instructor does not specify a required format in which to present your summary, then use the article's general headings or organization as your guide.

Here are some general questions for each of these four parts to help you summarize an author's work:

1. In the introduction and background, what is the main consideration (for instance, theoretical or practical) that leads the author to formulate this aim?
   - What is the author's aim (which may be worded as a purpose, thesis, hypothesis, problem, or question)?
   - What are the general concepts in the author's aim, and how are they defined or clarified?
2. Which specific methods and their design does the author use to study the aim?
   - What is the author's rationale for using those methods?
   - How does the author use those methods?

3. What is the general evidence (or results or findings) of the study?
    - How does the author analyze these results?
    - Can you state the most important arguments of the author's analysis as it pertains to the results?

TIPS Use the author's conclusion to help you determine the most import-ant arguments.

4. What are the author's conclusions between the aim and the analysis of the findings?
    - Which parts of the aim were supported by the findings and to what degree?
    - How does the author justify the support for the aim of the study?
    - How does the author rationalize the findings that did not support the aim?
    - Does the conclusion suggest a logical further study?

Knowing how to summarize an author's work competently and fairly helps to prepare you to add your evaluative comments. There are two general kinds of relat-ed evaluations that you can add to your summary of an article. They may be referred to as *internal* and *external* evaluations or critiques. Both kinds are usually included in a critique (without specifying which kind is being used). We use them here separ-ately to show you that learning more theories and research, as you progress in your courses and studies, will be a great source for improving your evaluations, especially external critiques. Both kinds of evaluations will also help you understand some of the processes involved in making those evaluations.

Internal Critiques

An *internal critique or evaluation* is concerned primarily with assessments (both posi-tive and negative) that focus on the article itself. This kind of evaluation is con-cerned mainly with arguments for each part of the article and the relationship of each part to the author's overall intended aim. If you are unfamiliar with the topic or subject matter contained in the author's work, then you may need to consult some reference sources to help you understand it.

TIPS For areas or aspects with which you might disagree with an author, consider wording your comment as a *suggested improvement* in-stead of simply stating your disagreement.

Your answers to the following questions will help you create some positive and negative internal arguments about an author's work:

- Is the author's writing of each part of the article clear and understandable, or are there vague and convoluted parts that can be improved on? Are there any gaps or omissions?
- Does each part relate consistently to the next, or are there some inconsistencies?
- What does the author assume in the article? Are such assumptions reasonable or unreasonable?
- Would clarifying some assumptions make the author's work more convincing?
- Is the author's aim developed rationally from the introductory background? What would improve it?
- Does the author use general concepts in a consistent way throughout the study? Are there any inconsistencies that need to be clarified?
- Is the method(s) clear and reasonable to investigate the aim? Are any short-comings clarified?
- Are the findings reliable and justified?
- Are the explanations of the results credible and persuasive arguments?
- Did the author convince you that the aim of the study was met successfully, or was it unsuccessful? What are the reasons for reaching your concluding opinion? What was crucial in convincing you?

External Critiques

In addition to positive and negative internal evaluations, there are also external evaluations to consider. An *external critique or evaluation* refers to positive *and* negative assessments that are predominantly outside of or peripheral to an author's work. The author's work is thus judged positively or negatively compared to other theories, research methods, research findings, and so on.

Here are some general external questions to address in making more evaluations:

> **Reminder**
>
> Throughout these external questions you may need to research *additional reference sources* to compare or contrast their theory and a nalysis of findings with the author's study.

- Is the author's introductory background a fair or inadequate summary of other works in developing the aim? (You will need to know these additional works.)
- Compared to other works, is the aim innovative or not very interesting? Who is more interesting and why?
- Does the author's use of general concepts compare favourably or not with other works? Is this justified for the study? How can it be improved compared to other works?

- Are there any other research methods, designs, or strategies that could improve the author's investigation?
- Do the results or findings of the study corroborate those of other studies? Are the results significantly similar to or different from those studies? What arguments might account for this?
- How does the author's analysis of the results compare with other theoretical arguments? Are the author's argumentative explanations relevant to other theories or not very meaningful?
- How do the conclusions compare to other studies in the insights provided? Do they advance our understanding? Are the implications of the conclusions worth pursuing?
- Could the conclusions be combined with those of other studies for useful research?

Most likely, you will *not* need to distinguish between the kinds of evaluations (internal or external) that you make. Use the preceding to help you determine the most important arguments that can be made to evaluate an author's work, and include both kinds. Use reference sources as necessary for both.

6.7.2 Write an Integrated Summary and Evaluation

An article critique that requires you to *integrate* a summary and evaluation of that article means that you are expected to express your opinions as you accurately and fairly present an author's work. This general kind of format for an article critique (or possible variation of it) assumes that you are able to summarize an author's study and can make internal and external argumentative evaluations of it (as presented in the previous section).

Gaining experience in writing a separate summary and evaluation will assist you greatly before undertaking a critique that requires you to integrate them. Now, you are expected to present your opinions on the topic of an author's work and to state the author's work fairly. That is, you should present how well or poorly the author's work contributes to the understanding of the general topic or issue. Many reviewers highlight the positive or negative aspects of an author's work as examples of how our knowledge about the subject matter or problem is enhanced or of limited value.

Your opinions are expected to be generally positive or negative arguments. A neutral stance for an article critique is generally not done. *Check with your instructor on what is expected before you start your article critique.*

The process for arriving at an overall opinion of an author's work is presented in the previous book review sections of this chapter. You can change or adapt this process to suit your instructor's requirements for a specific format for your article critique. If your instructor does not specify a format, then consider following the article's headings or organization.

The following questions are offered to you for your consideration in writing this kind of a critique. Answers to these questions combine internal and external evaluations. You should be able to recognize the internal and external focus of these questions from the previous section. (You may need to reread this section.) These questions are grouped into the same significant parts of an author's work as presented in the separate summary and evaluation section:

- Is the introductory background clearly related to a larger theory or issue? Does the author make similar acceptable or unacceptable assumptions that need to be clarified? What is the most important aspect about the introduction or background concerning the topic or problem?
- Do the introduction and background provide a clear or uncertain rationale for the aim?
- Is the aim presented clearly, or is it difficult to determine? What is the aim? Is the aim innovative or not very original compared to other studies in the field?
- Does the wording of the aim make it easy or somewhat difficult to determine the general concepts and their definition? What are the definitions or clarifications of the main concepts? Are they expressed clearly, or are the meanings vague?
- Are the definitions or clarifications of the overall concepts consistent with those of other authors, or do they depart significantly from generally accepted meanings? What are the implications for the current author's methods?
- Are the author's research design and methods appropriate for the study's aim and concepts? What are they, and are they presented clearly?
- Do the author's research methods correspond favourably with standard practice in the field, or are there some unclear aspects?
- Would the use of other methods significantly improve this study? Is the omission of these acceptable or unacceptable for the author's current purpose?
- What are the results and analysis of these results? Are the results as expected? Are they reliable and valid? Does the analysis of them present reasonable or unreasonable arguments? Is there anything that might improve the results?
- How do these findings and their analysis compare or contrast with similar studies? Do the results corroborate or cast doubt on the arguments of other studies?
- Would an explanation of the results that differs from that of the author's make sense or not?
- Is the conclusion between the aim and the analysis of the results rational, or are there uncertain aspects (and to what degree)?
- What are the main conclusions? Does the author convince you that the stated aim was achieved? What reasons or arguments can you give for being convinced or not?
- How do the conclusions from this author compare to arguments from other studies? Do the conclusions further our understanding of the aim or problem, or not?
- Does the conclusion contribute to and advance our understanding of the subject matter (or problem) in this field, or is this study of limited value?
- Are further logical investigations suggested? Do they appear useful, or would a different direction be appropriate?

You may need to consult references about the topic as well as other works for this integrated summary and evaluation of an article.

The referencing and formatting for an article critique are similar to that of a book review. For a suggested title page, see section 6.5 of this chapter and note the comment regarding ASA style at the end of the section. Confer with your instructor about the title page and any other information that may be unclear before submitting your article critique.

The suggestions for undertaking a review that were presented here were meant as a starting point on which to expand your knowledge.

Chapter Summary

Requirements before you start your book review (or article critique):

- Record the specific requirements from your instructor in the checklist.

Work on your book review outline:

- Create a book review outline using the First Social Science Outline in Appendix E.
- Start working with the first-priority items of the basic social science argumentative format and process.
- The aim will be your overall opinion of the work; the arguments will be your points and evidence about the work, including theory and research methods (either positive, undecided, or negative).
- Read the contents of the book and make notes about points and evidence that you felt were positive, undecided, or negative.
- Record your points, evidence, and page references from the book in the arguments section of the outline.
- Determine the aim of the book based on your completed arguments. (Were they mostly positive, undecided, or negative?)
- Research additional references and reviews by other authors and record them in your outline (as in-text citations and in references page, using APA, CMS, or ASA style).
- Consider writing a positive review for your first book review in order to learn to evaluate based on criteria and to become familiar with evaluative language.
- Confer with your instructor about the first-priority items of your review outline.
- Continue with the second-priority items of defining the general concepts in your aim, organizing your arguments, and drafting a conclusion (record additional references in outline).
- Consult with your instructor about your completed book review outline.

Write your book review draft:

- Writing skills: use correct spelling, grammar, punctuation, quoting, and appropriate language.
- Write your draft using proper sentences, paragraphs, and transitions.
- Three possible kinds of book reviews are positive, balanced, or negative.
- For a positive review, follow the basic social science argumentative format and process:
  - In arguments section, add one or two negative arguments to the majority of positive ones.
  - State that the negative ones have minimal impact on the overall positive aspect of author's work.
- For a balanced review, follow basic social science argumentative format and process:
  - Two variations in writing this review are as follows:
    1. Start by being neutral in introduction and aim, present positive and negative arguments, and then in conclusion favour one side over the other based on arguments presented.
    2. Start by being undecided in introduction and aim, present both sides in arguments, then remain neutral in conclusion.
- For a negative review, follow basic social science argumentative format and process:
  - In arguments section, add one or two positive arguments to the majority of negative ones.
  - State that the positive ones have minimal impact on the overall negative aspect of author's work.
- Consult with your instructor about your draft book review outline.

Revise book review:

- Set it aside for a day or two.
- Have a more experienced writer check it.
- Proofread it for errors in writing and in consistency.
- Double-space entire book review.
- Format references (if required) in correct APA, CMS, or ASA style.

Create title page (in APA, CMS, or ASA style) for book review (and article critique):

- Create proper title page as required.

Produce final copy:

- Make backup of book review in separate storage device before printing.
- For print submissions: print two copies (one to submit, keep the other one), staple top left corner, and submit at start of class.

- For online submissions: submit before deadline time and request instructor acknowledgement of receipt.

Suggestions for writing an article critique:

- Read and adapt all the sections in this book review chapter before starting your article critique.
- Two general formats for writing an article critique are a separate summary and evaluation or an integration of the summary and evaluation.
- A separate summary and evaluation format involves presenting a condensed version of an author's work followed by an internal and external critique or evaluation of it.
- An internal critique or evaluation means to make positive and negative assessments, mainly about the article itself (i.e., its clarity, consistency, and coherence).
- An external critique or evaluation refers to making positive and negative assessments mainly outside of or peripheral to the author's work (i.e., compared and contrasted to other theories, methods, and research studies).
- An integrated summary and evaluation format means to present your opinions about an author's work as you accurately present that work.

✔️ Checklist for Writing Book Review and Article Critique

Book review

Write book review draft:
- ☐ Did you make a copy of your outline to create a draft book review file?
- ☐ Did you make a backup copy of your draft book review file?
- ☐ Did you write your draft book review using correct writing skills, proper sentences, paragraphs, and transitions?
- ☐ What kind of book review did you write: a positive, balanced, or negative review?
- ☐ Did you follow the basic social science argumentative format and use transitions throughout to write your draft?
- ☐ Did you consult with your instructor about your draft book review and make any required revisions?

Revise book review:
- ☐ Did you proofread it for errors in writing, transitions, and consistency?
- ☐ Is your book review written as a coherent and unified whole?

continued

Format book review:
- [ ] Is your entire book review double-spaced, except long quotes (which are single-spaced)?
- [ ] Are your references in correct APA, CMS, or ASA style?

Create title page:
- [ ] Did you create a proper title page for book review (or article critique) by following APA, CMS, or ASA style?

Produce final copy:
- [ ] Did you make a backup copy of your book review in a separate storage device before printing?

  For print submissions:
  - [ ] Did you print two copies: one for your instructor and the other one to keep?
  - [ ] Did you staple the top left corner and hand it in the paper at the start of class?

  For online submissions:
  - [ ] Did you submit the paper before the time deadline and acknowledge receipt from your instructor?

Article critique

Write article critique:
- [ ] Did you read, understand, and adapt all sections involved in doing a book review before undertaking an article critique?
- [ ] For the separate summary and evaluation format of an article critique, did you write a fair summary of the author's work?
- [ ] Did you include internal and external evaluations of the author's work, suggesting how it might be improved?
- [ ] For an integrated summary and evaluation format, did you make internal and external evaluations as you accurately presented the author's work?
- [ ] Did you follow the book review process in completing your article critique, starting with "Revise book review"?

Recommended Websites

Massey University: *Te Kunenga ki Pūrehuroa* (New Zealand)
The OWLL (Online Writing and Learning Link)—article critique:
http://owll.massey.ac.nz/assignment-types/article-critiques.htm

Queen's University
Stauffer Humanities and Social Sciences Library—provides links to book reviews in the social sciences:
http://library.queensu.ca/research/guide/book-reviews/social-sciences/

Simon Fraser University
Library—Finding Book Reviews and Writing Book Reviews:
http://www.lib.sfu.ca/help/publication-types/book-reviews

University of Wisconsin at Madison
Libraries—provides links to book reviews in the humanities and social sciences:
http://researchguides.library.wisc.edu/bookreviews/

Recommended Readings

Johnson, Jr., W.A., Rettig, R.P., Scott, G.M., & Garrison, S.M. (2009). *The sociology student writer's manual.* (6th ed.). Upper Saddle River, NJ: Pearson.

Northey, M., & Timney, B. (2015). *Making sense in psychology: A student's guide to research and writing* (2nd ed.). Toronto, ON: Oxford University Press.

Appendix A

Answer Key to "What Do I Need to Know About Reading and Writing?"

The following are answers to the questions on pages 5 and 6 of the Introduction.

Spelling

1. The parents hid *their* alcohol from *their* kids.
2. *Their* teen did not *know* to phone home.

Grammar

3. A teen ran away from *home*.
4. Many teens ran away from their *homes*.
5. The family *are* worried about their runaway teen. (*Family* refers to members of a group acting individually and requires a plural verb.)
6. The family *is* worried about its runaway teen. (*Family* is referred to as a whole group and requires a singular verb.)
7. She does not like her parents going out drinking and partying, and staying out late. (This is one way to clear up the confusion of the pronoun *them* to refer to parents and not to *partying*, *drinking*, and *staying out late*.)
8. She was lying, cheating, and stealing to survive. (*Lying*, *cheating*, and *had to steal* were not parallel.)

Punctuation

9. A runaway teen may require food, shelter, and clothing.
10. The detox worker stated the policy clearly: "You must follow the rules of this clinic or you will not be allowed to stay."

Sentences

11. The family of the runaway teen is looking for her.
12. She ran away from home. She did not know where she would live or what she would be doing.

Appendix B

A Brief Grammar Reference

Parts of Speech

Every word in a sentence can be categorized as one of eight parts of speech depending on its function in that sentence. The eight parts of speech are as follows: nouns, pronouns, verbs, adjectives, adverbs, prepositions, conjunctions, and interjections.

Nouns

Nouns are words that name people (*Anichka, doctor*), animals (*Buster, dog*), places (*Kuala Lumpur, home*), and things—both concrete things, such as objects or substances (*hospitals, air*), and abstract things, such as qualities or concepts (*sorrow, intelligence*), measures (*metres, years*), and actions (*reading, writing*). In sentences, nouns act as subjects and objects.

Nouns may be classed as proper (beginning with a capital letter) or common (beginning with a lower case letter). Proper nouns start with capital letters because they name specific people, places, and things (*Dorothy Smith, Moose Factory, Mount Sinai Hospital*). All other nouns are common nouns and begin with lower case letters (*spatula, school, service*). Nouns may also be classified as countable (a hundred *excuses*) or non-countable (interminable *ennui*).

A noun that refers to a group rather than an individual (*team, company, herd*) is called a collective noun. Nouns made up of two or more words (*Parliament Buildings, father-in-law*) are called compound nouns. The words of a compound noun can be joined (*lighthouse*), separate (*light switch*), or hyphenated (*light-of-my-life*). Compound nouns change over time, often evolving from two words to a hyphenated word to a single word without hyphens. When in doubt about the correct form, consult an appropriate style guide or dictionary.

Pronouns

Pronouns substitute for nouns and allow us to avoid awkward repetition. The word a pronoun substitutes for or refers to is called its antecedent. In the sentence *Nikos forgot his keys*, the pronoun *his* refers to the proper noun *Nikos*, the antecedent.

There are six main types of pronoun: *personal, relative, demonstrative, indefinite, interrogative,* and *reflexive.*

Personal Pronouns

There are six forms of personal pronoun, as shown in the following chart.

Table B.1

	Singular	Plural
First person (person/s speaking)	I	we
Second person (person/s spoken to)	you	you
Third person (person/s spoken about)	she, he, it	they

First person refers to the person or people speaking (singular *I,* or plural *we*). *Second person* refers to the person or people spoken to (*you* for both singular and plural); and *third person* refers to the person or people or thing(s) spoken about (singular *she, he, it,* and plural *they*).

Relative Pronouns

Relative pronouns are used to link less important ideas to the main idea of a sentence. They include *that, which,* and *who* (also *whom* and *whose*). The relative pronoun thus performs two jobs at once: it joins a less important (or subordinate) clause to a main clause, and it refers back to its antecedent, the noun it substitutes for. The following examples show the relative pronoun underlined and the antecedent of the pronoun in italics:

> Here's the *book* that I promised you.
> She took the *train,* which was late.
> I had a *TA* who writes science fiction.

Demonstrative Pronouns

Demonstrative pronouns point out or indicate specific things. There are only four demonstrative pronouns: *this* and its plural form, *these*; and *that* and its plural form, *those.*

Indefinite Pronouns

Indefinite pronouns are numerous; like all pronouns, they refer to people, animals, places, and things but not to specific or particular ones. Table B.2 lists some commonly used indefinite pronouns.

Interrogative Pronouns

Interrogative pronouns, such as *what, why,* and *how,* are easy to recognize because they ask questions. The interrogative pronouns in the following examples are in italics.

> *What* would you like to do?
> *Which* do you prefer?
> *Who* was on the phone?

Table B.2

all	any	anybody	anyone	anything
both	each	either	enough	everybody
everyone	everything	few	less	many
more	most	much	neither	nobody
none	no one	nothing	one(s)	other(s)
several	some	somebody	someone	something

Whom did you invite?

Whose are these?

Reflexive Pronouns

Reflexive pronouns refer back to the subject and are also easy to recognize, because they always end in *-self* or *-selves* (*myself, yourself, himself, herself, itself, ourselves, yourselves, themselves*). Reflexive pronouns are used when the subject and object of a verb are one and the same, as in this sentence:

She cut herself.

Reflexive pronouns are also used for emphasis (sometimes called intensive pronouns):

I myself collected the data.

Verbs

The verb asserts something, expressing action or a state of being. It is the single most important part of speech since every sentence must have at least one verb, telling what the subject—the person, animal, place, or thing that the sentence is about—is doing, having, or being.

There are two main kinds of verbs: action verbs and linking verbs. Most verbs are action verbs: they express actions (although not necessarily physical ones, for example, *to think* is a kind of action verb). Linking verbs express something about the subject, either identifying the subject (*she is the singer*) or describing the subject (*she is talented*). The most common linking verb is the verb *to be* (in all forms: *I am, you are, she/he/it is, we are, you are, they are, I was, you were*, etc.). Other linking verbs include *appear, become, feel, grow, keep, look, prove, remain, seem, smell, sound, stand, stay, taste*, and *turn*. Most of these can be used as either action or linking verbs, as in the following examples:

Tamara appeared [*action verb*] in the doorway.

Tamara appeared [*linking verb*] upset.

The verb in a sentence may consist of a single word (*she sings*), but it may also consist of more than one word (*six months have passed, a week will have passed*). When the sentence verb is a phrase instead of a single word, then the last word—the one that indicates what is happening—is the main (or principal) verb; all the preceding words are auxiliary (or helping) verbs. For example, if I write *I go*, I have a verb made up of a single word, *go*. If I write *I have gone*, I have a verb phrase made up of the auxiliary verb *have* and the principal verb *gone*. The rule holds regardless of the number of auxiliaries. In the verb phrase *must have been leaving*, the principal verb is *leaving*, and all the other words (*must*, *have*, and *been*) are auxiliaries.

In addition to the verbs *be*, *have*, and *will*, which are used routinely to form certain tenses (*I am going*, *I have gone*, *I will go*), the following verbs are commonly used. They are called modal auxiliaries: *do*, *must*, *ought*, *let*, *used*, *need*, *shall*, and *should*; *will* and *would*; *can* and *could*; and *may* and *might*.

Tense refers to the time of a verb's action. Each tense—past, present, and future—has simple, perfect, progressive, and perfect-progressive forms. These convey a range of time relations, from the simple to the complex.

Table B.3

Tense	For actions . . .	Examples
Present	Happening now, occuring habitually, or true anytime	I walk; she walks
Past	Completed in the past	I walked; she walked
Future	That will occur	I will walk; she will walk
Present Progressive	Already in progress, happing now, or still happening	I am walking
Past Progressive	In progress at a specific point in the the past or that lasted for a period in the past	I was walking
Future Progressive	Of duration in future, or occurring over a period at a specific point in future	I will be walking
Present Perfect	Begun in past and continuing in present, or occurring sometime in past	I have walked
Past Perfect	Completed before others in the past	I had walked
Future Perfect	Completed before others in future	I will have walked
Present Perfect progressive	In progress recently, or of duration starting in the past and continuing in present	I have been walking
Past Perfect progressive	Of duration completed before others in past	I had been wallking
Future Perfect progressive	Underway for period of time before others in future	I will have been walking

Adjectives

An adjective describes or modifies a noun or pronoun (*a witty remark*, *a good one*), adding more information to make the meaning of the noun or pronoun more vivid, clear, or precise. The adjective can add information (*a red hat*, *a large house*, *a beautiful picture*), or it can limit the meaning to show which, whose, or how many (*this hat*, *Morgan's book*, *five pictures*). The words *the* and *a* or *an*—the definite and indefinite articles, respectively—are special kinds of adjectives. They belong in a category of words called determiners: words that show a noun will follow (*a house*, *an orange*, *the books*). (Other kinds of adjectives—possessive adjectives, for example—also act as determiners.) A determiner is a kind of marker (specifically, a noun marker). There are other kinds of markers: for instance, auxiliary verbs are verb markers, and adverbs are markers for adjectives and other adverbs. Finally, most adjectives can be compared, as in the following examples: *bright, brighter, brightest; dazzling, more dazzling, most dazzling.*

> Her *radiant* eyes made my heart melt.

[*Radiant* is an adjective that modifies or describes the noun *eyes*.]

> He was *thin* and *pale*.

[*Thin* and *pale* are adjectives modifying the pronoun *he*.]

> *One large brick* house stood on the hill.

[The adjectives *one, large,* and *brick* modify the noun *house*.]

Possessive words can function as nouns (*that bag is Zoe's*), pronouns (*this one is hers*), or adjectives (*Zoe's bag, her bag*). When possessives are used as adjectives, telling to whom or to what something belongs, they are called possessive adjectives. Notice that possessive nouns (*that is Dario's, this is the boy's*) do not change form when they are used as adjectives (*Dario's scarf, the boy's mitten*), but most possessive pronouns do: *the money is mine,* but *that's my money,* and so on (*yours/your, hers/her, ours/our, theirs/their*). In the following example, the possessive adjective *your* in the first part of the sentence and the possessive pronoun *yours* in the second part illustrate the difference:

> *Your* jacket is on the couch; *yours* is in the closet.

In the first part, *your* is an adjective because it has a noun to modify (*jacket*); in the second part, *yours* is a pronoun because it takes the place of a noun.

Adverbs

An adverb can describe a verb, an adjective, or another adverb; it can also describe a whole sentence or clause. When an adverb describes a verb, it shows when (time), where (place), or how (manner) something is done. When it describes an adjective or another adverb, it illustrates the extent or degree of some quality or condition. As noted above, when a verb is stated in the negative, the *not* is an adverb.

> The dancer moves *gracefully*.

[*Gracefully* is an adverb modifying the verb *moves*; it shows manner, how the dancer moved.]

> He has a *highly* intelligent daughter.

[*Highly* is an adverb modifying the adjective *intelligent*; it shows the degree to which the man's daughter is intelligent.]

> We studied *too* hard.

[*Too* is an adverb modifying another adverb, *hard*.]

> *Strangely*, the auditorium was empty.

[*Strangely* is an adverb that modifies or describes the whole clause, *the auditorium was empty*.]

Prepositions

A preposition is used to introduce a phrase (a group of words without a subject-and-verb combination). The main noun or pronoun in the phrase is called the object of the preposition. Here are examples of such phrases, with the prepositions in italics and the objects underlined:

up the escalator

down the road

into the oven

before the game

Prepositions don't *modify* words the way that adjectives and adverbs do, but in linking the words of the phrase to the rest of a sentence, prepositions show important relationships. For example, notice how the meaning varies when different prepositions are used with the same object:

on the desk

beside the desk

beneath the desk

to the desk

Recall that the noun or pronoun following a preposition is called the object. A prepositional phrase consists of a preposition and its object, often with an article (*the, a, an*) between them. (The definite and indefinite articles are considered adjectives because they always modify nouns or pronouns.) The phrase may also contain modifiers (*on the* comfortable *chair*). The whole structure—the preposition (*on*), the article (*the*), any modifiers of the object (*comfortable*), and the object noun or pronoun itself (*chair*)—is a prepositional phrase.

Additional words between the preposition and its object do not change the grammatical relationship: the preposition and its object form the backbone of the prepositional phrase.

Example:

The house in the *once-green* valley was destroyed *by a raging fire.*

In the first phrase, *in* is the preposition, and *valley* is the object of the preposition; *the* is the definite article, and *once-green* is an adjective modifying the noun *valley*. In the second phrase, *by* is the preposition, *fire* is the object of the preposition, *a* is the indefinite article, and *raging* is an adjective modifying the noun *fire*. The whole prepositional phrase includes the preposition, its object, and any modifiers.

Compound prepositions typically consist of two words, and sometimes three. The following are common examples:

Table B.4

ahead of	apart from	as for	aside from	away from
because of	belonging to	contrary to	due to	inside of
instead of	out of	owing to	rather than	together with
up at	up on	up to	in spite of	for the sake of
on account of	with reference to	with regard to		

A particle is a special kind of preposition that functions as part of a verb, forming something called a verb-particle composite.

Here are two examples:

He *looked up* the unfamiliar word in the dictionary.

She *ran into* an old friend.

Notice that the verb in verb-particle composites has a different meaning from that of the verb by itself: people who "look up" words in a dictionary are not looking over their heads, and "running into" old friends is not the same as colliding with them.

Conjunctions

Conjunctions connect words or groups of words in a sentence. Coordinating conjunctions (such as *and, yet, but, for, nor, or, either, neither, yet*) join elements of equal rank in a sentence (single words to single words, phrases to phrases, and clauses to clauses). Subordinating conjunctions (such as *if, since, because, that, while, unless, although*) join subordinate clauses to independent ones.

Conjunctions are indispensable, but they are often misused or treated carelessly. They help to express the logical connections between ideas, so care must be taken to use the right one. The choice of conjunction can radically change the meaning of a sentence:

Because she loved him, she had to leave.

Although she loved him, she had to leave.

Coordinating Conjunctions
The following examples illustrate coordinate elements, with the conjunctions in italics:

I enjoy apples *and* blueberries.

She looked in the closet *and* under the bed.

No one else was at home, *and* I answered the phone.

The first conjunction joins two nouns (*apples, blueberries*); the second joins two phrases (*in the closet; under the bed*); the third joins two independent clauses (*No one else was at home; I answered the phone*).

Subordinating Conjunctions
Subordinating conjunctions are used to show that one idea, expressed in the subordinate clause, leans on another idea, expressed in the independent clause. The following example illustrates this:

I answered the phone *because* no one else would.

Because no one else would is a subordinate clause. Unlike the independent clause, *I answered the phone*, it does not make sense by itself; it needs to be joined to the independent clause to form a complete thought. *Because* is the subordinating conjunction that does the job.

Correlative Conjunctions
Correlative conjunctions come in pairs (*both . . . and; neither . . . nor; either . . . or; not only . . . but also*), with each half of the pair introducing one of the two things being joined:

I love listening to music, *both* live *and* recorded.

I enjoy *neither* cooking *nor* cleaning the house.

I want *not only* to live well *but also* to act honourably.

Conjunctive Adverbs

A conjunctive adverb is an adverb that also performs the work of a conjunction, joining sentence elements. It can be used to join two independent clauses. Words used as conjunctive adverbs include the following:

also	anyhow	besides	consequently	furthermore
however	indeed	moreover	nevertheless	thus

Interjections

Interjections are used to express strong emotion and have no grammatical relation to the rest of the sentence. Some words are always used as interjections (*Hey! Wow! Ouch!*). Words that are generally used as other parts of speech may also be used as interjections (*Great! Oh, no! Too bad!*).

Punctuation

Punctuation is used to separate strings of words into manageable groups and help clarify their meaning. The marks most commonly used to divide a piece of prose or other writing are the period, the semicolon, and the comma, with the strength of the dividing or separating role diminishing from the period to the comma. The period marks the main division into sentences; the semicolon joins sentences (as in this sentence); and the comma (which is the most flexible in use and causes the most problems) separates smaller elements with the least loss of continuity. Parentheses and dashes also serve as separators—often more strikingly than commas, as in this sentence.

Period

A period is used to mark the end of a sentence that is not a question or exclamation. In prose, a sentence marked by a period normally represents an independent or distinct statement; more closely connected or complementary statements are joined by a semicolon (as here).

Periods are used to mark abbreviations (*Wed., Gen., p.m.*). They are often omitted from abbreviations that consist entirely of capital letters (*CBC, EDT, RRSP*) and from acronyms that are pronounced as words rather than sequences of letters (*Intelsat*). They are not used in abbreviations for SI units (*Hz, kg, cm*).

If an abbreviation with a period comes at the end of a sentence, another period is not added:

They have a collection of many animals, including dogs, cats, tortoises, snakes, etc.

But note:

They have a collection of many animals (dogs, cats, tortoises, snakes, etc.).

A period is used as a decimal point (*10.5%, $1.65*) and to separate the domains of an email or Web address (*http://www.oupcanada.com*). It is commonly used in British practice to divide hours and minutes in expressions of time (*6.15 p.m.*), where a colon is standard in North American use.

Semicolon

The main role of the semicolon is to join sentences that are closely related or that parallel each other in some way, as in the following:

> Many new houses are being built north of the city; areas to the south are still largely industrial.

> To err is human; to forgive, divine.

It is often used as a stronger division in a sentence that already includes several commas:

> Joanne and Emily went out for dinner, as they usually did on Wednesday; but when, upon arriving at the restaurant, they were told they would have to wait for a table, they went home and ordered Chinese.

It is used in a similar way in lists of names or other items to indicate a stronger division:

> I would like to thank the managing director, Jennifer Dunbar; my secretary, Raymond Martin; and my assistant, David Singh.

Comma

Appropriate use of the comma is difficult to describe as there is considerable variation in practice. Essentially, it is used to give structure to sentences, especially longer ones, in order to make their meaning clear. Too many commas can be distracting; too few can make a piece of writing difficult to read or, worse, difficult to understand.

A comma, typically followed by a conjunction (such as *and, but, yet*), is used to separate the main clauses of a sentence:

> Mario cooked a roast, and Jan baked a pie for dessert.

A comma is not used when the subject of the first clause is understood to be the subject of the second clause:

> Mario cooked a roast and baked a pie for dessert.

It is considered incorrect to join the clauses of a compound sentence with only a comma and without a conjunction:

> ✗   I like skating very much, I go to the local rink every day after school.
> ✓   I like skating very much, <u>so</u> I go to the local rink every day after school.
> ✓   I like skating very much<u>;</u> I go to the local rink every day after school.

It is also considered incorrect to separate a subject from its verb with a comma:

> ✗   Those with the smallest incomes and no other means<u>,</u> should get more support.
> ✓   Those with the smallest incomes and no other means should get more support.

Commas are usually inserted between adjectives preceding a noun:

An enterprising, ambitious person.

A cold, damp, poorly heated room.

However, the comma is omitted when the last adjective has a closer relation to the noun than the others:

A distinguished foreign politician.

A lush tropical forest.

An important role of the comma is to prevent ambiguity. Imagine how the following sentences might be interpreted without the comma:

With the police pursuing, the people shouted loudly.

She did not want to leave, from a feeling of loyalty.

In the valley below, the houses appeared very small.

Commas are used in pairs to separate elements in a sentence that are not part of the main statement:

I would like to thank you all, friends and colleagues, for coming today.

There is no truth, as far as I can see, to this rumour.

It appears, however, that we were wrong.

A comma is used to separate a relative clause from a noun when the clause is used to provide additional information about the noun but is not essential in identifying it:

The picture, which hangs above the fireplace, was a present.

In this sentence, the information in the *which* clause (a non-restrictive clause) is incidental to the main statement. Without the commas, it would become a defining or restrictive clause, forming an essential part of the statement by identifying which picture is being referred to:

The picture that hangs above the fireplace was a present.

Note that a restrictive clause is typically introduced by *that* rather than *which*.

Commas are also used to separate items in a list or sequence:

Emma, Sheilah, and Dorcas went out for lunch.

The doctor told me to go home, get some rest, and drink plenty of fluids.

It is acceptable to omit the final comma before *and*; however, the final comma has the advantage of clarifying the grouping if a composite name occurs at the end of the list:

I buy my art supplies at Midoco, Loomis and Toles, and Staples.

A comma is often used in numbers of four or more digits to separate each group of three consecutive digits starting from the right (e.g., $10,135,793$). In metric practice, a space is used instead of a comma to separate each group of three consecutive figures ($10\ 135\ 793$).

A comma is used to introduce a quotation of a complete sentence:

Nadia exclaimed, "Isn't he fabulous!"

It also substitutes for a period at the end of a quotation if this is followed by a continuation of the sentence:

"I've never seen such a remarkable athlete," said Stefan.

Colon

The main role of the colon is to separate main clauses when there is a step forward from the first to the second, especially from introduction to main point, from general statement to example, from cause to effect, and from premise to conclusion:

> There is something I forgot to tell you: your mother called earlier.
>
> It was not easy: to begin with, we had to raise the necessary capital.

It also introduces a list of items:

> This recipe requires the following: semi-sweet chocolate, cream, egg whites, and sugar.

A colon is used to introduce, more formally and emphatically than a comma would, speech or quoted material:

> I told them just last week: "Do not, under any circumstances, open this box."

It is used to divide hours and minutes in displaying time (*6:30 p.m.*, *18:30*).

Question Mark

A question mark is used in place of a period to show that the preceding sentence is a question:

> She actually volunteered to do it?
>
> Would you like another cup of coffee?

It is not used when the question is implied by indirect speech:

> I asked you if you would like another cup of coffee.

A question mark may be used (typically in parentheses) to express doubt or uncertainty about a word or phrase immediately following or preceding it:

> Jean Talon, born (?) 1625.
>
> They were then seen boarding a bus (to Kingston?).

Exclamation Mark

An exclamation mark is used after an exclamatory word, phrase, or sentence expressing any of the following:

- Absurdity (*That's preposterous!*)
- Command or warning (*Watch out!*)
- Contempt or disgust (*Your hands are filthy!*)
- Emotion or pain (*I love this song! Ouch! That hurts!*)
- Enthusiasm (*I can't wait to see you!*)
- Wish or regret (*If only I could fly!*)
- Wonder, admiration, or surprise (*What a caring, compassionate person she is!*)

Apostrophe

The main use of an apostrophe is to indicate the possessive case, as in *Justine's book* or *the boys' mother*. It comes before the *s* in singular and plural nouns not ending in s, as in *the girl's costume* and *the women's costumes*. It comes after the s in plural nouns ending in s, as in *the girls' costumes*. In singular nouns ending in s, practice differs between (for example) *Charles'* and *Charles's*; in some cases the shorter form is preferable for reasons of sound, as in *Xerxes' fleet* or in *Jesus' name*.

An apostrophe is used to indicate that a letter or series of letters has been removed to form a contraction: *we're, mustn't, Hallowe'en, o'clock*. It is sometimes used to form a plural of individual letters or numbers, although this use is diminishing. It is helpful in *dot your i's and cross your t's*, but unnecessary in MPs and *1940s*.

Quotation Marks

The main use of quotation marks is to indicate direct speech and quotations. Quotation marks are used at the beginning and end of quoted material:

> She said, "I have something to tell you."

In standard North American practice, the closing quotation marks should come after any punctuation mark, whether or not it is part of the quoted matter:

> They shouted, "Watch out!"
> "Leave me," he said, "and never return."
> They were described as "an unruly bunch."

Quotation marks may be placed around cited words and phrases:

> What does "integrated circuit" mean?

A quotation within a quotation is put in single quotation marks:

> "Have you any idea," he asked, "what 'integrated circuit' means?"

Note that in British practice, single quotation marks are often preferred, and the punctuation may be placed outside of the quotation marks when it does not belong to the quoted material:

> They were described as 'an unruly bunch'.
> 'Have you any idea', he asked, 'what "integrated circuit" means?'

Brackets (Parentheses)

The types of brackets used in normal punctuation are round brackets ( ), also known as parentheses, and square brackets [ ]. The main use of round brackets is to enclose explanations and extra information or comment:

> He was (and still is) a rebel.
> Congo (formerly Zaire)
> He spoke at length about his Weltanschauung (world view).

Brackets are also used to give references and citations:

> Wilfrid Laurier (1841–1919)
> A discussion of integrated circuits (see p. 38)

Brackets are used to enclose optional words:

> There are many (apparent) difficulties.
> [In this example, the difficulties may or may not be only apparent.]

Square brackets are used less often. Their main use is to enclose extra information added by someone (normally an editor) other than the writer of the surrounding text:

> Robert walked in, and his sister [Sara] greeted him.

Square brackets are sometimes used to enclose extra information within text that is already in round brackets:

> Robert and Rebecca entered the room, and Sara greeted them. (Robert and Rebecca had concluded a three-week driving adventure [through Quebec] and had not seen Sara in some time.)

Dash

A single dash is used to indicate a pause, either to represent a hesitation in speech or to introduce an explanation of what comes before it:

> We must try to help—before it is too late.

A pair of dashes is used to enclose an aside or additional piece of information, like the use of commas as explained above, but forming a more distinct break:

> He refused to tell anyone—least of all his wife—about that embarrassing moment during the medical exam.

A dash is sometimes used to indicate an omitted word or a portion of an omitted word, for example, a coarse or offensive word in reported speech:

> "We were really p— off," he said.

It may also be used to sum up a list before carrying on with a sentence:

> Chocolates, flowers, champagne—any of these would be appreciated.

Hyphen

The hyphen has two main functions: to link words to form longer words and compounds, and to mark the division of a word at the end of a line in print or writing.

The use of the hyphen to connect words to form compound words is diminishing in English. A hyphen is often retained to avoid awkward collisions of letters (as in *twist-tie*, *re-emerge*, or *miss-hit*) or to distinguish pairs of words (such as *re-sign* and *resign* or *re-creation* and *recreation*).

The hyphen serves to connect words that have a syntactic link, as in *soft-centred candies* and *French-speaking people*, where the reference is to candies with soft centres and people who speak French, rather than to soft candies with centres and French people who can speak (which would be the sense conveyed if the hyphens were omitted). It is also used to avoid more extreme kinds of ambiguity, as in *twenty-odd people*.

A particularly important use of the hyphen is to link compounds and phrases used attributively, as in *a well-known man* (but *the man is well known*), *water-cooler gossip* (but *gossip around the water cooler*), and *a sold-out show* (but *the show is sold out*).

A hyphen is often used to turn a phrasal verb into a noun:

> She injured her shoulder in the *warm-up* before the game.

Notice, however, that while a hyphen is used in the noun, the verb is still spelled without a hyphen:

> Stretching is a good way to *warm up* before a game.

A hyphen is also used to indicate a common second element in all but the last of a list, e.g., *two-, three-, or fourfold*.

The hyphen used to divide a word at the end of a line is a different matter because it is not a permanent feature of the spelling. The general principle to follow is to insert the hyphen where it will least distract the reader, usually at a syllable break.

Ellipsis

A sequence of three periods is used to mark an ellipsis, or omission, in a sequence of words, especially when forming an incomplete quotation. When the omission occurs at the end of a sentence, a fourth point is added as the period of the whole sentence:

> He left the room, slammed the door . . . and went out.
>
> The report said: "There are many issues to be considered, of which the most important are money, time, and personnel. . . . Let us consider personnel first."

Capitalization

A capital letter is used for the first letter of the word beginning a sentence:

> She decided not to come. Later she changed her mind.

A sentence contained in brackets within a larger sentence does not normally begin with a capital letter:

> I have written several essays (there are many to be written) and hope to finish them tomorrow.

However, in the following example, the sentence is a separate one, and so it does begin with a capital letter:

> We have more than one option. (You have said this often before.) For this reason, we should think carefully before acting.

A capital letter is used to begin sentences that form quoted speech:

> The assistant turned and replied, "We think it works."

The use of capital letters to distinguish proper nouns or names from ordinary words is subject to wide variation in practice. Some guidelines are offered here, but the most important criterion is consistency within a single piece of writing. Capital letters may be used for the following:

- The names of people and places (*Terry Fox, Prince Edward Island, Robson Street*)
- The names of languages, peoples, and words derived from these (*Inuktitut, Vietnamese, Quebecer, Englishwoman, Americanism*)
- The names of institutions and organizations (*the Crown, the Senate, the Department of Health, the National Museum of Natural Sciences, the Law Society of Upper Canada*)
- The names of religions and their adherents (*Judaism, Muslim, the United Church*)
- The names of months and days (*June, Monday, New Year's Day*)
- Nouns or abstract qualities personified (*a victim of Fate*)

Note that *the Anglican Church* is an institution, but *the Anglican church* is a building; a *Democrat* belongs to a political party, but a *democrat* simply supports democracy; *Northern Ireland* is a name with recognized status, but *northern England* is not.

A capital letter is used by convention in many names that are trademarks (*Xerox, Cineplex, Arborite*) or are otherwise associated with a particular manufacturer. Verbs derived from such proprietary terms are often not capitalized (*xeroxing, googled, skidooing*).

Capital letters are used in titles of courtesy or rank, including compound titles, when these directly precede a name (*the Right Honourable Lester B. Pearson, Dame Emma Albani, Brigadier General Daigle, Prime Minister Stephen Harper*). It is not necessary to capitalize a title when it is not placed directly before a name or when it is set off by commas (*an interview with Stephen Harper, prime minister of Canada; an interview with the prime minister, Stephen Harper*).

A capital letter is used for the name of a deity (*God, Father, Allah, Great Spirit*). However, the use of capitals in possessive adjectives and possessive pronouns (*in His name*) is now generally considered old-fashioned.

Capital letters are used for the first and other important words in titles of books, newspapers, plays, movies, and television programs (*The Merchant of Venice, Who Has Seen the Wind, The Vertical Mosaic, Hockey Night in Canada*).

Capital letters are used for historical events and periods (*the Dark Ages, the Enlightenment, the First World War*); also for geological time divisions but not for certain archaeological periods (*Devonian, Paleozoic*, but *neolithic*).

Capital letters are frequently used in abbreviations, with or without periods (*CTV, M.B.A.*).

A capital letter is used for a compass direction when abbreviated (*N, NE, NNE*) or when denoting a region (*cold weather in the North*).

Appendix C

Answer Key to Writing Samples in the Introduction

Here are answers to the writing samples in the box called "Can You Recognize the Concept, Definition and Evidence/Example in These Samples?" on pages 8 to 9 of the Introduction.

Sample 1

Maureen Baker (2008) writes the following:

Concept: household
Definition: refers to people sharing and dwelling, whether are not they are related by blood, adoption, or marriage
Evidence/Example: a boarder might be part of the household, but not necessarily part of the family. Table 8.1 shows the percentage of Canadians living in various family types in 2001, compared to 1981.

Sample 2

Myers (2014) writes the following:

Concept: adolescence
Definition: the years spent morphing from child to adult
Evidence/Example: starts with the physical beginnings of sexual maturity and ends with the social achievement of independent adult status

Sample 3

Macionis and Gerber (2011) write the following:

Concept: a global perspective
Definition: the study of the larger world and our society's place in it
Evidence/Example: the position of our society in the larger world system affects everyone in Canada. Consider Canada's ambivalent relation to the United States—the destination of 85% of our exports—and our nation's attempts to come to terms with the economic powers of China and India

Sample 4

Steckley and Letts (2013) write the following:

> *Concepts*: socialization, primary socialization, secondary socialization
> *Definition*: a learning process, one that involves learning how to be a social person in a given society, and it brings changes in an individual's sense of self
> *Evidence/Examples*: childhood (generally known as **primary socialization**); later in life, (which is sometimes known as **secondary socialization**)

Note: The writing sample by Steckley and Letts here is more complicated.

- The **main concept** is socialization, which they define and give examples of childhood and later life.
- Once they have presented each example, they then go on to define socialization in childhood as *primary socialization* and socialization in later life as *secondary socialization*. These are **secondary concepts**.
- These secondary concepts are dependent upon and part of the main concept. This is similar to having a main heading and a second level heading in a textbook chapter.

Appendix D

Tips on Selecting Appropriate Academic Sources for a Research Paper

To find appropriate academic sources for your research, you will need to evaluate them. A number of tips or suggestions are provided here to help you evaluate research sources so that you can decide if they are suitable for an academic research paper. There are two general steps you should use. First, use the criteria that are presented to evaluate your research sources. Second, record all the relevant information of your appropriate sources in your term paper outline.

1. How Do I Evaluate My Research Sources?

In searching for appropriate, academic sources, you will have to decide whether or not a research source is acceptable. Some suggestions have already been presented in Chapter 2. You can also use the CRAAP test developed by the Meriam Library of California State University, Chico (2014), to evaluate your sources. Evaluating research sources includes websites, books, and articles. Here is an adapted version of the CRAAP test organized according to the building blocks: concept, definition, and example.

Table D.1 The CRAAP Test for Evaluating Appropriate Academic Sources

Concept	Currency	Relevance	Authority	Accuracy	Purpose
Definition	*Timely information*	*Importance to your needs*	*Source of information*	*Content reliability, truthfulness, and correctness*	*Reason for information*
Example of Questions	Time of publication?	Information relates to topic or question?	Determine author, publisher, source, sponsor?	Source and evidence of information?	Information is to inform, teach, sell, entertain, or persuade?
	Revised or updated information?	Audience-appropriate information?	Author's credentials or organization affilliations?	Reviewed or refereed information?	Clear purpose or intention of author or sponsor?

continued

Table D.1 *continued*

Concept	Currency	Relevance	Authority	Accuracy	Purpose
	Functional links?	Compared with other sources?	Relevance of URL to author or source?	Verifiable information from other sources?	Is informa-mation fact, opinion, or propaganda?
				Emotional-free tone? Grammatical errors?	Objective or impartial point of view? Political, cultural, or religious biases?

Source: Adapted from Meriam Library of California State University, Chico, 2014.

1.1 Books

Start the search for books on your topic in your academic library. Here are some suggestions:

- Use the words of your topic, the various search terms and strategies, in your library website catalogue. You can also search for authors on your topic if you know any.
- Evaluate the books for their academic appropriateness. Publishers of academic books: e.g., Oxford University Press, Pearson, Sage, plus publishers from various universities, e.g., University of Toronto Press, Chicago University Press.
- For an e-book, you will get the link to it. For a printed book, you will need the call number, the location (which campus library in which it is located), and to check to see if it is available.

For example, here is one suitable result in an academic library catalogue for a search on street kids:

> Kristina E. Gibson. 2011. *Street Kids: Homeless Youth, Outreach, and Policing New York's Streets.* New York: New York University Press. The call number in the library catalogue is: HV1437.N5 G53 2011.

You use the call number to find this book in your library stacks or request it through interlibrary loan. If you have any problems, contact a librarian to assist you. Record this source, including the library call number, in the references portion of your research outline.

1.2 Articles

To search for articles, you will need to be acquainted with your libraries' databases. Libraries subscribe to companies that provide databases for research. Some of these companies are: EBSCO, ERIC, INGENTA, INTUTE, JSTOR, LexisNexis, ProQuest, and SSRN.

Some specialize in certain areas, such as ERIC in educational sources. Most are multi-disciplinary. Some will also include books, government documents, and so on.

These companies provide the databases that you use for research to find articles on your topic. Your goal is to find and then search the databases that match your topic in your subject discipline or program (ask librarians to help you use databases if you are unfamiliar with them). Some of these databases are as follows:

- AnthropologyPlus
- Bibliography of Native North Americans
- Gender Studies Database
- International Political Science Abstracts
- Social Sciences Index
- Sociological Abstracts

Use your search terms and the way to search with them in these databases, and others not listed here, to find the most relevant articles (and other sources) on your topic.

The results you get will contain the title of the article, the name of the journal, the year, the volume and issue number, and the author(s). Evaluate the quality of each article to see if it meets the criteria for an academic source (the CRAAP test). If you decide that it does, then request the full text version. This may involve obtaining a printed version through interlibrary loan, so do this early in your research.

Avoid using the first number of sources you find that fulfill your instructor's requirements. Continue your search for appropriate academic sources for your topic.

Another way to search for articles (including books and other sources) is to use subject guides or program guides that use different databases from which to search. This may take you through several screens until you narrow your search for your topic. For example, research data sources in the disciplines of sociology and psychology will mean going to sociological abstracts PsychINFO or PsycARTICLES. You then search for articles on your topic in these databases.

Here is an example of an appropriate academic article using EBSCOhost. This involved selecting one of their databases called Academic Search Premier and clicking Connect. By typing in "street kids," using quotation marks, and pressing Search, a number of results were produced. The left side of the results allows you to limit or refine your search, such as years of publication and refereed journals, from which to search. The right side of the results allows you to chat with a librarian should you encounter problems. Here is an example of an appropriate academic article that you can copy and paste into your research outline:

> Scivoletto, Sandra; da Silva, Thiago Fernando; Rosenheck, Robert Alan. Feb. 2011, Child psychiatry takes to the streets: A developmental partnership between a university institute and children and adolescents from the streets of Sao Paulo, Brazil. *Child Abuse & Neglect*. Vol. 35 Issue 2, p89–95. 7p. DOI: 10.1016/j.chiabu.2010.11.003.

By selecting the article you will get detailed information about it, such as the abstract. As well, a number of commands appear to the right, including the word *Cite*, which will provide the information of this article in a general referencing style, such as APA. (You may need to double-check the citation that is provided—see Chapter 3 in this book—to make sure that it is actually accurate). There are more commands available for you, including importing this information into referencing software.

At the bottom of the article you should find the word *subjects*. This heading provides more related words that you can use to search on your topic.

Your goal is to obtain quality scholarly research sources. The more time you spend on your research, the better the quality of your sources. Ask librarians to help you if you have any problems. They can teach you how to do your own research and to become a skilled researcher.

2. What Should I Include about My Research Sources (Books, Articles, Websites, and So On) in My Outline?

There is considerable work, time, and effort involved in searching for and finding appropriate academic sources for your term paper. To avoid having to repeat your searches, make sure that you record all the information about your sources in your outline and make a backup copy.

Here are some final suggestions:

- Study Chapter 3 to learn what information to include in your reference sources. Use Chapter 3 to help you decide what information to copy and paste when you are actually examining a source.
- You can always include extra information, for now, such as library call numbers and URLs. This is to help you locate your source should you need to do so.
- You can easily delete or leave out the extra information in your outline until you finalize your References list.
- Remember to include all in-text citations in your outline from your reference sources.
- Once your term paper has been written, then format your References list according to your instructor's required style. Only those research sources you used in writing your term paper are included in your References unless your instructor states otherwise.

You should now be ready to evaluate and record your research sources in your outline.

Recommended Websites

California State University, Chico
Meriam Library on evaluating information by using the CRAPP test (a summary is in Appendix D):
http://www.csuchico.edu/lins/handouts/eval_websites.pdf

Meriam Library on distinguishing different kinds of scholarly articles:
http://www.csuchico.edu/lins/handouts/scholarly.pdf

Appendix E

The First Social Science Outline

_____

Tentative Title of Term Paper

by

_____

Student Name (if required add student number)

_____

Course Name, Number, and Section Number

_____

Instructor

_____

College or University

_____

Date submitted

The First Social Science Outline

General Topic

_____

Introduction

_____

Aim (what will be demonstrated)

_____
_____

Definition of Concepts (concepts from the aim that will be defined and their sources)

_____
_____
_____

Organization of Arguments (the sequence of arguments)

1._____
2._____
3._____
4._____
5._____

Presentation of Arguments (the points and evidence to support each point and their sources)

1.   **Point:** (Include concept, definition of concept, and source.)

_____

Evidence:

_____
_____

2.   **Point:** (Include concept, definition of concept, and source.)

_____

Evidence:

_____
_____

3. **Point:** (Include concept, definition of concept, and source.)

_____

Evidence:

_____

_____

4. **Point:** (Include concept, definition of concept, and source.)

_____

Evidence:

_____

_____

5. **Point:** (Include concept, definition of concept, and source.)

_____

Evidence:

_____

_____

Conclusion (Restate aim and how each argument supported the aim.)

Aim (past tense)

_____

_____

1. Argument:

_____

Supported aim:

_____

_____

2. Argument:

_____

Supported aim:

_____

_____

3. Argument:
_____
_____

Supported aim:
_____
_____

4. Argument:
_____
_____

Supported aim:
_____
_____

5. Argument:
_____
_____

Supported aim:
_____
_____

References (APA, CMS, or ASA style: list all books, periodicals, and other reference sources)
_____
_____
_____
_____
_____
_____
_____

Appendix F

The Second Social Science Outline

This outline starts with Step 1 and is revised until Step 3. Always save a copy of your outline before revising it to work on the next step.

> Step 1: Start with the First Social Science Outline to Create Individual Arguments (See Appendix E)
>
> Step 2: Create Headings/Themes from Individual Arguments of Appendix E. Note: It is important to complete Step 2 before starting Step 3.
>
> Step 3: Organize Headings/Themes (and Points & Evidence) & Complete the Second Social Science Outline

---

Tentative Title of Term Paper

by

Student Name (if required add student number)

Course Name, Number, and Section Number

Instructor

College or University

Date submitted

Step 2: Create Headings/Themes from Individual Arguments of Appendix E

Introduction

_____

Aim (what will be demonstrated)

_____

_____

Definition of Concepts (concepts from the aim that will be defined and their sources)

_____

_____

Organization of Headings/Themes (the sequence of headings or themes for groups of arguments)

_____

Presentation of Headings/Themes (the wording of each heading/theme and their points and evidence to support each point and their sources: may contain subheadings and an individual argument)

_____

(Use more/fewer points and more/less evidence as required for each Heading/Theme below.)

1. Heading/Theme:
1. Point:

_____

Evidence:

_____

2. Point:

_____

Evidence:

_____

2. Heading/Theme:
1. Point:

_____

Evidence:

_____

2. Point:

_____

Evidence:

_____

(Create more **Headings/Themes** with points and evidence, as necessary, like the ones above.)

Conclusion (Restate aim and then state how each heading or theme of arguments, including subheadings, supported the aim.)

_____

_____

Aim (past tense)

_____

_____

References (APA, CMS, or ASA style: list all books, periodicals and other reference sources)

_____

Step 3: Organize Headings/Themes (and Points & Evidence) & Complete the Second Social Science Outline

General Topic

_____

Introduction

_____

_____

Aim (what will be demonstrated)

_____

_____

Definition of Concepts (concepts from the aim that will be defined and their sources)

_____

_____

Organization of Headings/Themes (the sequence of headings or themes for groups of arguments)

_____

(Use more/fewer headings/themes as necessary.)

1. Heading/Theme:

_____

2. Heading/Theme:

_____

3. Heading/Theme

_____

4. Heading/Theme

_____

Presentation of Headings/Themes (the wording of each heading/theme and their points and evidence to support each point and their sources: may contain subheadings and an individual argument)

_____

(Use more/fewer points and more/less evidence as required for each Heading/Theme.)

1.   Heading/Theme:
1. Point:

_____

Evidence:

_____

_____

2. Point:

_____

Evidence:

_____

2.   Heading/Theme:
1. Point:

_____

Evidence:

_____

2. Point:

_____

Evidence:

_____

3.   Heading/Theme:
1. Point:

_____

Evidence:

_____

2. Point:

_____

Evidence:

_____

4.   Heading/Theme:
1. Point:

_____

Evidence:

_____

2. Point:

_____

Evidence:

_____

(Create more/fewer Headings/Themes with points and evidence, as necessary, like the ones above.)

Conclusion (Restate aim and then state how each heading or theme of arguments, including subheadings, supported the aim.)

Aim (past tense)

_____

_____

_____

(Create more/fewer individual Headings/Themes and how each supported aim as necessary.)

1. Heading/Theme:

_____

Supported aim:

_____

2. Heading/Theme:

_____

Supported aim:

_____

3. Heading/Theme:

_____

Supported aim:

_____

4. Heading/Theme:

_____

Supported aim:

_____

References (APA, CMS, or ASA style: list all books, periodicals and other reference sources)

_____

_____

References

Alfano, C.L., & O'Brien, A.J. (2011). *Envision: Writing and researching arguments* (3rd ed.). Boston, MA: Longman.

American Psychological Association. (2010). *Publication manual of the American Psychological Association* (6th ed.). Washington, DC: Author.

American Sociological Association. (2010). *American Sociological Association style guide* (4th ed.). Washington, DC: Author.

Baker, M. (2008). Families and intimate relationships. In L. Tepperman, B. Curtis, & P. Albanese (Eds.), *Sociology: A Canadian perspective* (pp. 218–241). Don Mills, ON: Oxford University Press.

Booth, W.C., Colomb, G.G., & Williams, J.M. (2008). *The craft of research*. Chicago, IL: University of Chicago Press.

Brym, R.J., Roberts, L.W., Lie, J., & Retina, S. (2013). *Sociology: Your compass for a new world* (4th Canadian ed.). Toronto, ON: Nelson.

Campbell, M., & Gregor, F. (2008). *Mapping social relations: A primer in doing institutional ethnography*. Toronto, ON: University of Toronto Press.

Corbett, E.P.J., & Connors, R.J. (1999). *Classical rhetoric for the modern student*. New York, NY: Oxford University Press.

Davis, R., Davis, L.K., Stewart, K.L., & Bullock, C.J. (2013). *Essay writing for Canadian students with readings* (7th ed.). Toronto, ON: Pearson.

Dunn, S.D. (2004). *A short guide to writing about psychology*. New York, NY: Pearson.

Engkent, L., & Engkent, G. (2013). *Essay do's and don'ts: A practical guide to essay writing*. Don Mills, ON: Oxford University Press.

Gibson, K.E. (2011). *Street kids: Homeless youth, outreach, and policing New York's streets* [Kindle e-book]. Available from http://ezproxy.viu.ca/login?url=http://muse.jhu.edu/bo oks/9780814733370/

Gooch, J., & Seyler, D. (2013). *Argument!* (2nd ed.). New York, NY: McGraw-Hill.

Henderson, E., & Moran, K.M. (2010). *The empowered writer: An essential guide to writing, reading, & research*. Don Mills, ON: Oxford University Press.

Hudd, S.S., Sardi, L.M., & Lopriore, M.T. (2013). Sociologists as writing instructors: Teaching students to think, teaching an emerging skill, or both? *Teaching Sociology 40*(1) 32–45. doi:10.1177/0092055X12458049

Gibaldi, J. (2003). *MLA handbook for writers of research papers* (5th ed.). New York, NY: The Modern Language Association of America.

Johnson, Jr., W.A., Rettig, R.P., Scott, G.M., & Garrison, S.M. (2009). *The sociology student writer's manual* (6th ed.). Upper Saddle River, NJ: Pearson.

Kirszner, L.G., & Mandell, S.R. (2011). *Introducing practical argument: A text and anthology.* Boston, MA: Bedford/St. Martin's.

Kirszner, L.G., & Mandell, S.R. (2012). *Patterns for college writing: A rhetorical reader and guide* (12th ed.). Boston, MA: Bedford/St. Martin's.

Macionis, J.J., & Gerber, L.M. (2011). *Sociology* (7th Canadian ed.). Toronto, ON: Pearson.

Messenger, W.E., de Bruyn, J., Brown, J., & Montagnes, R. (2012). *The Canadian writer's handbook: Essentials edition.* Don Mills, ON: Oxford University Press.

Murray, J.L., Linden, R., & Kendall, D. (2011). *Sociology in our times* (5th Canadian ed.). Toronto, ON: Nelson Education.

Muth, F.M. (2006). *Researching and writing: A portable guide.* Boston, MA: Bedford/St. Martin's.

Myers, D.G. (2014). *Exploring psychology* (9th ed.). New York, NY: Worth.

Northey, M., & Timney, B. (2011). *Making sense in psychology: A student's guide to research and writing.* Toronto, ON: Oxford University Press.

Norton, S., & Green, B. (2011). *Essay essentials with readings* (5th ed.). Scarborough, ON: Thomson/Nelson.

Reinking, J.A., von der Osten, R., Cairns, S.A., & Fleming, R. (2010). *Strategies for successful writing: A rhetoric, research guide, reader, and handbook.* Toronto, ON: Pearson.

Ritzer, G. (2010). *The McDonaldization of society* 6 (6th ed.). Thousand Oaks, CA: Sage.

Schaeffer, R.T., Smith, E., & Grekul, J. (2009). *Sociology* (2nd Canadian ed.). Toronto, ON: McGraw Hill.

Smith, D.E. (2005). *Institutional ethnography: A sociology for people.* Lanham, MA: Altamira.

Smith, D.E. (Ed.). (2006). *Institutional ethnography as practice.* Lanham, MA: Rowman & Littlefield.

Steckley, J., & Letts, G.K. (2013). *Elements of sociology: A critical Canadian introduction* (3rd ed.). Don Mills, ON: Oxford University Press.

Stewart, K.L., Allen, M., & Galliah, S. (2009). *Forms of writing: A rhetoric, handbook, and reader* (5th ed.). Toronto, ON: Pearson.

Szuchman, L.T. (2013). *Writing with style: APA style made easy* (6th ed.). Scarborough, ON: Wadsworth/Cengage.

Turabian, K.L. (2010). *Student's guide to writing college papers* (4th ed.). (Revised by G. G. Colomb, J.M. Williams, & University of Chicago Press Editorial Staff). Chicago, IL: University of Chicago Press.

The University of Chicago Press. (2010). *The Chicago manual of style* (16th ed.). Chicago, IL: Author.

Wilson, A., & Pence, E. (2006). U.S. legal interventions in the lives of battered women: An indigenous assessment. In D. Smith (Ed.), *Institutional ethnography as practice* (pp. 199–225). Lanham, MA: Rowman & Littlefield.

Index